IN SEARCH OF ENGLAND

IN SEARCH OF
England

H. V. MORTON

DA CAPO PRESS

Cataloging-in-Publication data for this book is available from the Library of Congress.

First Da Capo Press edition 2002
Reprinted by arrangement with Methuen Publishing Ltd.
ISBN 0–306–81105–7

Published by Da Capo Press
A Member of the Perseus Books Group
http://www.dacapopress.com

Da Capo Press books are available at special discounts for bulk purchases in the U.S. by corporations, institutions, and other organizations. For more information, please contact the Special Markets Department at the Perseus Books Group, 11 Cambridge Center, Cambridge, MA 02142, or call (800) 255–1514 or (617) 252–5298, or e-mail j.mccrary@perseusbooks.com.

1 2 3 4 5 6 7 8 9—06 05 04 03 02

CONTENTS

IN SEARCH OF ENGLAND

INTRODUCTION TO
THE DA CAPO EDITION

When this famous book was first published, in 1927, it introduced a vast new reading public to an old and honored genre. Down the centuries innumerable writers had chronicled journeys around England, that oldest and most charismatic of nation-states, from the chatty seventeenth-century patrician Celia Fiennes or the indefatigable Daniel Defoe, to William Cobbett the social reformer or the peregrinating theorist Arthur Young, who was more concerned with crop rotations and ploughing methods than with the sights and sounds of a nation.

Henry Vollam Morton, however, then in his thirties and new to the writing of books, did something quite new with the form. In England there was already a huge mass readership for fiction, first tapped by Charles Dickens long before, but earlier writers about place had generally addressed themselves to particular social groups, whether cultivated bibliophiles of the leisured classes or specialist intellectuals. Morton set out to introduce a universal audience to the delights of travel writing—and travel writing not about exotic destinations, long made fashionable by the sensational memoirs of explorers, soldiers, and adventurers, but travel writing about *home*, about the people next door, the town up the road, local traditions that survived, often enough, half-forgotten in the reader's own experience.

It was above all the pleasure of travel writing that was his forte. He was a popular journalist by trade, and he aimed at easy reading, gentle jokes, personal reminiscences of the kind that made one chuckle rather than guffaw. Morton had soldiered in the Great War that had so recently ended, but the carnage of Flanders feels a million miles away, if not a million years, from this happy serendipitous amble through the beloved English landscapes.

In Search of England is most decidedly a period piece, and that is half its charm. Foreigners who may be tempted to use it as a guide to modern England—even as a guide to the contemporary English flavor—will be stupefyingly disillusioned. This is the England of *Masterpiece Theatre*, not of Thatcher or Blair! Not much that Morton describes or suggests is recognizable in today's England, beyond the bare bones of it, or the echo.

It is true that even today they dance the weird Furry Dance through the streets of Helston in Cornwall, and that Ely can still feel, as Morton thought, "like a floating Camelot." Clovelly is as determinedly quaint as ever. At a pinch even twenty-first-century Stonehenge can seem, to a sufficiently impressionable visitor, "inexpressibly remote." But little of it feels quite natural any more—the Tourist Board is always present and there is likely to be a television crew around the corner. The invariably rosy-cheeked farmers' wives that Morton meets, the archetypal squires, the plethora of "characters" always to hand—all have vanished from the face of the country, and a totally new breed of English men and women, not half so English, not half so rosy-cheeked, gentlemanly or colorful, has emerged to sustain the age-old heritage.

However Morton's vision of his country can strangely move one too. We are seeing in the pages of this work, portrayed with unfailing freshness, immediacy, and enthusiasm, a myth in its own lifetime. It is an idea of a great country that was perfectly true in its time, evolved out of a thousand years of insular independence. The England of 1927 had seen no foreign invaders since the eleventh century, and very few foreign challengers. Its history was one of unexampled success, and its way of life, its attitude to the world at large, had grown out of unquestioning national self-confidence. No alien example could corrupt its habits and its values. The English then knew themselves for certain to be the best, serene and ever-victorious, and they saw no reason to modify their ways or restrain their peculiarities. Winston Churchill was in his fifties then, and when he was urged that talking to some Indians might modify his views on the future of the British Empire in India, he replied: "I am quite satisfied with my views on India, and I don't want them disturbed by any bloody Indians."

Few English people nowadays, after half a century of national decline, view themselves or the world with the same blithe assurance. They have lost that empire since 1927, they have been weakened and belittled by history and overtaken by younger and richer powers. Their island culture is no longer invulnerable. Nor are there many observers at work with the same guileless benignity as Morton—a chronicler without cynicism, seeing the best almost always and responding with an open-hearted simplicity. The style may sometimes jar upon modern susceptibilities, but it is touching too, because it expresses emotions that have curdled since his day, and perceptions that are lost.

We know better than the author ever could how fragile was the matter of his descriptions. How could he have guessed that the proud society he celebrates would so soon be pitifully unsure of itself, or that the great imperial sovereignty it underlay would be left high and dry among the nations, searching decade after decade for its role in a new world? Nor could he imagine that he himself, buoyant with the optimism of youth, would seem in 2002 like a writer from another age, expressing himself in a prose that ironically still seems fresh chiefly because its manner is so utterly of a lost time.

But of course there is more to it than that. Morton was a writer *sui generis*, and that style was altogether his own. His prevailing air of innocence, which so often seems to hover on the brink of naivete, is profoundly English, but English in the most unassuming, un-Churchillian kind. It was a yeoman Englishness. There was no cynicism to it, no arrogance, and there were none of the worldly devices which made so many of his contemporaries sound as though they were writing for an upper-class clique of their own. Morton wrote for the English people at large, and seemed to speak with the very voice of middle England itself, as it spoke in the 1920s before disillusionment crept in.

Later in life Morton was to develop more sophisticated attitudes, and the writing of his universally admired last books appealed to a more demanding readership. It is the lasting charm and strength of *In Search of England*, though, that it seems to reflect at once in its material and its manner the spirit of a lost society—of a lost culture, perhaps. England is not like this any more, and nobody writes nowadays as the young H.V. Morton wrote 75 years ago. The Englishness he represented, like the England he described, lives on only in myth, longing, and literature, and in his own engaging cadences.

Jan Morris
January 2002

INTRODUCTION

THIS is the record of a motor-car journey round England.

Any virtue it may possess, and all its sins, spring from the fact that it was written without deliberation by the roadside, on farmyard walls, in cathedrals, in little churchyards, on the washstands of country inns, and in many another inconvenient place. I have gone round England like a magpie, picking up any bright thing that pleased me. A glance at the route followed will prove that this is not a guide-book, and a glance at the contents will expose me to the scorn of local patriots who will see, with incredulous rage, that on many an occasion I passed silently through their favourite village. That was inevitable. It was a moody holiday, and I followed the roads; some of them led me aright and some astray. The first were the most useful; the others were the most interesting.

A writer on England today addresses himself to a wider and a more intelligent public than ever before, and the reason is, I think, that never before have so many people been searching for England. The remarkable system of motor-coach services which now penetrates every part of the country has thrown open to ordinary people regions which even after the coming of the railway were remote and inaccessible. The popularity of the cheap motor-car is also greatly responsible for this long-overdue interest in English history, antiquities, and topography. More people than in any previous generation are seeing the real country for the first time. Many hundreds of such explorers return home with a new enthusiasm.

The roads of England, eclipsed for a century by the railway, have come to life again; the King's highway is once more a place for adventures and explorations; and I would venture to prophesy that within the next few years we shall see a decline in the popularity of the seaside resort, unfortunate as this may be, and a revival of the country inn.

The danger of this, as every lover of England knows, is the vulgarization of the countryside. I have seen charabanc parties from the large manufacturing towns, providing a mournful text for an essay on Progress, playing cornets on village greens and behaving with a barbaric lack of manners which might have been outrageous had it not been unconscious, and therefore only pathetic. This, however, is exceptional. The average townsman of no matter what class feels a deep love for the country, and finds there the answer to an ancient instinct.

Against the vulgarization of the country we must place to the credit of this new phase in the history of popular travel in England the fact, already mentioned, that thousands of intelligent men and women are every year discovering the countryside for themselves. The greater the number of people with an understanding love for the villages and the country towns of England the better seems our chance of preserving and handing on to our children the monuments of the past, which is clearly a sacred duty. Time is already having its way with many a cathedral whose roots are in Norman England and with many a famous stronghold like Durham Castle, and, in parts, with Hadrian's Wall, which should at once be made an official 'ancient monument' and preserved from further decay by a top-dressing of concrete. When the public really feels that these signposts along the road which the English people have followed in the course of their development are not dead shells of the past but a living inspiration to the present, to the future, and, in addition, that they possess a personal interest to them as part of a common racial heritage, then we shall have advanced a long way and – perhaps the petrol engine will have atoned for a few of its sins!

There is another and a very interesting aspect to this question. Since James Watt invented a new world on Glasgow Green, the town and the country have grown apart. They do not understand one other. Since the so-called Industrial 'Revolution'   evolution is surely a better word – English country life has declined, agriculture has fallen on bad times, and the village has been drained to a great extent of its social vitality.

It is difficult at first for the unaccustomed eyes of the townsman to understand that behind the beauty of the English country is an economic and a social cancer. An old order is being taxed out of existence; 'our greatest industry' – as the experts call it – employs fewer men than those on the dole, and, struggling along, is facing insuperable difficulties with a blundering but historic stolidity. While our cornland is going back to grass year after year, our annual bill to the foreigner for imported foodstuffs is four hundred million pounds. Everywhere is the same story: mortgages on farms; no fluid capital; the breaking up of famous estates when owners die; the impossibility of growing corn because of the expense of labour and danger of foreign competition; the folly of keeping cattle when the Roast Beef of Old England comes so cheaply from the Argentine.

'Why should the towns be expected to understand the complex problems of the countryside? We have our own troubles. The countryside must lick its own wounds!' That is the view of the town, and I submit that it is an ignorant and a short-sighted view. The towns should understand the problems of agriculture, because as the life of a countryside declines, as in England today, and the city life flourishes, the character and physique of a nation deteriorate. History proves to us that a nation cannot live by its town alone: it tells us that the virile and progressive nation is that which can keep pace with the modern industrial world and at the same time support a contented and flourishing peasantry.

The 'Back to the Land' cry is a perfectly sound instinct of racial survival. When a man makes money he builds himself a country home. This is the history of our great families – town wave after town wave – since the earlier nobility committed suicide in the Wars of the Roses. And any man who wishes his family to survive has at some time to take it and plant it in the country. Where are the town families? Where are the Greshams of London? The Whittingtons, the Philipots?

'The Grenvilles are country squires,' wrote Langton Sandford in his *The Great Governing Families of England*, 'who for five hundred years vegetated on slowly increasing estates in Buckinghamshire.' For five hundred years! In half that time the average city family has disappeared into racial anaemia.

I have introduced this note in a book which is pitched in a much lighter key because I feel that help for the woes of our agricultural districts may, quite unexpectedly, come from the cities. Political power is today all on the side of cities. They have a four-fifths majority in the electorate, and the countryman has no legislative tradition. His vision is bounded, as it always has been, by the line of his own hedges. But granted that a healthy countryside is necessary to a nation, it is then surely the duty of every man to ponder these problems and to enter into them. If those men and women who, as my letter-bag so clearly proves, are starting out in their thousands to discover rural England will see it not merely as a pretty picture or as an old battlefield whose drama has long since departed, but as a living thing, as important today as it was when all men drew their bread from it, we may be a step nearer that ideal national life: on one hand the wealthy industrial cities; on the other a happy countryside, ready to give its new blood to the towns, guarding the traditions of the race, ready always to open its arms to that third generation from the city in need of resurrection.

We may not revive the English village of the old days, with its industry and its arts. The wireless, the newspaper, the railway, and the motor-car have broken down that perhaps wider world of intellectual solitude in which the rustic evolved his shrewd wisdom, saw fairies in the mushroom rings, and composed those songs which he now affects to have forgotten. Those days are gone. The village is now part of the country: it now realizes how small the world really is! But the village is still the unit of development from which we have advanced first to the position of a great European nation and then to that of the greatest world power since Rome.

That village, so often near a Roman road, is sometimes clearly a Saxon hamlet with its great house, its church, and its cottages. There is no question of its death: it is, in fact, a lesson in survival, and a streak of ancient wisdom warns us that it is our duty to keep an eye on the old thatch because we may have to go back there some day, if not for the sake of our bodies, perhaps for the sake of our souls.

To
T. C. T.

You will remember, lady, how the morn
Came slow above the Isle of Athelney,
And all the flat lands lying to the sky
Were shrouded sea-like in a veil of grey,
As, standing on a little rounded hill,
We placed our hands upon the Holy Thorn.

Do you remember in what hopeful fear
We gazed behind us, thinking we might see
Arthur come striding through the high, bright corn,
Or Alfred resting on a Saxon spear?
And as the cold mists melted from the fields
We seemed to hear the winding of a horn.

You will remember how we walked the Vale
Through Meare and Westhay unto Godney End;
And how we said: 'Time is an endless lane
And Life a little mile without a bend. . . .
Behind us what? Before us, if we ran,
Might we not be in time to see the Grail?'

'But the Glory of the Garden lies in more than meets the eye.'
RUDYARD KIPLING

CHAPTER ONE

I go in search of England. Describes how I leave the Place Where London Ends, meet a bowl-turner, stand beneath a gallows on a hill, enter Winchester, accept the wanderer's dole at St Cross, and ends quite properly, with a maiden in distress

I

I BELIEVED that I was dying in Palestine. There was no woman to convince me that the pain in my neck was not the first sign of spinal meningitis, so that, growing rapidly worse, I began to attend my own funeral every day. My appetite, however, remained excellent.

In the black depths of misery, I climbed a hill overlooking Jerusalem, unaffected by the fact that this has been considered the best of all places to die, and, turning as accurately as I could in the direction of England, I gave way to a wave of home-sickness that almost shames me now when I recollect it. I find it impossible in cold blood, and at this distance, to put into words the longing that shook me. I have forgotten the pain in the neck, but never will I forget the pain in my heart.

As I looked out over the inhospitable mountains I remembered home in a way which, given any other frame of mind, would have astonished me. I solemnly cursed every moment I had spent wandering foolishly about the world, and I swore that if ever I saw Dover Cliffs again I would never leave them. I had by this time made myself too ill to realize that it is this rare stay-at-home sanity which justifies travel. Perhaps in instinctive contrast to the cold, unhappy mountains of Palestine, there rose up in my mind the picture of a village street at dusk with a smell of wood smoke lying in the still air and, here and there, little red blinds shining in the dusk under the thatch. I remembered how the church bells ring at home, and how, at that time of year, the

I

sun leaves a dull red bar low down in the west, and against it the elms grow blacker minute by minute. Then the bats start to flicker like little bits of burnt paper and you hear the slow jingle of a team coming home from fields. . . . When you think like this, sitting alone in a foreign country, you know all there is to learn about heartache.

But does it seem strange that a townsman should in his extremity see this picture? Would it not be more reasonable to expect him to see his own city? Why did I not think of St Paul's Cathedral or Piccadilly? I have learnt since that this vision of mine is a common one to exiles all over the world: we think of home, we long for home, but we see something greater — *we see England.*

This village that symbolizes England sleeps in the subconsciousness of many a townsman. A little London factory hand whom I met during the war confessed to me, when pressed, and after great mental difficulty, that he visualized the England he was fighting for — the England of the 'England wants you' poster — as not London, not his own street, but as Epping Forest, the green place where he had spent Bank Holidays. And I think most of us did. The village and the English country-side are the germs of all we are and all we have become: our manufacturing cities belong to the last century and a half; our villages stand with their roots in the Heptarchy.

I was humiliated, mourning there above Jerusalem, to realize how little I knew about England. I was shamed to think that I had wandered so far and so often over the world neglecting those lovely things near at home, feeling that England would always be there whenever I wanted to see her; and at that moment how far away she seemed, how unattainable! I took a vow that if the pain in my neck did not end for ever on the windy hills of Palestine, I would go home in search of England, I would go through the lanes of England and the little thatched villages of England, and I would lean over English bridges and lie on English grass, watching an English sky.

2

I opened my window to an April night and, looking down into the London square, saw that new leaves were silver-white in the lamplight. Into my room came an earthy smell and the freshness of new grass. The top boughs of the trees were etched against the saffron stain of a London sky, but their boles descended into a pool of darkness, silent and remote as the primeval forest. The fretful traffic sped left and right against the railings, and beyond lay that patch of stealthy vitality older than London. What an amazing thing is the coming of spring to London. The very pavements seem ready to crack and lift under the denied earth; in the air is a consciousness of life which tells you that if traffic stopped for a fortnight grass would grow again in Piccadilly and corn would spring in pavement cracks where a horse had spilt his 'feed'. And the squares of London, so dingy and black since the first October gale, fill week by week with the rising tide of life, just as the sea, running up the creeks and pushing itself forward inch by inch towards the land, comes at last to each remote rock pool.

The squares of London, those sacred little patches of the country-side preserved, perhaps, by the Anglo-Saxon instinct for grass and trees, hold in their restricted glades some part of the magic of spring. I suppose many a man has stood at his window above a London square in April hearing a message from the lanes of England. The Georgians no doubt fancied that Aegipans and Centaurs kicked their hoofs in Berkeley Square, and I, above my humbler square, dreamt a no less classic eclogue of hedges lit with hawthorn, of orchards ready for their brief wave of pink spray, of fields in which smoky-faced lambs pressed against their dams, of new furrows over which moved slowly the eternal figure bent above a plough.

This, then, is my adventure. Now I will go, with spring before me and the road calling me out into England. It does not matter where I go, for it is all England.

I will see what lies off the beaten track. I will, as the mood takes me, go into famous towns and unknown hamlets. I will shake up the dust of kings and abbots; I will bring the knights and the cavaliers back to the roads, and once in a while, I will hear the thunder of old quarrels at earthwork and church door. If I become weary of dream and legend I will just sit and watch the ducks on a village pond, or take the horses to water. I will talk with lords and cottagers, tramps, gipsies, and dogs; I will, in fact, do anything that comes into my head as suddenly and light-heartedly as I will accept anything, and everything, that comes my way in rain or sun along the road.

2

All good knights, pilgrims, sons in search of fortune, seekers after truth, and plain ordinary fools, turn towards the city they have left and take farewell according to their natures. This is a full moment in all journeying, the time when girths are tightened in preparation for the miles that lie ahead. Some cities, such as Durham, which stands on a hill, or Salisbury, which, if I remember it, lies in a snug hollow, lend themselves to apostrophy and appear to have been designed by man and nature to encourage the gentle art of valediction. But London is too big: by the time you reach the fringe of her there is no London to be seen; and you cannot waste sentiment on a suburban gasworks.

Of course, no living man has seen London. London has ceased to be visible since Stuart days. It was then possible for the last time in history to stand among the water meadows at Westminster and to see London riding on Ludgate Hill, escorted by her church towers and spires. Plantagenet London must have been the best of all the Londons for the purpose of a farewell speech: a city behind its wall, something definite to see and to address. Today, even if you climb to the dome of St Paul's, you see not London the City State but London the labyrinth. The nearest approach to a real view of London is that from the tower of Southwark Cathedral or, better still, from a boat on the Thames at night when darkness lends an ancient enchantment to the roof lines.

However, a man contemplating a farewell address to London finds that all enthusiasm has evaporated by the time he reaches the Place Where London Ends.

Now London ends at a public-house.

Outside the public-house stood an old man wearing silver side-whiskers and a peevish expression which suggested to me that some one had promised to stand him a drink in '85 and had never turned up.

'Hallo,' I said to him, but he looked the other way and spat rudely.

In a line with the public-house were new shops. In a field some way off the high road were scared-looking, pink and white villas, each one possessing a bald garden and a brand-new galvanized dustbin at the back door. Wives as new as the gardens and the houses busied about their work and took frequent peeps through the front windows to make sure that the baby was still on the safe side of the garden fence. The most significant item on the landscape was an empty omnibus standing in a weary attitude opposite the public-house. There were London names on the indicator board, but they seemed as unlikely as the Italian names on the French expresses at Calais.

The history of London is the moving on of that red omnibus another mile along the road; more pink and white houses; more shops; more wives; more babies.

'Good morning,' said I to the ancient man.

'Straight on,' he replied.

'Good morning,' I ventured again.

'About seven miles,' he retorted.

I felt that we were going to be great friends.

'Will you have a drink?' I asked.

Even this failed to bring us together, so I went right into his silver side-whiskers and shouted 'Beer!', whereon he sprang smartly to attention and walked into the bar. By shouting slightly to the right of his left ear I found myself in touch with a personality not only charming but also interesting.

He asked me where I was going in that little blue motor car.

'Anywhere,' I told him four times.

Like so many old men who stand thinking (or just standing) outside public-houses, he had been in the Navy, and was therefore fitted by experience to understand my vivid state of mind.

'I feel,' I told him, 'exactly as I used to feel when school broke up in July, or when the Armistice was signed. No troubles and no duties: nothing to do but to go on and on, to stop and talk when I feel like it, to loiter when the mood takes me, and to hurry when I want to.'

I told him that all the towns and villages of England were before me; and he confided to me that he had a brother who once upon a time lived in Bolton.

We were just warming up to one another when a tremendous throbbing rose outside – the engine of the omnibus had started! I went to the door. It was a moment for which I had been waiting. The conductor flung away his cigarette, the driver climbed up to his seat, an old woman in black sat inside, and a young man in a belted macintosh climbed aloft, the driver put in his clutch, and the last red link with London started off down the road.

'Good-bye, London!'

That was all I said. There comes a moment in all travel when you know that you have really started. It may be weeks before you start or weeks after you have started; it is a spiritual emotion, a turning towards the future with an eager heart; and this is how I felt when the last omnibus went back to London, leaving me alone at the Place Where London Ends. . . .

I started the engine. I felt that I had seen the last of London.

'Good-bye,' I said to the old man.

He wiped his mouth and looked the other way. I think he did not hear.

I sped on into a green tunnel of a lane, with England before me; and the keen air was like wine to me, and the green of the young leaves was like music.

The river looked delicious at Datchet. . . . Eton was slumbering behind elms in well-bred reticence. . . . Two scarlet sentries marched up and down the steep slope before the entrance to Windsor Castle. . . . Two pretty girls stood with a white sealyham pup at the very beginning of Reading; and on I went and on into green Berkshire till I came to a little lane with a bend in the middle that seemed to say, 'I dare you!'

'This looks good!' I said.

The cart tracks were full of water and the lane led up to a hill; and the earth of this lane was the colour of amber. At the top of the lane was Bucklebury Common aflame with gorse. Tall trees stood up from this gorse, making lovely green patterns against a windy sky.

3

As I was trying to decide which lane had the best turning, there came towards me over the wet, sandy road a scholarly-looking, middle-aged man. I hailed him (as I intend to hail everybody), and we fell into conversation. He was, I observed, carrying a wooden bowl.

'Perhaps you know these lanes,' I said. 'I seem to be lost, but before I find my way out is there anything worth seeing here?'

'Well,' he replied, holding up his wooden bowl, 'what do you think of that?'

I looked at it curiously, unwilling to admit that I saw nothing remarkable about it. His bowl had a marvellous grain, a fine smooth finish, and two neat lines round the outer rim.

'That,' he said, 'is the work of the last bowl-turner in

England. He lives over the hill at Bucklebury. A most interesting survival. Quite remarkable. You ought to look at his workshop, for you will never see another one like it!'

I had a suspicion when first I saw him fondling the bowl that this stranger was an antiquary, and when he proceeded to deliver a lecture on 'treen', standing there with his feet in a puddle, I knew it for certain.

'Before people used pewter for plates and tankards,' he explained, 'wooden trenchers, drinking cups, and bowls – called "treen" – were used by everyone. I hope I am not boring you? Well, in Elizabethan times pewter came in fashion and wooden things were used only by poorer people. Then came china and glass. They knocked out pewter, and the demand for "treen" dwindled to almost nothing, but the art of making it never quite died out. Now there is only one maker of "treen" left, and he turns bowls exactly as they did in the days of Alfred the Great. . . .'

A sharp shower of rain interrupted, and he went on his way, and I in search of the last 'treen' man.

The gorse flung itself in a sheet of flame across Bucklebury Common, and the birds were singing like mad in the rain.

How often in London rain weighs on the spirit and soaks itself into the very soul; but in the country it seldom saddens you – in fact, there is a kind of country rain that exhilarates and causes you to sing aloud.

I would not care to be the postman at Bucklebury. The cottages hide one from the other; the hamlet is spread generously over little hillocks, so that a man in a motor car has a fair chance of finding himself in Stanford Dingley or Yattendon or Frilsham, or even Beenham, before he discovers his object in this gorsy labyrinth. And why not? These names have quality. These lanes are so friendly. I was thinking more or less in this way, half deciding to take the road to Yattendon and give up the quest for the 'treen'-maker, when I came to a tumble-down hut on a green knoll. Enormous elm logs stood piled outside the door; inside, a man was sharpening a long knife on a whetstone. He glanced up and admitted that his name was William Lailey. He looked to me like a shy, middle-aged faun. His cheeks were red, and his healthy country face was shaded by a floppy green hat. He asked me in, and went on sharpening his knife, his back towards me, an attitude which delighted me because it was, from him, so sincere; his knife meant more to him than I did, and he was – I looked at his hands – a craftsman.

No; there wasn't much to see next door, where he worked, but he'd show me! Yes, he loved making bowls better than anything! He never felt happier than when he was holding a good bit of elm to the lathe! His father taught him to make 'treen', and his grandfather taught his father; and so it went back to goodness knows when. . . .

Talking like this, he opened the door to his workshop.

To say that eight hundred years seemed to have stopped at the door conveys nothing. The room was an Anglo-Saxon workshop! probably the same sort of shed existed also in Ancient Egypt. It seemed, at first sight, that Heath Robinson had fitted it up with all manner of pulleys and strings. The floor was deep in soft elm shavings, and across the hut was bent a young alder sapling connected to a primitive lathe by a leather thong.

'No other kind of lathe will do,' explained William Lailey, stepping down into a wicker-work pen. 'The sapling takes off the strain. You watch! I'm going to turn an elm bowl.'

He picked up a chunk of wood and, putting it to the lathe, worked a foot pedal and held a sharp bent knife to the rapidly revolving wood. With surprising speed he cut the outer shape of the bowl; then, taking a different knife, he cut out the inside as you might cut out the inside of a turnip. The bowl was roughly finished.

'It wants titivating up, of course,' he explained, 'and the inside will make another smaller bowl.'

The alder sapling sprang back, vibrating: a clumsy, primitive, marvellously efficient invention, and in it – and many more now lost to us – the secret of those beautiful handicrafts of antiquity which remain to astonish us and to confound our modern machinists.

'Boys won't learn like this now,' he said. 'It's not as easy as it looks, and unless you learn when you're a lad you can never catch the knack of it.'

He uncovered a pile of beautifully turned bowls of all sizes in a corner of the hut. I saw what the man in the lane was so proud of: each bowl had the individuality which only a man's hands can give to an object.

'You could make a lot of money if you wanted to,' I told him.

'Money?' he said with a slow faun-like smile. 'Money's only storing up trouble, I think. I like making bowls better than I like making money.'

'Will you say that again?'

He leaned against the door of the hut, his homely brown face shaded by his green floppy hat, and said it again, slightly puzzled, and feeling, I think, that I was in some way 'getting at him'. But you will have guessed that I wished to hear for the second time the voice of a craftsman, the lover of his job, the proud creator of beautiful, common things; a voice that is now smothered by the scream of machines.

I went on down the green hill feeling that my search of England had started well.

4

Newbury, in Berkshire, where the children, I am told, still place flowers in those mounds where Cavalier and Round-head sleep together as they fell together in the Civil War, is, like all towns which have traffic with race-horses, a knowing-looking, bandy-legged town. It is the twin of Newmarket: both seem to have their fingers laid against their noses, one eye shut and the other on the stable door.

I went into the old Cloth Hall, which is now a museum, and looked at the Egyptian antiquities presented by the late

Earl of Carnarvon, whose body lies nearby on the bare, chalk summit of Beacon Hill – the most lonely grave in all England. . . .

Late in the afternoon I set off to cross the high chalk downs into Hampshire with the vague idea of reaching Winchester by bed-time. (You gather that I am no racing motorist.) Several side roads got in the way, so that in no time I found myself lost in a tangle of up-and-down lanes which connect village to village. When taking my bearings I saw on the summit of the highest down an object which I took to be a flagstaff. But why a flagstaff on the bald head of a great hill? I took out binoculars and saw a gallows standing up there, a mark for several counties, firm and unmistakable, as if ready for a hanging.

A gibbet!

Before climbing the steep road I thought that I would ask a few questions. I stopped a labourer on a bicycle.

'What is that on the hill?'

'Gallows,' he said suspiciously.

'Who was hanged there?'

'Dunno.'

'When was it last used?'

'Dunno.'

'Have you ever heard any story about it?'

'No.'

I discovered that he had been born and bred in the shadow of Inkpen Beacon, which is the name of this hill. The next man was just as negative; so was a third. Dusk was falling. I thought that I would waste no more time. The road climbed round and round: to the right lay a misty panorama of distant green fields, dark clumps of trees, tiny white roads like threads intersecting them, the whole view shut in by low-sailing, dark clouds. I left the car at the end of the road and struck off over grassland.

Soon the top of the gallows showed itself, outlined against the pale sky as I advanced, and in a few moments I was standing on a high mound; before me was a great dip in which, a thousand feet below, lay Hampshire, like a green table.

No gallows I have ever read of has been complete without wind whistling through it. Combe Gallows lives up to the tradition. The wind tore through it, screamed past it, so that I had to hold on to it; it vibrated slightly in the wind. It was eerie standing up there so near the slow-moving clouds, with dark falling and no one near, only the low bushes bent forward in the wind, and a few drops of falling rain.

What grim crime was commemorated by this old cross? I noticed that the wood was not of one date. The gallows had been repaired in fairly recent times. That struck me as curious. A white paper fluttered in the wind from four nails. Suppose this told the history of the crime! I read with difficulty – for it was almost dark – the following words: 'Teas can be obtained at Combe.'

That sent the skeleton back to the bushes! I laughed and went back along the grass to the car.

Now this is the story of Combe Gallows, unravelled later in Winchester Library. On March 7th, 1676, a man and a woman were hanged on this gibbet, and their bodies exposed as a warning to all sinners. Their names were George Brownman and Dorothy Newman, and they were hanged for the brutal murder of two children which the woman had by a former husband. The children's bodies were discovered in the little hill-pond near the gallows.

This pond was in Inkpen parish, but the authorities repudiated it and refused either to arrest or to go to the expense of punishing the murderers. The parish of Combe, in which the man and woman lived, took the case into its own hands, drew a new parish boundary to include the scene of the crime – twenty-five acres and a pond – erected the gibbet, and exposed there the bodies of the murderers.

The strange part of the story is this: the gallows owes its existence to a clause in the lease of Eastwich Farm, at the foot of the hill. The tenants of this farm have for two hundred and fifty years been obliged to keep the gallows in repair. The present gibbet is the third erected on the site. I am told that a charity in Combe owes its existence to the upkeep of the gallows. If the gallows disappears so does the charity. A rather different version of this tragedy is given by W. H. Hudson in *Afoot in England.*

I must tell you that as I dipped into Winchester at eight o'clock they were ringing the curfew from the Guildhall – a bell that had been ringing for eight hundred and sixty years. Such a snug, friendly old town – a town full of bells, for it was practice night at the cathedral.

By bedtime a hush had fallen over Winchester, and I put my head out of the window in the hope of seeing King Alfred's ghost riding down the street, but it was raining and the street was empty.

5

The rain ceased in the night and, awakening early as one does in a strange room, I saw a brightness behind the blind that told me the sun was shining. Winchester was not yet awake. It was that lovely time in early spring when the world, it seems, is swept and garnished for a festival. As I walked through the empty streets, I wondered when the citizens of Winchester, now snuggling down into that last self-indulgent half-hour of bed, would realize their folly and, opening their doors, come tumbling out to go a-Maying. A thrush was singing in the cathedral limes and the sun, still low in the east, played early morning tricks in the streets, gilding unexpected places, casting improbable shadows. It was mellow over that old school which has sent so many men clearly labelled into the world. You can generally tell them at a glance, especially in the law courts, when they rise for the prosecution and, with a kind of cold pleasure, stab the rhetoric of the defence with an intellectual instrument forged at Winchester – 'aut disce, aut discede, manet sors tertia caedi'; some one who knew Winchester (it may have been Wren) carved that on the wall of 'School' in 1683.

I went on, thinking that if one were looking for the germ of the British Empire, it is to be found in this quiet little city of Winchester. The princes of this city emerged as the Kings of Wessex, after their long war with the Danes, and later became the Kings of England; and it was the royal city of Winchester which was truly the very heart of England until Westminster Hall and the Abbey gathered round them the royal city of a new England.

And, sitting on a sunny wall, I tried to look back into a time when many a poor swineherd raked the embers of his fire over a Roman pavement. The fern and the elder tree were pushing asunder the walls of London, and I wondered how many strange tales of ghosts in the old dead city on the hill were whispered beyond the walls at night. Did any man prowling those empty streets by day rest a while upon the statue of a fallen Caesar, and hold in either hand a statue of Christ and Isis and wonder what they were? Such a mist it is into which a man looks from a wall in Winchester. 'The era of Celt, Saxon, and Dane is like Macbeth's battle on the blasted heath,' says Mr G. M. Trevelyan in his *History of England*. 'Prophecy hovers around. Horns are heard blowing in the mist, and a confused uproar of savage tumult and outrage. We catch glimpses of giant figures – mostly warriors at strife. But there are ploughmen, too, it seems, breaking the primeval clod, and we hear the sound of forests crashing to the axe. Around all is the lap of the waves and the cry of seamen beaching their ships.'

Surely there was also, as the prophetic mist blows aside a little, a glimpse of men walking the old Roman roads of England bearing a cross, the legions returning with shaven heads? Surely the most important sound in that mist was the sound of chanting; surely the most gigantic figure, greater than Guthrum with his shield and sword, was the holy man under an oak tree talking to a bearded king about something strange and wonderful that happened long ago in

Bethlehem? I think so. For Rome conquered England twice; once with a sword and once with a story, and as horns blew in the mist, and the warriors roared together at the palisades, the monasteries locked their doors on all that was left of civilization or fled with their relics, still along the roads of Rome, conscious that they guarded the little flame of a new world. And it seems, as we look into this mist, that these men from Rome, from Wales, from Ireland, ran through England, over the wild heathland, through the dark forests, crying their good news in the half light as boys run laughing through the streets of a city in the first hour of the New Year.

The cathedral bell began to ring; and the birds were singing in the lime trees.

6

I went to see the Great Hall of the Castle of Winchester, all now left of the royal palace that stood on the traditional Castle of King Arthur. How the prestige of Winchester endured! When Henry VII wished to strengthen his hereditary claim to the throne in 1486, he could think of nothing better to his purpose than to bring his queen to Winchester in order that the heir to the throne might be born in the Castle of King Arthur.

I expected to see Norman work, but it is Early English, aisles, dormer windows, and high, slim pillars of Purbeck marble. In Winchester Great Hall, and in how many other halls, castles, abbeys, earthworks and monasteries throughout England, the imagination halts before the richness of their associations. If I were the curator of a hall, an abbey, a castle I would be driven to madness by my anxiety to make people see the part such buildings had played in the long pageant of history.

The Round Table of King Arthur has hung for over five hundred years on the walls of Winchester Hall. It is first mentioned by John Hardyng in 1378:

IN SEARCH OF ENGLAND

*The rounde Table of Wynchester beganne
And there it ended and there it hangeth yet.*

Henry VIII brought the Emperor Charles V, when he was visiting England in 1522, to see this table, which he exhibited as one of the most interesting sights in the kingdom. It cannot, of course, be the Round Table of legend, but it is a most fascinating piece of carpentry. It was repainted in Tudor times, and it shows King Arthur sitting crowned in Tudor robes. A point in favour of the legend is that it is quite large enough to seat the king and his twenty-four knights.

7

He was standing in the choir of Winchester Cathedral surrounded by the first tourists of the year. He was a clean-shaven man with the mobile face of an actor, shrewd, humorous eyes, and white hair brushed straight back over his head. I learned afterwards that he is well known in America.

Vergers as a class are not likeable. The profession of verging appears to induce mousy manners and complete ignorance of history. When I saw the verger of the cathedral of the Kings of Wessex, I edged up to the group miserably, thinking:

'I might write something about the balderdash these fellows hand out like cold muffins. . . .'

In two minutes I had discovered that the man was alive! He had imagination, magnetism; he had a real sense of history and a good technique; he threw out ground bait, and then began from the beginning and built up. A fat, middle-aged motorist who, I judged, had been too busy making money all his life to be more than eight years old in other things, stood gaping on the edge of the crowd; he seemed to be struggling reluctantly with a new point of view.

'This chap's good,' he whispered, 'isn't he? I expect he's pulling our legs a bit. He talks about the old days as if he had been there. . . .'

As the man with the white hair talked in the silent choir of Winchester – before him the long sweep of that marvellous nave, on either side those lovely Norman transepts soaked in a pale gold light – he moved his hands in time to his words, and his eyes went over the group to each listener. There was not a shuffle. He had gripped them! They had come prepared to be bored; they stayed strangely thrilled by this man's enthusiasm and by the pictures he called up. That was it, he humanized the history book. . . .

We saw as he talked, down a long tunnel of time, the Kings of Wessex riding through a country that was not yet England; we saw the long boats of the pirates pointed to our shores; we saw the Roman cities desolate on their hills. Darkness and fighting. We saw the monk from Rome come walking over English meadows; Saint Augustine, preaching beside the pagan wells, bringing the Cross from Rome again, telling the world's greatest story to king, to noble, to common man. So the seed of all cathedrals was sown. The speaker then rebuilt Winchester stone by stone. The old story, like all old stories told properly, took on a new importance, became dramatic and somehow near at hand. The crowd had heard it before at school; but they had never *seen* it before.

'Who's coming up to the roof with me?' said the verger. 'Come on, and you'll have the treat of your lives, and on the way I'll let you walk where the monks walked who day and night guarded the golden shrine of St Swithin which once stood where you are standing.'

Up spiral staircases we went, holding on to ropes, feeling the smooth face of the stone in the dark, till we came to a dim, dusty tunnel crossed by a narrow wooden platform. We were walking above that lovely vaulted nave of

Winchester. Above was the roof, and crossways stretched vast oak beams that uphold the structure.

'Just look at them!' he said. 'Eight hundred years old, and as good as new. The architect who was here the other day says that all they need is a little lead treatment. And those giant oaks were felled by the Normans! Come on. Mind your heads!'

We came to that eerie spot where the great bells of Winchester tick off time so patiently, and here this amusing verger lined us up – solemn elderly women, fat men, thin men, and little children – gave each one of us a bell, delivered a lecture on bell-ringing, numbered us off from the right, and pointing to each one in turn as he wished him to ring, drew forth from the unpromising assembly 'Abide with Me.'

We were delighted with ourselves.

Up we went again, and round and round, till we bent under a little stone doorway and came out on the roof of the cathedral; below us lay London's old rival – Winchester.

We looked down on the tops of feathery lime trees, on the river and the distant hills, the little town lying pleasantly in a blue haze of smoke from its chimneys, Winchester!

'I love it,' said the verger. 'You ought to come up here on a moonlit night and look down. You can imagine things: you can see ghosts. . . .'

'You must,' I said, 'have devoted your life to this.'

'When I was appointed verger, the spirit of Winchester gripped me and I knew that I had found my right job. I love every stone of this cathedral.'

'Who are your most intelligent listeners?' I asked him.

'American women over forty!' he replied instantly.

Down we all trooped over those sheer corkscrew stairs and out into the lime avenue. We found that we all knew each other. We all shook hands before we parted. Such is the power of one man's enthusiasm.

I was walking between Compton and Winchester in the morning when I came upon a tattered old man sitting by the side of the road. He was, he told me, 'looking for odd jobs', but there was something about his personality which told me that if an odd job showed itself he would look keenly enough, but in the opposite direction.

He had the slow, steady slouch of the tramp. He told me that he had once lived in Hounslow, but beyond that he was not giving away the secret of his life. I could get nothing out of him. I discovered by touching on safe current topics that he knew literally nothing of events: his hazy opinions of the world were gathered from the pieces of newspaper in which people sometimes gave him food.

When we came to the outskirts of Winchester he caught sight of another shabby figure ahead, and began to hurry.

'I don't wanter miss my beer,' he mumbled.

'Your beer?' I said. 'You can't get beer now; it's not yet ten o'clock.'

'I can get beer all right,' he told me, 'as long as those blinkin' —— [he was a nasty-mouthed old man] don't swill it all down first!'

We came to a lane that led to the Itchen, and at the end of the lane was a lovely grey gatehouse leading to a courtyard, beyond which stood a second gateway framing a gracious picture of green trees and old greystone buildings – rather like the Charterhouse.

Round the porter's hatchway at this second gate were two or three seedy-looking men, drinking out of horn mugs and eating dry white bread. My unpleasant old friend hurried up, pushed through the group, rapped on the door, which was opened by an aged porter, and said:

'Gimme the wayfarer's dole!'

Immediately the porter handed out a horn full of ale and a big slice of white bread.

'Won't you offer me the wayfarer's dole?' I asked.

The porter put his head out.

'We never offer the wayfarer's dole,' he replied. 'You have to ask for it.'

'Well, please give me the wayfarer's dole!'

Promptly appeared his hand, holding a horn of ale and a slice of bread.

I went in through the gateway to the Hospital of St Cross.

If souls in heaven gain any pleasure from looking through the golden bars to earth, men like old Thomas Sutton, who planted the Charterhouse in Smithfield, and men like that much more distant philanthropist, Bishop Henry de Blois, the grandson of William the Conqueror, who planted this hospice of St Cross in Hampshire, must feel an overwhelming happiness. The seed has grown and borne fruit century after century. Time, which wrecks the greatest monuments, has left such works unchanged – good deeds still shedding kindness in the world.

In the year 1136 Henry de Blois founded the Hospital of St Cross to shelter 'thirteen poor men, feeble and so reduced in strength that they can hardly or with difficulty support themselves without another's aid'. They were to be provided 'with garments and beds suitable to their infirmities, good wheaten bread daily of the weight of 5 marks, and three dishes at dinner and one at supper suitable to the day, and drink of good stuff'. The hospital was also to give food and drink to poor wanderers who came to its gates.

This has been going on for seven hundred and ninety years. The hospital still retains its ancient charter and its buildings. The poor Brethren of St Cross are still sheltered by the ancient walls; the poor men still come from the King's highway and are not refused.

St Cross is the oldest almshouse in England.

Such places are so steeped in the peace of unhurried years that they seem out of the world: you feel that the worries of life have ceased at the gates. On the west side of the lawns stand the houses of the Brethren, distinguished by tall chimneys, each house containing, like those of the

Carthusians, two rooms, a pantry, and a garden. Over the smooth grass, in the shadow of the gracious grey stones, walk the ancient Brethren of St Cross, each one in a long gown, with a silver cross worn on his breast. When a Brother dies his silver cross is cut from his gown and placed on a red velvet cushion, which is placed over his heart in the coffin. Then it is removed, and the Master of St Cross fastens it on the gown of the next Brother, thus admitting him into the hospital.

'There's a waiting list as long as your arm,' said a smiling old Brother. 'We are very lucky to end our days here. Would you care to see the church?'

We went into one of the finest Transition-Norman churches I have ever seen: a calm, majestic, splendidly proportioned church, with great stone columns down the nave, vast as giant oak trunks. When the church was restored recently traces of colour were found on the stones, and this colour has been renewed. The church is a mass of geometric patterns in red and blue and yellow. It was painted in 1866 and the colours used reproduce those discovered beneath the limewash which at that time covered the church. Few people, so the Brother told me, like this colouring, but I do: it has brought the church to life in an amazing way; there is nothing cold and unclothed about it.

The Brethren's Hall, where, for centuries, old men have eaten their 'mortrell' of 'was-tell' and milk, or herring pie and, sometimes, 'plum broth', not forgetting, of course, their 'galiones' of small beer, is a building which dignifies the word charity. A study of charity through the ages is a good subject for a man with the taste to write it; and in this hall we are in touch with an age which gave nobly and gladly. Side by side with hideous cruelty and callousness existed this pious love for 'the poor of Christ'. There is a raised hearth in the centre of the hall round which the Brethren gathered at a charcoal fire. At one end of the room is a delicious gallery in which the minstrels played on great occasions.

When passing through the gateway on my way out, I stopped to talk to the porter about the wayfarer's dole.

'Every day,' he said, 'we give away two gallons of beer and two loaves of bread, divided into thirty-two portions. It's just a snack, but a very old one, for it goes back over seven hundred years.'

About thirty wayfarers – mostly tramps who appreciate the horn of ale – receive the dole each day.

In the lane I met a tramp hurrying along with an anxious face.

'It's all right,' I shouted. 'You're in time!'

And I thought what a strange sight it would be could one assemble all the men, and the women too, who have hurried down that lane with empty stomachs in nearly eight centuries of wayfaring.

9

I was bowling down the hill, thinking not of women but of spare wheels, when I found myself heading for a small stone bridge on which a girl was leaning, gazing, like Melisande, into the water. On the steep slope of the bridge a small but stubborn motor-car had coughed, sighed, and stopped. Now I must explain to you that it was a magic morning: the rain had ceased; the sun was warm; the trees were well furnished with singing birds, and a rich, gentle happiness lay smoothly over the world.

I wondered, in the second at my disposal, what to do. If, I argued, that girl happened to be leaning over the bridge because she liked watching the water go past, she would consider me impertinent if I offered to help her on the assumption that her car had broken down. If, on the other hand, I argued, her car really had broken down and she was hating the water as it went past, she might hate me if I also went past; she would certainly consider me a boor. Fortunately I had no time to decide whether it is better to be considered impertinent or boorish, for the girl, in the amazing way women have of settling life's little uncertainties, stepped out into the middle of the road and held up her hand, just like a policeman.

I stopped.

She smiled.

I smiled.

She smiled again.

I cut off the engine and raised my hat.

'Could you,' she said, flickering her eyes in a way she knew was fascinating (and had probably practised in a mirror), 'could you lend me half a pint of petrol?'

She was distinctly charming, especially when she flickered. She was wearing a small brown hat into which a diamanté arrow had been shot by an unerring Bond Street jeweller. She was neat as a doe, and rather deer-like in a brown tweed costume – with speckly stockings ending in brogues. A tight string of small pearls was round her neck, and her blouse was tangerine colour.

As soon as she asked for half a pint of petrol I was immensely relieved: I was as relieved as most knights-errant were, I am sure, in days of the older romance, when, on examining the maiden in distress, they saw no trace behind her of a large and unpleasant dragon, but were requested merely to free a skirt from a bramble or to chase away a toad.

You see, I had visualized the dragon: I had seen myself plunged in the entrails of that small but stubborn car, pretending, for such, under a woman's eyes, is the terrible vanity of man, to be a mechanic, blundering round its interior with a careless and ignorant spanner; and probably cutting myself, losing my temper, swearing, and doing something quite serious and expensive to that small but stubborn machine.

But half a pint of petrol. . . .

'I could not *lend* you half a pint of petrol,' I said sternly. (And she said 'Oh!' just as I wanted her to.) 'But,' I continued, 'I could, and will, *give* you two gallons.'

When I had said this it seemed to me, looking at her, that two gallons was a miserable quantity: I should have said — how does it go?

Two pints one quart,
Four quarts one gallon,
Nine gallons one firkin,
Eighteen gallons one kilderkin,
Thirty-six gallons one barrel. . . .

I should have said:

'Allow me to give you a barrel of it, or at least — for I have a long way yet to go — a mere firkin!'

However, as I clambered out over the side, feeling rather paltry, I heard her say:

'Oh, but really I couldn't!'

I looked at her.

'Really,' she said (and those eyes flickered three times), 'I couldn't accept it — really I couldn't.'

I knew that she could and that she would, so I unlimbered the tin and advanced on the bonnet of the small bath-like car.

'Honestly, I can't accept it, you know,' she said.

A thrush joined in:

'Silly ass, silly ass, silly ass!' it said.

'Hear that?'

'What?' she asked.

'The bird!'

'You must let me pay you for it?'

'Nonsense,' I replied; and gurgle-gurgle went the two gallons into the small but thirsty car. The deed was done!

She had been to a Point-to-Point, I think, because there was a shooting-stick in the car. . . .

'How much is petrol?' she asked (flicker, flicker), groping in a bag.

'I honestly forget.'

'Oh, but *do* tell me.'

I wanted to say:

'Lady, the essence of chivalry is the joy of performing a

24

service for an entire sex – your sex, of course – because had you been a man I would have called you a glaring ass to travel on a dry tank and have charged you double. Also, had you worn spectacles, been spotty, or possessed rabbit teeth or legs like a Norman nave, I would still with almost the same alacrity have given you two gallons of petrol. The fact that you are utterly delicious and can flicker your eyes so charmingly adds pleasure without altering the ethics of this act.'

What I really said was:

'Forget it, please do! It's nothing really!'

'It's too sweet of you!' she said, with a flicker, closing the bag.

What I wanted to say then, with a bow, was:

'Lady, I do not wish you to feel under any obligation to me, neither am I a garage, so I will not take money from you; but it has been a privilege since chivalry elevated you to the pinnacle from which you try so hard now and then to descend for us to look after you. Really it is I who am in your debt. Don't take away the warm and unusual glow of feeling that I am really a member of the stronger sex.'

What I really said was:

'Well, are you all right?'

'Quite, thanks!' she replied with a flicker. Such blue eyes!

'Topping day!'

'Too marvellous!'

'Well – goodbye, and good luck.'

'Bye-bye and – thanks most awfully!'

She flickered adorably three times, and then the stubborn little tin bath shot over the bridge, and she was gone. I waited a while before I started off along the same road.

What is Romance? Surely it is just feeling that things are a bit more marvellous than they are, women more beautiful, yourself braver, the grass a sharper green. . . .

'Silly ass, silly ass, silly ass!' said the thrush.

'Thank you,' I whispered. 'That was very good of you.'

CHAPTER TWO

I explore the Nunnery at Romsey, watch a liner leave for America, lose myself in the New Forest, talk about ghosts in an abbey, and attend a Point-to-Point

I

ROMSEY, in the magic county of Hampshire, is the ideal small market town. Lord Palmerston, with bronze hair turned green by years of rain, stands importantly on a plinth in the market-place; a policeman in an easier attitude stands near him; there is a full cake-shop opposite; everything is slowed down to a reasonable pace; men in leggings stand on the kerbstone with the expressions of deep thinkers; now and then a man and a cow cross the square.

A little distance from the road, standing back among trees is Broadlands, the big white house that once belonged to Palmerston; and over Romsey broods a mellow restfulness as if the place has done its bit in nineteenth-century politics and is now content to retire from all kind of passion.

Overshadowing all, as in so many similar little English towns, is the weathered bulk of the great grey nunnery built in Saxon times, destroyed by the Danes, rebuilt in 1130, and bought by the citizens of Romsey (good judges of a bargain) for £100 when Henry VIII collected the Dissolution windfall.

All typical of England, from Palmerston with his green head, the town constable, the cow, to the grey abbey with its feet in the Heptarchy.

I was sitting on the churchyard rails, looking through a feathery green screen of new elm leaves at the Norman clerestory windows, the squat grey tower, and the weather-cock on which, says Romsey, a jackdaw perches whenever it is going to rain. (The bird must be tired out, for I looked in vain for it!)

Three small girls in white pinafores were nursing dolls in

26

the graveyard; a butcher's boy in a blue pinafore cycled past with mutton, and down the elm walk there came an elderly man holding a posy of wallflowers in his right hand. We talked together, first of history and then of life. He was a churchwarden. I was surprised to learn that he is seventy-six years of age. There was nothing to indicate it, and his pale blue eyes showed pleasure when I told him, quite sincerely, that I would have put him down as fifty-five.

'And never a day's illness in my life!' he said. 'I don't feel seventy-six. I'm happy – perhaps that's why! I think the secret of health, and of living as long as I have lived, is a contented mind.'

'You have, of course,' I said, 'never had to run to catch a bus!'

He smiled:

'It is quiet here,' he replied. 'Very peaceful! Nothing much ever happens. Come round the church: it is shut really, but I can take you in.'

We went down the elm avenue together.

Here, in a grey light reflected from old stone, in the splendid strength of Norman pillar and rounded arch (if you love Norman architecture, see this abbey), in this cold hush, I met a lady, the Lady Ethelflæda, third Abbess of Romsey. They tell beautiful stories about her. They say that she was so holy that clothed only in darkness she would steal out of the abbey to stand naked in a stream near by till she had recited the psalms of the day.

That, I think, is as pretty a story as the one Coventry tells about Lady Godiva.

She was rewarded as she deserved to be. One night as she was reading the lesson to her nuns in church, the candle flames shook and went out, but she continued to read by a pale, soft light that shone from the tips of her fingers. That, too, is a lovely picture. It is difficult to imagine this holy lady in the grip of a financial crisis, but legend says that once, having been entrusted with a large sum of money, she was suddenly filled with compassion for the poor and with brimming eyes gave it all away, although not hers to give. When the day of settlement arrived she fell on her knees in prayer and lo! the empty bags filled again . . . fortunate, holy Ethelflæda . . .

One night drama, very near to tragedy, came to Romsey.

William, the Red King, who, it is well known, was a most unpleasant person, knew that if he married Ædgyth, the beautiful Saxon princess then in the wardship of the abbess of Romsey, he would strengthen Norman rule in England by linking the new monarchy with the old. So one night there was a great waving of torches and a clatter of hooves on the cobbles; and up rode the Red King, ready to take the girl. The abbess, who had no intention of giving up her ward, hurriedly dressed the princess in a nun's habit and told her to kneel at an altar.

The King was received. The abbess told him that the girl whom he wished to marry had taken vows of chastity and now belonged to Christ. Through the dim colonnade he walked, and we can imagine how the knees at the altar trembled as his steps came up the nave! Pausing at a chapel, the Red King saw a young nun bent in prayer, and he walked out of the church and rode away.

There is in Romsey Abbey, in a locked box, a tress of auburn hair. It was found during excavations in the year 1839 in a leaden coffin of Saxon date under the floor of the south aisle near the abbess's door. The coffin was otherwise empty and the hair had been placed in a box of oak that rested upon a wooden stand. What, I wonder, is the story? How often a mystery like that hangs in the mind when the greatest monuments in a church have faded from remembrance.

The Norman stone still stands, grey and lovely, in Romsey Abbey. In the little whisperings and creakings that go on when an old church has shut its doors you can fancy old memories are stirring, so that you almost expect to meet Ædgyth, pale and trembling, or holy Ethelflæda, cloaked like Monna Vanna, going to her cold bath with a psalm book.

We came out, the old warden and I, into the elm grove, very silent.

2

I stood on the Bar Gate at Southampton and looked down over the town of Sir Bevis. It was a clear morning. There was a bustle along the narrow streets. The tramcars went past beneath the gate, clearing it as by a miracle, and in the air was the nearness of great ships.

As I stood there trying to trace the line of the ancient walls I thought: 'Shall I write about the Lion Heart who sailed from Southampton in 1189; or about the *Speedwell* and the *Mayflower* which set off to found Broadway a little later; or about that last most glorious of Southampton epics when the long troop-trains came in, one after the other, that August night in 1914, before most people knew of the thing that was to change our lives and our thoughts?'

What a puzzle it is to write a few words about a town in which every stone tells a story.

So I went down, and towards the docks, still wondering, thinking about the giant Ascupart whose painted figure rests in the Bar Gate with that of Sir Bevis, and about God's House (or the Hospice of St Julian) which holds another different story. Then on the quayside at Southampton I came upon a live drama: the thing at the very heart of this town.

An Atlantic liner lay at the dockside. Over the gangways swarmed porters carrying luggage. Men shouted and cleared a space as the huge cranes swung round lifting piles of cabin trunks. There was the throb of imminent departure. Men looked at watches. Each second had its value. Smoke came from the funnels of the monster whose bulk was lifted above me, deck piled on deck. The sides of this ship were like the side of a cliff. From the high portholes gazed here and there a face like the face of a caveman looking down into a valley.

Someone shouted my name from the top of the mountain. Looking up, I saw a rich man known to me.

'Get a pass and come aboard!' he shouted.

In a few minutes I was sitting in a dove-grey boudoir like the reception-room of an exceptionally famous actress (only tidier), which this man called his cabin. He had an oxidized bed. A door led to a marble bathroom of the latest design full of oxidized taps and gadgets, cold showers and hot showers. He had paid £200 for all this.

'A sailor's life is a hard one,' I suggested.

'Pity you can't come over,' he said, with an idiot disregard of time and duty which is characteristic of those unhappy people with too much money.

We went on a tour of inspection down endless paint-smelling corridors. He told me how many yards long they were, but I have forgotten. We went into a vast palm lounge, into a dining-room bigger than the dining-room of any hotel, into a swimming pool, into a gymnasium full of electric horses, camels, rowing boats, cycles and machines designed to pommel the horrid stomachs of fat men. (I would like to have interviewed Columbus in this ship.)

Gold lifts shot up and down. Stewards ran here and there. Dazed-looking passengers wandered about wondering how they had taken the wrong turning and if they would ever find the way back to their cabins.

My friend, who is swiftly bored, left me: and I went down and down into the bowels of this grotesque hotel.

Hundreds of men and women in shabby clothes were huddled together with bundles, bags, boxes. They were like a herd of scared cattle. There were Irish, English, Jews, and Italians; whole families with all their possessions packed in a box setting out to make a new start in life – the steerage!

There is no more heart-aching sight than this in any country. It seemed to me that the gold lounges upstairs were a crazy dream, and that here in the unseen, neglected, unthought-of lower deck I had touched the reality. Some of these people were dumb and dazed; others were voluble and excited. No body of people could have looked less like adventurers, and yet – think of this adventure of theirs: starting again in a strange country, making a new beginning, taking a second throw in the gamble of life.

A girl opened a paper bag and gave a sandwich to an old man, obviously her father. She put her arm round him, and he patted her hand as it lay on his shoulder.

I knew that there would be hysterical laughter and tears in this place soon. . . .

A siren blew.

'Visitors on shore, please!'

The great ship was ready to cross the Atlantic.

I met my friend near the restaurant.

'I don't feel hungry,' he said sadly. An orchestra was tuning up.

The purser was smoothing down a ruffled woman who had, it seemed, lost a whole bathroom which she had paid for. On the gangway stood a man and a girl with that pale, insecure smile of parting trembling on their lips.

'Goodbye!' he said. 'Write a bit each day and post it from New York.'

The siren blew again. A ship's officer shouted. The girl dabbed her eyes with a handkerchief and smiled. The young man walked down the gangway, and I knew – remembering ancient agonies – that he felt the ship to be an inhuman monster dragging her away from him; that every blast of the siren was like a burst of devil's laughter, and that the endless miles between them began as soon as his foot touched shore. A mile or so above, her tiny white face looked down at him, and I felt sorry for both of them.

The siren laughed again with fiendish hoots; and slowly – so slowly – the ship moved with two tugs beneath her great bows.

The inch between her and the dockside widened to a

yard. From the point of view of parted lovers she was now already in New York! The young man stood there with a white face watching, as in the slow, drawn-out agony the liner found her way inch by inch into Southampton Water. Twice he tried to leave the spot, but could not.

I stood beside him, entirely in sympathy, thinking of those poor, forgotten ones and their pathetic bundles, wondering whether they were laughing, crying, or praying as the great ship moved to sea. . . .

A telegraph boy stood on the quay with his fist full of undelivered envelopes and his eyes, following the liner, full of injury and resentment. He was as ridiculous as a frog feeling annoyed about a volcano. But he whistled, jumped to his bicycle, and pedalled back with his bundle of pink farewells into the grey Town of Goodbye which men call Southampton.

3

Here, in Beaulieu – they pronounce it Bewley – nothing happens or, it seems, could happen except the coming and going of the tide in the river, the budding and the falling of the leaves, the rising and the setting of the sun and the moon. . . .

This is a strange, lonely place in the middle of the last of England's great forests. I am inclined to think that it is one of the strangest places I know. The people are slow Saxons, well-mannered, deferential people, with their wits about them and their tongues padlocked. Their ancestors most wisely took to cover when William Rufus came crashing through the bracken in search of the stag which – as you remember – led to a grave. They are still good at taking cover behind the barriers of their reticence. The place, like the people, encourages a delicious slowness. You feel that London with all its fret is not quite so important in the ultimate scheme of things as Mr Smith's new litter of pigs;

and it seems to you, as you lean against a fence in a portentous silence, that those things which men break their hearts upon are not worth so much in the long run as the sight of the moon tangled up in the boughs of a young birch wood. Heresy, of course!

It would be fatal to stay too long in Beaulieu; you would wish for nothing better than to lean over Mr Smith's pigsty or to stand by the mill-stream and watch the stars grow bright in the evening.

I have been wondering, in the spell of this village, whether it is possible for the odour of Sanctuary to cling to a place.

This tiny hamlet with its magnificent abbey ruin was from 1204 till 1539 one of the chief places in England to which the murderer, the thief, the plotter, and the general fugitive from justice flew literally for his life. Once within the wall no one could touch him: 'the peace of the Church' was over him like a shield, and the sheriff might bang on the great gates as loud as Judgement Day and the knights might ride round the wall for as long as they liked with their swords drawn, but the fox had gone to holy earth; he was as safe as though he had never sinned!

Through the Middle Ages, Beaulieu must have entertained one of the world's record assemblies of rogues and vagabonds; men who dared not take one step outside the walls. The white monks farmed the land and fished the river, singing High Mass every day in the lovely abbey church; and I suppose no one was startled or excited at so usual a sight as that of a man on a winded horse riding full tilt at the gate to join this queer brotherhood of the hunted. I imagine that the Abbot of Beaulieu owned a visitors' book rather like Scotland Yard's file of wanted faces!

All that remains of this old storm is a tall ruin in the light of that same moon on the banks of that same river. The evil seems to have gone from Beaulieu, but the feeling of Sanctuary remains: the feeling – it may seem a strange thing to say – that 'the peace of the Church' is still over the fields, making something more than solitude.

I thought in this way one evening when the tide was going out and the sun was setting. It was low in the west behind trees, lost in a blaze of sudden, unexpected splendour.

There were two layers of cloud, one low and moving, the other high and stationary. The low clouds were indigo blue and stormy; the high a soft, apricot pink colour. The west was burning with gold light, and the edges of the dark clouds were etched with thin lines of fire. The pageant moved, changed . . . the river against the sun was a sheet of dull silver on which a jet-black duck moved noiselessly; a swan, silhouetted as if cut in black paper, swam with his neck beneath the water; a wind came fretting the river, blowing a handful of pale blossoms into the grass. The hush of evening deepened. I could hear a dog barking far away; and the words of two men talking over a lichened wall were clear as bells.

Yes, said one, his garden could do with a week of sun, that it could. . . .

Click! went his spade against a pebble.

The water shivered in the fretful wind, the gold in the sky deepened and dulled; above it extended a pearly greyness, not so much the death of light as the birth of a new, unearthly light. . . .

There is one moment at sunset in the country when the whole visible world seems to gather itself in prayer, and it seems to you strange that men should move on unconscious of this with spades over their shoulders, instead of falling on their knees in the grass; for in that hush, in that benediction of seconds before the first star shines, the universe seems waiting for a revelation, as if the clouds might part and Man know something of his destiny. . . .

Lights shine in windows, there is the sound of steps on the road, someone laughs loudly, night falls, and – the dream is gone.

4

On a sunny afternoon there is no place known to me in which you would be more likely to see a ghost in daylight than the ruins of Beaulieu Abbey. But it would not be a horrid spectre; it would be a pleasant lay brother walking to the ruins of the laundry with a basket over his arm, or sauntering slowly in the direction of the kitchen carrying a platter of shelled peas, stopping to steal one and to wiggle a stone from the toe of his sandals. It is a quiet place, full of kind ghosts.

Tall trees lean from soft grass, and little blue flowers grow in clumps from the ruined cloisters. There is a colony of primroses over the walls of the chapter-house. When the sunlight slants from the grey stone walls the air becomes lazy with the drone of bees. Perhaps the most ghostly thing of all is the field in which the abbey church once stood. Henry VIII allowed the monks' building to remain, but he ordered the church to be pulled down, so that not one stone stands upon another; yet the shape of the great abbey remains in a field. In this green meadow you instinctively raise your hat, for it still seems holy ground. There is a huge cross in the grass, the arms formed by the site of the transepts. A little path like a sheep-track, only dead straight, runs up the centre of that which was the nave, leading to a wooden cross, where the high altar of the King's Beaulieu once rose blue in incense.

What a spectre of a church: the sky its vault, the thrush in a yew-tree its choir; the dews of night its benediction.

I am told that the villagers of Beaulieu believe the place to be haunted, and that no one sits out among the ruins when they have a dance in the Domus, or dormitory of the monks, which is now used as a kind of parish hall. I heard it said that the vicar, who has looked after the soul of Beaulieu for over thirty years, is on excellent terms with the spirits of certain Cistercians; but that, of course, may be gossip.

The one person who ought to know is Miss Aimée Cheshire, a young woman who lives alone in the ruins of the abbey. She occupies a vast, dark, oak-beamed stone room, with a bedroom above, in the ruins of the old dormitory. She has electric light in the large room, or I think that even she would be hard put to it to spend a night there with candlelight shaking over the stone walls and making the blackness deeper. When night falls the abbey is locked up: Miss Cheshire is as sundered from the world as if she were in the middle of the desert. She looks through her deep, stone windows upon the moonlit cloisters, with dark shapes of the yews lying over the grass; the stone walls shine in the moonlight, the vaulted arches rise up fractured; the grass and the wallflowers stand like black hair growing on the top of tumbled walls. She is alone with seven hundred years; three hundred and thirty-five of them – from 1204 till 1539 – years of active life within the ruins, years not of quiet prayer, but years of storm and sin; as I have said, the Abbey of Beaulieu opened its arms to all sinners, except, of course, those guilty of heresy or sacrilege.

'And you are never nervous here alone?' I asked Miss Cheshire.

'No,' she replied. 'Not now. Two years ago, when I decided to live here, people begged me to have someone to keep me company on the first night, but I refused. I knew that if I funked the first night I would funk the first week; then, of course, it would be all up with me.'

We sat in the big monastic room, the little lead-paned windows bright with sun and flowers, a tame robin, flirting his tail and his head on one side, perched on top of a screen.

'Few women would dare to live alone here. You only require to be a bit run down to imagine things.'

'Things do happen, of course,' said Miss Cheshire in a matter-of-fact voice, 'but I won't have anything to do with them. I just turn over and go to sleep.'

'What sort of things?'

'Well, I often hear steps and the sound of a key in the night. The monks used to sleep here in cells, and someone used to come and awaken them in the small hours to sing

36

matins. Several people, when in these rooms, have heard a choir singing: it comes not very often, sometimes by day and sometimes by night, as if one had "tuned-in" to something – if you know what I mean. But, as I say, I won't become interested in it, because I do not think it right, and I know so many people who have ruined their health in spiritualist inquiries.'

'You – forgive me – don't imagine things?'

'No, I am not the kind of person to imagine things. If I did, living here all alone as I do, I would see things, or imagine I did, and that would be the end of such peace of mind as I possess. The singing of the monks has been heard by two friends of mine who came to scoff. It came on suddenly while we were sitting here one night after dinner, and I said nothing in order to see which one of them would hear it first, or if they would hear it at all. Oh, yes, they heard it. . . .'

The robin flew across the room, jumping me, I admit, for it was eerie to sit listening to this woman in this room talking in such cold blood about the other world.

'I have put my piano over there by that old window,' she said, 'because of a very vivid dream. That window was the window of the cell of a Brother Ambrosius, who was a musician.'

Saying goodbye, I walked down a flight of old stone steps into the monks' walk with the feeling that if I slept alone in Beaulieu Abbey, I would see and hear much more than Miss Cheshire claims to have done. But only for one night, because I would hate to be awakened for matins.

5

The port of the little kingdom of Beaulieu is some three miles south along Beaulieu River; and it is called Buckler's Hard.

Buckler is the name of a man who lived there centuries ago, and Hard refers to the character of the river bank in this locality. Now, when you enter Buckler's Hard you feel at once the queer atmosphere which clings to a place in which men have expended great energy; the village seems to be resting after effort. The street, as wide as Regent Street, is only one hundred yards long! It ends, as if cut off suddenly, in green hummocks and mounds on which cattle graze.

Below this single street standing among fields, the ground falls gently to the banks of the Beaulieu River. The stream is wide at full tide, and at low exposes a great tract of shallow, reedy bank. Beyond the river, wood lies piled on wood to the sky-line.

When you walk beside the river you notice once again that evidence of a dead village buried under grass. Here are more green hummocks and mounds. Great timbers go down into the water, rotting and covered with weed. In the field are gigantic dips and hollows full of lush grass and flowers.

In those dips and on those rotting slipways once rested the stout oak-built ships which helped to found the British Empire. This unknown, forgotten village in Hampshire was once loud with the sound of forge hammers, here thousands of great oak trees were formed into ships of the line; and into the water of Beaulieu River was launched in 1781 the *Agamemnon*, a 64-gun ship of 1,384 tons burden, in which Nelson lost his right eye at the siege of Calvi.

The history of Buckler's Hard is, apart from its interest as a dead village which played its part in Empire, well worth telling; for it shows how swiftly time and fate can alter a place.

One hundred and fifty years ago, John, Duke of Montagu, then lord of the manor, owned the sugar-producing island of St Vincent in the West Indies. His manor was stocked with fine oak trees, and his little port of Buckler's Hard was a free harbour – a legacy inherited from the old abbots of Beaulieu. What prevented his land from becoming a great centre of West Indian trade?

John Montagu, a keen business man, thought it would be a fine thing could he steal a little of the shipbuilding trade from Southampton and transplant it to Buckler's Hard. He already had oak there and ironworks at Sowley Pond. All he required were shipbuilders. He got them. He offered quay frontages on a ninety-nine years' lease, at a yearly rent of six and eightpence! For every house erected he gave three loads of timber. The noble duke used to stride the hill and rejoice in the sound of the builders' men; for the dream of his life was to create a great seaport in this sheltered wilderness, and he rechristened the village Montagu Town.

Henry Adams, the veteran shipbuilder, settled here, and soon the country was loud with hammers knocking against the wooden walls of England.

Between 1745 and 1808 about forty-four men-of-war were built and launched at Buckler's Hard. Here were built the *Agamemnon*, the *Swiftsure*, and the *Euryalus*, whose guns thundered at the battle of Trafalgar.

When a ship was launched, this now desolate little village was the scene of great excitement. Sometimes as many as ten thousand came from far and near to see the launching. Many came in tumbrels and farm wagons. Scaffolds were erected, and the great crowd waited – the ship on the slipway – watching for the tide to become full. It must have been an amazing sight: one bank of the little river buzzing with life and colour, the other peaceful and green, the woods stretching to the horizon. Then there would be shouting, 'Off she goes – off she goes!' and a big 74-gun man-of-war would move slowly to the water with a band playing 'God Save the King'.

The wooden children of Buckler's Hard found their way about the world, and they discovered in their travels plenty of fighting. They carried the Union Jack into every quarrel that was going, their great keels cut foreign waters and met the French on every sea.

John, Duke of Montagu, who died at his house in Privy Gardens in 1749, five years after the hammers came to

Buckler's Hard, went to Heaven with the belief, perhaps, that in Montagu Town he had founded another Portsmouth.

Time stepped in.

The wooden walls gave place to the iron, the sail to the funnel. Gradually fewer and fewer ships were launched in Beaulieu River. Swift as had been the rise of the village, as swift was its fall. Its old name came back; and now the grass has come back; the wildfowl cries where once the caulking hammer sounded, and the heron perches on the great oak pathways from which ships of the line stepped majestically into our naval history. . . .

A ghostly place! When the last slipway cracks and falls into the water I would like to think that some old native will see, faint as if spun in mist on Beaulieu River, a gallant ship, her sails glimmering, her colours shot to shreds, come creeping home to Buckler's Hard to fade like a night fog into the English grass which gave her birth.

6

We will attend that characteristic event of an English spring – a hunt Point-to-Point.

It is afternoon. It has stopped raining, and the sun has come out; so has the entire country. Those lonely mansions set upon a hill, or lying snug in woods, which six days out of seven appear dead prove to be inhabited by colonels, majors, Sir Alfred This and Lord That. It is a startling coming-to-life. The recently desolate roads are alive with limousines – luncheon baskets on top, the girls inside, and the major driving – and in a side-lane opposite the gate leading to Farmer Sweetbread's field stands the village bobby, hot and bothered, tied up with Fords and Rolls-Royces, to say nothing of Lady Snatcher's hunter, Pinch o' Ginger, favourite for the Hunt Cup, who moves restlessly amid the mudguards with a mustard-coloured blanket on his back and a groom making soothing noises at his head.

A distracted yokel at the gate collects ten shillings from the gentry towards the restoration of Farmer Sweetbread's meadow as each car churns in over the muddy entrance and bumps through a sweet scent of bruised grass and daisies to the car park.

The clouds are big over the green backs of the hills: enormous sailing gold clouds; and there is a sharp wind. From the hill the country falls away into a crystal-clear patchwork of acres cut by sharp green hedges, with here and there little scarlet flags, which mark the course, fluttering in the wind.

On the hill overlooking the course the motor-cars are drawn up on the grass, and near them thirty bookmakers shout and bellow. Behind the bookmakers is an outraged-looking thatched cottage; to the left of the cottage shines a white marquee, the weighing-in tent, and opposite, behind rails, is the paddock.

Here is 'the county'.

The field is as rich in types as Piccadilly. There are old men with monocles and lined, sagging faces, like blood-hounds. They wear fawn bowlers, and smoke thin cheroots held between fingers in yellow gloves. They wear check clothes that would strike the observer dead in a city; the green grass seems to tone them down. There are still older men bent double, who cup their ears with a hand when addressed, and reply with an asthmatic cough:

'Oh, lord, yes . . . damn good horse! Look at his legs!'

Then there are young men, loose-limbed creatures, who are bred, not born; they are bred to ride horses, so that nature falls into line and fits them out with exactly the kind of legs you need to ride a horse. There is nothing but 'horse' in their minds, and when they die surely they become centaurs. Everybody's collar-bone has been broken.

Then the girls. Nowhere in the world will you see such trim, neat girls. They sit on shooting-sticks. They wear tweed clothes as perfectly as their brothers wear riding breeches. When quite young their noses have freckles. Most of them have the beauty that comes with health and simplicity, and they stride across a field magnificently, discussing 'fetlocks' and 'withers' with the man of their choice. They never hesitate at a fence; they are neat-limbed, lovely things. . . .

A flash of colour in the paddock!

Three young men in pink coats ride off over the fields to the starting-point.

'Good luck, sir,' says the groom.

'Thank you, Tom.'

"E'll win it!' says Tom to the chauffeur.

More riders trot out; the crowd streams away after them. . . .

Here they come! A line of horsemen rises and dips over the first brushwood jump; they take the second and disappear. Nothing happens for five minutes . . . ten . . . fifteen . . . twenty; then:

'Here they are! "Strike-me-Pink" leading. . . . No, no, it's "Harkaway". Come on, sir; come on "Harkaway"! Ride him; come on – oh, *bad* luck, he's down! – come on "Strike-me-Pink".'

Over the top of the big water-jump appears the head of a horse, there is a crackle of brushwood, a splash of water, a top-hat floating, a rider catching at the reins, then another horse – a flying horse that clears the jump and thunders to the winning post.

Now luncheon!

The colonel superintends the spreading of an oil sheet on the grass.

'Come on, you gals. Dashed good race, what? Any feller here care for a gin and bitters? Good! John, where's the bottle? Who's that good-lookin' woman old Barrowdale's takin' around. A snorter, what? By Jove, what a rip-snorter!'

The 'gals' sit down. The feast begins. A tin sandwich box circulates.

'Anchovy underneath, chicken on top!'

A horse passes.

Everyone stops eating as at the approach of a god. It goes.

The colonel comes back to life:

'Good-lookin' woman old B.'s cartin' about. . . . I've got a treat for you, my children!'

He goes to the car and comes back with a bottle of sloe gin and a plum-cake.

'Dashed good-looker, that woman!' he mutters. 'I say, any feller got a corkscrew?'

And over the hill the big gold clouds wheel and change pattern slowly; dropping away to a green sky line, the fields, sharply cut in the sunlight, lie cosily between hedges. . . .

Old Sir Timothy Heavy walks past, still on his crutch. Bad luck! He missed two of the best runs of the season, and – oh, bad luck! – they say he will never be able to hunt again.

He might as well be dead. . . .

Poor old Tim.

CHAPTER THREE

Tells how I was waylaid at Christchurch, how the sun rose at Stonehenge, how George III's bath lies in a Weymouth garden, and how I climbed up into the cradle of London. I meet an American at Exeter, sit on Plymouth Hoe, and watch the making of a battleship at Devonport

I

BOURNEMOUTH puzzles me. I have looked at the smooth, sunny sea and I have been worried; I have admired the gardens in the same frame of mind; also the pear, with the usual fringe of strong men smoking pipes near lines which once every three hours become attached to an infantile plaice the size of a postcard. Confound it! What is it about Bournemouth that eludes me?

I have looked at the up-to-date shops; the neat arcades; the retired colonels in their retired gardens; the massed bands of the brigade of tulips – for Bournemouth is ruled by gardeners – the girls who walk up the cliffs and down the cliffs; the old people who sit in Bath-chairs drawn by ponies, and . . . what on earth is nagging at me? Something I cannot quite grasp.

I have motored up the hills to Boscombe and to Branksome, and I have seen the astonishing growth of Bournemouth, which involves the murder of the pines. One by one the scented high woods are marked down as desirable building plots, so that if Bournemouth does not wish to relinquish one of her proudest boasts she will soon have to make it a penal offence to kill a pine tree.

But – what is this vague, mental toothache of mine?

I was sitting on a seat watching a small boy sail a boat on the modest little Bourne which tinkles through the Pleasure Gardens. He wore a grey shirt and short grey trousers, and a floppy grey hat, and he held a stick. He was dying to take

44

off his shoes and become beautifully wet, but a nurse sat within disciplinary distance, hemming a pillow-slip.

Whenever I see a small boy sail a boat I long to join in. I can never see him without wondering whether boys still have the heavenly time with boats that I have had. As I watched him I remembered how once I built a small island in the middle of a rain-water tank on top of a stables, and there I marooned (with every modern comfort) two delightful mice, saved from the murderous hands of the gardener.

Each morning a grey clockwork gunboat would leave for the island, bearing cheese and bread. The mice would come to the water's edge and tuck in. By splashing the water it was often possible to dislodge the gunboat from land and send the exiles for a short circular tour round the tank and back home again. There were lush forests of grass on this sugar-box island, and marvellous caves of mud, through whose fastnesses, as I hung over the tank with torn trousers, I followed them in a million great adventures. How I longed to shrink myself to the size of a tin soldier and go out with the food-ship to Mouse Island, there to swap yarns with the two explorers and to wander with them in green jungles! I tried to colonize a frog to be a kind of faithful hound, but the frog had more ambitious ideas and must have leapt the galvanized boundary into a wider world.

(If the little grey boy with the boat, I thought, prods it in my direction I will push it back and make friends, and no doubt he will like me to show him how to build a harbour of stones.)

That did it!

I recalled this Bournemouth memory.

Twenty-four years ago a nurse said to a horrid, scrubby little boy in this town, 'Now, for goodness' sake, Master Henry, don't put any more candles on it or it'll sink!' and I remember this boy sticking thin twisted green and red Christmas-tree candles all over a big grey destroyer which was to take part in the children's illuminated regatta on this very stream.

I walked down with the big grey ship beneath my arm; and I recall the still, hot August night in these gardens with not a breath moving the dark trees, the red glow from Chinese lanterns and fairy lamps over the flushed faces of other children as they leaned above the spangled waters to their twinkling craft. They gave me a prize for this grey ship, for I made a harbour of stones for it, and an Eddystone light on the tallest; and there it lay at anchor, a proud, lovely thing. It was the first prize I had pulled out of life, and I have forgotten what it was; but I remember the pride of it and the dreadful thing I did in the stillness of that night, when, stretching my hand from bed, I felt the grey ship on a chair beside me, and, getting up, took the night-light, and lit the last candle, sitting up in ecstasy to watch it splash in green grease and gutter on the deck.

I felt a sudden tenderness for Bournemouth, for all the old people in Bath-chairs, for the discreet gardens and the shaven lawns and the tulips and the town clerk, the mayor and the corporation, even for old colonels with enlarged livers in enlarged check suits, and for all the bored married people of whom the hotels are full. . . .

Then, just as the grey little boy in the floppy hat was near me, and I thought how good it would be to put my arms round his thin, scraggy little body; just as I was preparing myself rather timidly to meet myself in him over twenty-four long years with a hearty 'That's a jolly fine boat of yours', the nurse – vile woman – locked her needle in the pillow-slip, removed her spectacles, said, 'Come along, Master John; it's time for lunch', and rose. He went away, striding conversationally beside her, a grey ship under his arm. . . .

So in the Pleasure Gardens of Bournemouth, where nothing out of the ordinary, it seems, could ever happen, a man met with a little grey ghost small enough to stand beneath his arm but big enough to fill his heart.

2

Fight as I may, I have never been able entirely to conquer the belief that women are in all situations honest. All men I suspect; all women I trust; for – I believe in living dangerously!

In Christchurch, near the Priory, is a short, narrow street full of tea-shops. It is so full of tea-shops that several charming waitresses and proprietresses – for this street seems entirely a feminine endeavour – picket the doors and say with a smile, if you appear to linger bunwards, 'Oh, wouldn't you like some tea?' And you think, 'Oh, probably I would!' and so you become deflected from the Priory. Goodness alone knows how many religious pilgrims have been lured to repletion in this street of the sirens.

I was walking on with a soul full of Norman transepts when a maiden stood before me and looked. She had the greyest eyes.

'Would you,' she said, 'like a lobster?'

I observed her closely and realized that she was serious. Behind her lay in negligent attitudes dozens of lobsters on a table among roses. It was 4.30 p.m. It had never occurred to me that people eat lobster at tea-time. In fact, there is to my mind something almost indecent about it. I was so embarrassed that I said 'Yes', whereupon, giving me no time to repent, in the manner of women, she picked up a big scarlet brute and disappeared, leaving me to slink miserably to a chintz chair, with a clammy foreboding of great evil.

'Tea?' she asked.

I made a feeble protest, but she assured me that China tea 'goes' with lobster. I wanted to ask whether this experiment had ever been tried before by man, but I was given no time. When the shell was empty some devil entered into me and urged me to reply 'Yes' to everything this girl said (and she was a good talker), with the result that basins of Dorset cream, pots of jam, puffy cakes oozing sweetness, ramparts of buns and crisp rolls became piled up behind the rose-bowl. The only thing I missed at this tea-party was the Mad Hatter.

We of London hear stories of West Country excesses: of creamy dawns and jammy eves. Was this, I reflected, an unofficial welcome to Dorset and Devon! I looked round to ask the hovering one, but she was outside luring a curate with a *langouste*.

I stood up heavily and strode out up the green avenue to the ancient Priory, feeling rather ashamed of myself.

Lobster and Dorset cream are not the right food for pilgrims. I believe the Crusades could have been stopped by a Dorsetshire tea. I found myself mooning round the Priory, wondering stupidly why they call it the 'richest' -- a most unpleasant word – Norman nave in England.

In one of the transepts – which are the poorest part of this lovely building – I found an elderly verger named Mr Hyde, who has for thirty-seven years been the custodian of Christchurch. He made me forget the orgy in the side street. As we walked round together he revived my enthusiasm for life. I discovered that during his career he has, so to speak, collected royalties and distinguished people. Half the crowned heads of Europe have visited this remote corner of Hampshire. In an old visitors' book he showed me the signature of the Kaiser in letters two inches high, and beneath it the name Louis Raemaekers. An interesting juxtaposition. How on earth did the War Lord and the man who was destined to do him so much harm with a pencil manage to sign the same page?

'It was like this,' explained Mr Hyde. 'In 1907 the ex-Kaiser, who was staying at Highcliffe Castle, near here, came with his suite. Every now and then the Kaiser would make some remark and turn to each member of the suite, and ask if he agreed with him, and the answer was always "Yes". He was interested in the curious carving in the choir under the misereres. One represents Richard III crowned. On either side the devil and the devil on a woolsack which,

I explained to him, was a satire on the Lord Chancellor of the period. The Kaiser turned to Prince von Bulow, then Chancellor of Germany, and repeated what I had said, adding some personal remark, for they both laughed heartily. The Kaiser then signed the visitors' book, and said he hoped to come again. It would be interesting,' reflected Mr Hyde slyly, 'to know what kind of a visit he had in his mind, for he signed his name in English!

'That was in 1907. During the war a man came here, and noticed the Kaiser's signature. He took out a pen. "If I might," he said, "I'd like to put my autograph close to his, because he is a friend of mine, and knows me very well!" I was curious! It was not usual for anyone to claim friendship with the Kaiser during the war, so I allowed him to do it! He wrote: "Louis Raemaekers", and there it is . . .'

We examined the Lepers' 'Squint' in the small chapel set apart for these poor outcasts in the Middle Ages, so that they might see the priest elevate the Host.

'When the King and Queen of Norway visited the church in 1887,' said Mr Hyde, 'they were interested in this. The King told me that his people were today suffering from a similar disease. He thought it must be the same kind of complaint. He knew that Christchurch is noted for salmon, and no doubt it was a common food in the district in the Middle Ages, and was the cause of a skin disease mistaken for leprosy. . . .'

At the back of the Priory, on the way down to the River Stour, I found one of the most delicious lanes I have seen in Hampshire. The trees formed a green gloom over it, and there were weathered grey stones and long green grass. . . .

On the way back through the narrow street a maiden stood before me and looked. She had the greyest eyes.

'Would you,' she said, 'like a lobster?'

I saw that she was still serious, and so was I. . . . I passed on down the street, looking neither to creamy left nor jammy right.

3

In the chill morning before sunrise I took the road out of Salisbury and made for Stonehenge. Inexpressibly remote those great stones seemed, standing up there in the faint light that was not the light of moon or sun but the spectral half-light that comes before day. I was reminded of Egypt. There is in this prehistoric circle the same carelessness for human labour that underlies the gigantic works of Egypt. It is not, I think, known how these early men built Stonehenge, why they built it, or whether the stones were carried from Wales or Brittany; but that does not lessen the grandeur of their effort, for they worked with their naked hands.

But Stonehenge, unlike Egypt, is dead. I would sleep on the high altar without a tremor, but there is not one temple in Thebes in which a man would not be haunted. How impossible it is to feel any sympathy or understanding for the distant builders of Stonehenge. It is a gloomy temple. One feels that horrible rites were performed there, even more terrible, perhaps, than the burning of pretty Berkeley Square ladies in wicker-work cages as depicted by the Victorians. Stonehenge is like a symbol of all the dark beliefs at the root of ancient theology. Here is a fitting sanctuary for the Golden Bough.

Even so, it is lifeless. The ghost of the priest-king has been laid long ago. The wind whistles mournfully between the monoliths, and sheep crop the grass on the ancient barrows which lie in the shadow of the dead temple.

The sun rose. A thin streamer of pink light lay across the east. The stones were jet-black against the sky. The grey clouds that had so recently moved across the stars now caught fire and became gold arrows in the heavens. The light grew second by second, the pink turned to a dull red, then to mauve, a veritable furnace of light blazed up above it, and in the midst of this the sun came up over Salisbury Plain.

I was going back over Larkhill of many memories. I

stopped my car and got out, waiting. There was not long to
wait. There it came, silver-clear in the morning: a bugle
playing reveille! How strange it seemed to be standing there,
a free man, listening to reveille on the Plain . . . away over
at Bulford they were playing the same call. (How the whole
Plain rang with distant bugles during the War.) I thought I
caught the sound of the cavalry reveille from Netheravon,
but that must have been imagination, I think, even on a
windless morning.

I looked over the smooth sweep of the Plain, remembering so many mornings just like this, recalling to mind so
many good fellows, so many bad days. How sharp the air
was before breakfast . . . the sound of hard boots on cobbles,
the smell of stables, the feel of riding a horse bareback at
morning exercise over the basket jumps. . . .

I went back thoughtfully into Salisbury.

4

Salisbury is, I imagine, the only example in England of a
town established upon a hill which suddenly packed up,
lock, stock, and barrel, and marched into the plain to begin
again. When the Romans came they fortified the hill known
as Old Sarum and called it Sorbiodunum. The Britons
seemed to have shortened it into something like Sarum. The
Saxons, conquering it, gave it the name of Searesburh (as if
it were the burgh founded by Sear), and the Normans
corrupted it to Searesbyrig, from which is a short step to
Salisbury. What adventures words can encounter in a few
centuries of invasion!

I wandered about the ruins of this first Salisbury,
prodding the earth with a stick in the hope of finding a piece
of that shining Samian pottery which on the most unlikely-
looking dunghills all over the world proclaims the presence
of Rome. But there was nothing. Why did the people of Old
Sarum march into the plain? History says that there was a
difference between the soldiers and the Church which

reached a climax one cold, windy night when the monks, returning from a Rogationtide procession, discovered themselves locked out of their church. 'Let us,' said one of the canons, 'in God's name descend into the level. There are rich champaigns and fertile valleys abounding in the fruits of the earth, and profusely watered by living streams. There is a seat for the Virgin patroness of our church to whom the whole world cannot afford a parallel.'

I like the old story which says that Bishop Poore, who led the descent into the plain in 1219, ordered an arrow to be shot from the heights of Old Sarum into the valley below and where it fell he built the Salisbury Cathedral of today.

You cannot help feeling as you explore the mounds of the ruined city of Sarum, that overcrowding and lack of a good water supply must also have entered into the question. The hill was probably adequate for a camp and a small Saxon stronghold, but when the first cathedral and its outbuildings rose up, what room could there have been for anything else?

Salisbury is surely the most peaceful cathedral city in England. It seems that all its tragedy was packed into the history of Old Sarum and with its removal into the valley came a delicious uneventfulness. I like to go out some few miles and look down on Salisbury, its thin spire, the finest in all England, rising from the plain, the smoke of its chimneys throwing a faint blue mist over the city. It is one of the cosiest English views. It is interesting, too, to note that Bishop Poore anticipated American town-planning. The streets of Salisbury do not wind like a number of glorified village lanes as do the streets of most medieval towns. Was the Bishop original in this or did some memory of the Roman Camp linger on in Old Sarum?

I had two great moments in Salisbury. It was market day. The cattle market was loud with mooing and bleating. Country gigs stood in the square and over the pens leaned the burly, red-faced Wiltshire farmers. Many a Tess went off with a basket over her arm to buy – lisle-thread stockings, I suppose! I looked at the crowd and heard their bargaining, I met them in Ox Row and Blue Boar Row and Oatmeal Row, I watched them come from tap-rooms wiping their mouths with the backs of their big hands and – the railway might never have invaded Salisbury.

The other moment? It was evening and the sun was setting behind the cathedral. In that walled close nothing it seemed could ever hurt: the soft green grass, the mighty church pointing its slim finger to the sky, and the old grey cloistered buildings dedicated to centuries of peace. I went inside. It is not, to my mind, one of the loveliest of our cathedrals, but it is one of the most chastely dignified; it sings on the same note. St Paul's in London, Truro Cathedral, and Salisbury Cathedral, stand alone, I think, as the work of one generation. . . .

A little whisper of organ music lost itself in the grey arches. When it was dark I visited the old inns of Salisbury and walked through quiet streets which are the streets of Barchester.

5

There is something about Weymouth that suggests a big travelling carriage swinging along between the sand-hills near the sea, the postilions with dust on their eyebrows, their wigs awry, the horses in a lather; and inside, against the cushions, His Majesty King George III, very ill and tired, trying to forget the word Whig, hoping there will be Dorset dumpling for dinner.

Weymouth has not yet recovered from the surprise that George III discovered it as a health resort. It looks patchily Georgian, as if trying to live up to the ugly statue of that monarch on the 'front'. You cannot be here for more than ten minutes without hearing something about George III, and I rather like this about Weymouth in a world of short memories. The hotel lounge, which has a loud speaker and many naval officers dotted about it, was once the reception-room of Gloucester House, the royal residence, and I am

53

told that many important Cabinet meetings have been held there. In the garden is something that looks like a stone coffin. They tell me that it is the bath of George III. Weymouth has no museum, so they have put the King's bath in the garden where the sparrows can enjoy it.

Weymouth is rich in natural endowments, and it could, if it cared to forfeit its air of happy reminiscence, become either a Margate or a Bournemouth. Of course, it is much more delightful in its present state of indecision. On a sunny day its bay really has a look of Naples; I could never tire of the harbour where the ironclads lie at anchor; and, just out at sea, vague and mysterious in mist, queerly impressive in sunlight, is a great mountain of stone, sacred to all who love London, the strange Isle of Portland, the most interesting spot I have yet discovered, and the least written of.

But to return to George III.

Fanny Burney, whose *Diary* I have been re-reading in bed, was one of Queen Charlotte's maids of honour when the King went to Weymouth in search of rest. Precious little rest the poor man found! All George III wanted to do, I take it, was to potter round quietly, throw a few stones in the sea, take walks with his humdrum family, and find out the recipe for Dorset puddings.

That loyalty, however, which blinded England to the comedy of the Hanoverian Succession, went right to the heads of the natives. It must be terrible to be a king. Every time he broke cover they gave tongue, and he could seldom escape from the National Anthem. It followed him even into the sea. Fanny Burney's description of His Majesty's first bathe makes me smile:

'They have,' she says, 'dressed out every street with labels, "God save the King". The bathing-machines make it their motto over all their windows, and those bathers that belong to the royal dippers wear it in bandeaus on their bonnets, to go into the sea; and have it again in large letters round their waists, to encounter the waves. Think of the surprise of His Majesty when, the first time of his bathing, he had no sooner popped his royal head under water than a band of music concealed in a neighbouring machine struck up "God Save Great George our King"!'

There was another sensation when the mayor came to present an address of welcome to His Majesty. He had been told to kneel, but at the critical moment and to the astonishment of all present, he remained standing and took the royal hand 'in a common way'

'You should have knelt, sir!' he was told by an outraged equerry.

'Sir,' answered the mayor. 'I cannot.'

'Everybody does, sir!'

'Sir,' replied the mayor, 'I have a wooden leg!'

One of the most impressive seascapes in England is, I imagine, that of the Chesil Bank from the high, western end of Portland. The Chesil Bank is unique. It is, with the exception, perhaps, of a beach on the Baltic, the longest pebble beach in Europe. For seventeen miles the sea has flung up a great barrier of pebbles, which varies in height from fifty to sixty feet. As the beach goes west, so the pebbles, owing to the action of the currents, become smaller and rounder. Fishermen tell me that if they land on the Chesil Bank in a fog they know exactly what part they have struck when they examine the shape and size of the stones. In storms ships have been lifted right over the bank.

It was a sunny day as I stood on the heights of Portland and looked west towards Bridport. The bank was like a thin gold crescent at the edge of an intensely blue sea. There was a fine, white line of foam edging the gold, and then the broad, blue water streaked across with pale green streamers, marking currents. Against the sky, perfecting this lovely bird's-eye view, lay the green downs, with gold clouds slowly sailing up over the edge of the horizon.

Quite near Weymouth is a wishing-well at a place called Upwey. It lies behind a farm gate tucked away at the edge of a wood. The water bubbles up, ice-cold, within ancient moss-covered masonry, and I imagine that the Georgians, those great spa finders, believed that it had healing properties. A girl who seemed to be in charge of the magic waters dipped a cup for me, and said all in one breath:

'Turn your back on the wishing-well, wish and take a drink and throw what's left back into the well over your left shoulder, and then your wish'll come true!'

'Are you sure?' I asked.

She looked alarmed, as though she might be asked to sign a guarantee.

'George III used to drink it,' she replied sturdily.

'And did his wishes come true?'

'I don't know,' she said, very confused and pink.

So I wished and drank and threw what was left into the well. A few natives gathered round, but they were all dumb, with the exception of one woman.

'The King, when he was Prince of Wales, once had a wish here,' she said.

'And what did *he* wish?'

'He wouldn't tell us!' An old man who lives down in the village shouted out: "What are you wishing for; a beautiful princess?" But he wouldn't tell us!'

They all smiled at the recollection of the old man's audacity. I passed through the farm gate to the main road and so back to Georgetown.

6

'That,' said the quarry foreman, as he included the landscape in a sweep of his hand, 'is where St Paul's came from!'

I looked down toward the sea from a high cliff on the eastern side of the Isle of Portland. I saw a valley gouged out of the hillside: a dead, desolate wilderness; a cutting away of high stone cliffs as if some race of giants had scooped out the stone to its bed, leaving exposed the grey, jagged roots of the rock, now covered here and there with grass and wild flowers.

The foreman turned, pointing downwards towards a cosy bay that lay between steep cliffs with the waves breaking on a shingle beach.

'Some of the City churches came out of that great hole! All these old quarries on the east side were worked by Sir Christopher Wren when he rebuilt London. We often find stones quarried in his time and bearing his mark, but rejected for some reason and never shipped to London. Look! This old pillar is said to have been cut for St Paul's Cathedral; but it never got there!'

I turned to look at a grey pillar that might have stood on Ludgate Hill, lying covered in brambles that clung closely, as if trying to console it for its failure. We walked on together over roads so white with powdered Portland stone that the dust clung like flour to our clothes and formed a grey film on our hands. My guide pointed to a long gash in the rock.

'The Cenotaph!' he remarked casually.

We went on.

'I helped to choose some of the stones for the Cenotaph,' he continued: 'the top ones with the wreath on them. We picked the purest white stone in the island.'

We came at length to a quarry near the sea, in which men were cutting Portland stone. They worked below on stone ledges, driving iron bars beneath the stratum; for Portland stone lies in convenient layers. A crane dropped a chain into the quarry. It was attached to the iron wedges, then the crane worked, pulling at the bars till the stone broke into a rough square slab.

On top of the quarry men were shaping these slabs: huge creamy slabs. Portland stone is not white until it has weathered, as you can prove for yourself in the Strand any day by comparing new Bush House with ancient Somerset House. Some day Bush House will lose its look of sunburn and grey down to the silver monotone of London.

'Where is all this stone going?' I asked the foreman as we passed between walls of it.

'That,' he replied, 'is Regent Street!'

Apart from their sentimental interest to all Londoners, the Portland quarries are strange places in which to prowl. You look at a hillside, and see, plain as in an architect's sectional plan, the strata of which the island is formed. First comes a thin top-dressing of soil, below is a deeper stratum of waste stone never used for building which is broken up and thrown into the sea; so that another smaller isle of waste Portland stone four hundred feet high has formed on the west end of the island.

Immediately below the waste is a stratum called by the quarrymen the 'dirt bed' – a curious grey, knobby mass like concrete. It is full of fossil fish and trees. I picked out many fine stone mussels, a stone oyster the size of a tea-plate, and the bough of a tree which waved over Portland millions of years ago, so convincing (apart from its weight) that a short-sighted person examining the plainly-marked knots might easily mistake it for wood.

The roots of many of these trees are in the 'dirt bed', but the boughs rise up to the stratum of waste stone. Below the dirt bed begins the strata used for building, lying in regular layers.

If you would like to examine the fossils in Portland stone you will see many in the plinth of the King Charles statue at Charing Cross: it is full of sea-shells.

'Will we ever cut the island to the sea level?' repeated my guide, with a laugh. 'Not in our time, sir! We reckon that there's enough stone here to last the whole world for another five centuries!'

I thought, in my vanity, that I knew London.

I realize now that no one understands London until he has explored the significant chasms of this white island: this mother of London. How would you analyse the beauty of London? Surely it is due to the changefulness of this island stone that gathers smoke shadows on its windless side as trees gather lichen. On dull days it looms, remote and grey, as if withdrawn into some region of thoughtfulness, and in the sunlight it blazes in sudden whiteness, so that you feel London has as many moods as a woman.

Somerset House, St Paul's, the Bank, the Royal Exchange, the Mansion House, the Law Courts, the British Museum, all the Wren churches – one could extend the list to the end of the chapter – have left their caves, gullies, and gaps in the Isle of Portland. What an unforgettable experience it is to walk in the mighty bed from which, at the command of Wren, St Paul's arose to stand guard on Ludgate Hill.

As I walked along the dusty roads of the island, which dazzle the eyes like snow in sunlight, I thought not only of the buildings which Portland has already given to London, but of the London to be which we will never walk, that slumbers still in darkness in the womb of this pregnant Isle. The new Bank of England came out of here. There are new streets to be cut out of the hills. I had the queer fancy that perhaps my footsteps might echo down to the London of tomorrow, stirring it from its prehistoric slumbers, giving it an uneasy nightmare of destiny.

And this I thought: that never again will I look on London with quite the same eyes. Always at the back of my mind will be, as I walk the streets of London, knowledge of a white island lying out to sea like a great whale. When I see Portland stone in London I shall think of the sea breaking against high hills; I shall hear the scream of the gulls; the suck back of pebbles on the little stony beaches; the white dust lying over the road in the little mysterious Isle of London.

7

He was standing in the Cathedral Close at Exeter, reading his guide-book like a good American, ready to be friendly on the slightest provocation. . . .

I was thinking that if you close your mind to detail, the

cathedral cities of England are deliciously alike – they have grown up on the same pattern out of the same past. I like the invariable narrow entrance to the precincts; the green trees which look as if each one is valeted; the close-cut grass; the bright chatter of sparrows; the slow chime of bells; the discreet Georgian doors with heavy brass knockers which mark themselves out as the barriers between the world and the dean's dignity. Each close is drenched in the same air of ancient peace; high above dream the grey walls and towers, whose every stone proclaims an age of boundless faith. . . .

The American entered Exeter Cathedral, and I followed.

Here is a piece of perfectly balanced architecture – a beautiful, but to me, unemotional cathedral; each arch the exact echo of another arch, each pillar the replica of its opposite. It is like a problem in mathematics set to music. It is almost too perfect! At one moment it seems that the whole fragment might fly up to heaven or dissolve in cold, formal music. The thing that keeps Exeter Cathedral firmly rooted to earth is the organ erected in an unfortunate position above the choir, so that you cannot see beyond to the great east window. This is Exeter's anchor of ugliness.

I know that it is a marvellous organ; that, because Exeter is the one cathedral in England with transeptal towers, there is no other place for it. That does not lessen the shock.

'Say,' said the American. 'Can you tell me what a recorder is?'

'A magistrate.'

'No; it's some kind of musical instrument! This book says that the angels carved on the minstrels gallery are playing a viol, a harp, bag-pipes, a trumpet, an organ, cymbals, and – a recorder!'

We went up together and looked at the earliest English stone orchestra I know of.

'That's a recorder!' I suggested. 'That instrument played by the third angel from the left.'

'That's a kind of old English saxophone.'

'It *is* rather like a saxophone!'

'Well, that's pretty cute; saxophones in heaven!'

We walked out into the close, talking. He had 'stopped off' the 'boat' at Plymouth, and was, as he put it, 'just tickled to death' by Exeter.

'I don't know a darned thing about England yet,' he said, 'but I'm getting a line on her, sure enough. If it's all like this – well, I'm glad I came over!'

I asked him what 'tickled' him about Exeter.

He replied thoughtfully: 'Do you know America?'

'I regret to say I have never been there.'

'Well, we kind of sneer at tradition, but, believe me, under our skins we admire it and wish we had it. We don't know what it is to have roots. Now this morning I went to a place, the City Hall here – the Guild-hall they call it – that old place with a top story hanging over the main street. There's a guy there dressed like a cop. They call him a sergeant-at-mace. He told me things about this town till I was dizzy. You've had a lot of kings in England! That fellow balled me up with William the Conqueror, King Charles and a queen called – wait while I look at my diary – Henrietta, and then he took me upstairs and showed me the mayor's chains and things. Proud as Lucifer that guy was, because something or other was older than something or other in London! And I saw a sword covered in old black cloth. I said to him, jollying a bit, "Why don't you get all that stuff off it; what's the idea?" He looked at me kinda shocked. I could see him thinking: "You poor Yank; you poor ignorant fish!" "That sword, sir," he said, "was put in mourning for King Charles the First, and it's still in mourning for him!" Well, gee, I just walked right out. . . .'

'The motto in this town is "always faithful"!'

'Sure! This history means a whole lot. I can imagine how it feels to have a city like Exeter in the family. I'm a New Englander, so I guess I've got English blood in me, and maybe that's why this old stuff gets me going. Now look at this crazy old shop.'

We went into a bookshop, where I bought a map of Cornwall.

'I don't know,' said the bookseller shyly, 'whether you two gentlemen would care to step upstairs and see my old room.'

'You bet your life!' said the American.

We went up a dark staircase, and entered a low room that overhung the High Street. The floor was uneven, the ceiling was Stuart, the walls were panelled in oak, and the windows were small and leaded.

'Prince Rupert lived here when Exeter was held for the King!'

'Well, what do you think of that?' said the American.

We went down again.

'I don't know who Prince Rupert was,' whispered my friend, 'but – that was just bully! Well, mighty glad to know you. Goodbye! What gets me is that sword! Can you beat it?'

Really, when you come to think of it, you cannot.

These snug old towns of ours, these Exeters, so quiet, so assured, have known their own minds for so long, have fought and won, or, equally gloriously, lost their battles for so long that no man can be insensible to their dignity and their power.

They seem to sleep; and that is where you are liable to go wrong! In 1914 they proved how swiftly their old eyes can look into the present; how quickly their experienced hands can feel their grip still firm upon a hilt.

8

Every boy in England should be taken at least once to Plymouth. He should, if small, be torn away from his mother and sent out for a night with the fishing fleet; he should go out in the tenders and meet the Atlantic liners; he should be shown battleships building at Devonport; he should be taken to the Barbican and told the story of the

Mayflower and the birth of New England, and most important of all, his imagination should be kindled by tales of Hawkins and Drake on high, green Plymouth Hoe, the finest promenade in Europe.

It was evening when I went up to the Hoe. Darkness was falling. In every town there is one place where youth and beauty parade at night under the glum influence of the spirit of natural selection. The girls walk two by two, the boys in vague bands. Now and then there is a little sociability known as 'clicking'. If a youth after passing and repassing a particular maid for about ten miles eventually says, 'Good morning!' and she stops and replies, the youth is said to have 'clicked'. This parade of mutual suspicion goes on every night in every high-street; in Plymouth it takes place on the spot where Francis Drake is said to have been playing bowls when they told him that the Spaniards were in sight.

Far below, the grey waters of the Sound lay smooth between sheltering cliffs. The breakwater was a faint, grey line on the sea. There were lights on Drake's Island; lights on Mount Edgcumbe; lights on a grey destroyer steaming towards the dockyard at Devonport. From the right came the distant sound of hammering against metal: a vigorous touch in this peaceful scene; a reminder that Plymouth is more than ever Plymouth. . . .

Straight out at sea, fifteen miles away over grey waters, snapped a light, the most famous light on the British coast: the light of the Eddystone.

I am sorry for the man who can stand for the first time on Plymouth Hoe without a tingling of the blood.

I sat and looked out to the fast-fading seascape; and I thought about Southwark. There is a link between this lovely Devon hill above the sea and that grim region of warehouses on the south bank of the Thames: the one means Shakespeare, Marlowe, Ben Jonson; the other Drake, Hawkins, Cooke, Sir Humphrey Gilbert; Southwark, the centre of the Elizabethan revival in literature; Plymouth, linked for ever with the Elizabethan discovery of the world.

It seemed to me as night fell over Plymouth Sound that I could imagine those grim old swashbucklers who went pirating along the Gulf of Mexico, calling on God to take a hand with them in the slave traffic. They planted a few flags for us! I remembered a number of disjointed stories: how Cochrane sailed into the Sound with three golden candle-sticks taken from a Spanish galleon lashed to his mast-head; how three ships came home from Nombre de Dios, full of plate and Spanish pieces somewhere about 1573, with a man on deck who from the top of a tree had taken a first sight of the Pacific, and had sworn to sail an English ship in those waters.

At the back of me the statue of Francis Drake was black against the sky. He stands with one hand on the globe and the other above his sword-hilt.

'If Drake played bowls on the Hoe, did he play uphill or down?' I asked a man sitting next to me.

'Well,' he replied with that kindly Devon smile, 'in his day they say the Hoe was not so bumpy. He is supposed to have been playing on a green which stood where his statue is now. Whether he finished the game or not when the Armada came in sight I don't know. I was in the Army during the war, and I imagine that there must have been considerable "wind up", don't you?'

'Do you, as a Devon man, really suggest that Francis Drake ever had the wind up?' I asked, horrified.

'I wouldn't be surprised.'

My companion was interested, as most Plymouth men are, in the history of his town, and we sat together on the Hoe attempting to drag the year 1588 out of the past.

The last promenader departed.

A chill wind blew from the sea. In our imagination we saw the fleet of a hundred sail set out from Plymouth to meet the ships under Don Alonso Perez de Guzman, Duke of Sidonia, who had decided that when he had conquered

64

England he would take Mount Edgcumbe, at Plymouth, for his English residence. It must have been a great moment on the Hoe as the Spanish galleons came slowly, heavily, from the Lizard up Channel . . . the hundred little English ships going out into the blue to meet them.

'I would rather have lived in that age than any other,' said my companion. He was a frail-looking man, as frail-looking almost as Nelson.

'The world must have seemed such a big place then. If one could have only gone with Drake in 1577 in the *Golden Hind*!'

'Ah! Now the *Mauretania* is due tomorrow!'

'Yes.' He sighed.

'How,' I said, 'would you like to have burnt up Vera Cruz, to have sacked the churches, and have driven the natives below the hatches, and then held a church parade?'

'Splendid!' he whispered. 'That was the spirit of the time. . . . Well, I must be going home.'

He said good night, and I watched his lank, dyspeptic, blood-thirsty figure fade into the distance.

Beyond the breakwater a liner passed far out at sea, her lit portholes like a string of pearls on the water. A ship's siren called at the mouth of the harbour . . .

Fifteen miles south the Eddystone snapped and winked, a little pin-point of light directing the traffic, saying every minute: 'Here, my children, is Plymouth, but, for goodness' sake, steer clear of *me*!'

9

I went to the Barbican to see the spot from which the *Mayflower* sailed, expecting to find all the Americans in the West of England standing round in reverent attitudes. Instead, I found a lame old sailor sitting on a wooden seat smoking a stubby pipe.

'Good morning,' I said.

"Mornin', zur,' he replied, removing his pipe and spitting neatly into Sutton Pool.

'The sun feels good!'

'That it do, zur!'

We watched the fishing fleet unloading at Sutton Wharf. The trawlers had been out for over a week in stormy seas, and they had slipped in on a calm tide with the salt caked to their smoke-stacks and a week's auburn whiskers on the crews. The wharf was slippery with fish-scales and crushed ice. Strong-voiced Devon men stood above limp piles of dead fish – such enormous skate the size of card-tables, dog-fish, soles, plaice, crabs, and purple lobsters. The fishermen clip-clopped over the stones in thigh boots, their faces the colour of Spanish mahogany, their bodies in blue jerseys, their legs in brown trousers. A lovely colourful picture in the bright sun of forenoon. . . .

'So the *Mayflower* sailed from here?'

The old sailor pointed to the head of the jetty with his pipe.

'That it did, zur, in 1620, as you can see from that stone.'

He got up and limped over to a stone set in the roadway.

'*Mayflower*, 1620,' was the inscription.

'If you was an American you'd ask me to take your photograph on it,' said the old man. 'And quite right too. If it hadn't been for the *Mayflower*, where would America be now? Thank you, zur!'

He brightened considerably.

'See that house – No. 9, the Barbican – that's the house where the Pilgrim Fathers slept the night before they sailed.'

'What? The whole hundred and twenty?'

'Well, zur, as many as could, maybe.'

I went over to No. 9, the Barbican.

It may be one of England's undiscovered treasures. It is one of the few remaining Elizabethan houses on the Barbican. As one hundred and twenty Pilgrim Fathers had to find bed and breakfast as near the jetty as possible on September 5th, 1620, it seems highly probable that some of

66

them slept at No. 9. Anyhow, it would not be difficult to make out an argument for it! The ground floor of the house is now a coal-agent's office.

'I believe,' said the man behind the counter, 'that unless they can prove that the Pilgrim Fathers really did sleep here, this house may be pulled down in a slum improvement scheme.'

It is surely the duty of Plymouth to solve this problem.

'It's strange that not many Americans know this house. It is not, I think, mentioned in the guide-books. We call it "Mayflower House", and the tradition here on the Barbican is that the pilgrims put up here, and in other houses now pulled down, while their ships were overhauled.'

I asked him if I might explore the old place.

'An old lady lives upstairs,' he replied. 'You might ask her.'

I mounted a dark staircase. At the top, in a gloomy little room, an old woman was peeling potatoes. I told her I was interested in 'the Mayflower'. She dipped a potato in the water.

'I'm busy,' she said.

I saw that quite a large pile of potatoes separated me from historical investigation.

'I can't show you over now,' she said, 'or what'll my men say if they find their dinners not ready?'

'Quite right,' I said.

The work of the world must come first.

'You can take it from me,' remarked the old woman, with an air of finality which no man would dare to question, 'this is "Mayflower House". There's no doubt about it. I know it is.'

'I begin to feel it is too,' I said.

'Do you?' she replied. 'Well, if you come back some other day when I'm not busy maybe I'll take you over it; it's a rare queer old house.'

She bathed another potato and assaulted it with a knife.

I went down the dark stairway into the Barbican. . . .

67

A narrow flight of stone steps leads up to Plymouth Hoe. I mounted them. The sailing of the *Mayflower* was one of the most dramatic events of the last three hundred years. Think how much was storing up for the world when that little ship went Westward Ho!

As I stood overlooking the sea, an unforgettable thing happened. A queenly Cunarder, prompt to the minute, steamed slowly into the Sound and lay at anchor beyond the breakwater. Fussy little tenders steamed beneath her mountainous sides. There was great activity on her decks. The mails were lowered, the tender sped back with them towards Plymouth. . . .

Slowly the long, slender ship moved out to sea again on her way to Southampton.

When I reached the hotel, I found it full of Pilgrim Fathers.

'Oh, say, get some ice water, and waiter, three dry martinis. Gee, lookit here! What's this chickfeed? Is this a sixpence?'

I had a swift vision of the first Pilgrim Fathers kneeling on the shores of Mass., returning thanks for their safe arrival. You know the picture? The wind blowing their hair; their broad felt hats in their hands; beyond the inhospitable dunes so soon to blossom with safety razors and sock suspenders.

'Here's mud in your eye!' said one of the modern pilgrims, tossing down his martini.

It is seldom that life is so artistic.

10

I have read somewhere that when women make a garment they take a paper pattern, place it over the material, and cut it out. Battleships are made like this too. It seems incredible that the Fleet has been cut out on the same principle as (forgive me) a petticoat. . . .

I went to Devonport Dockyard from a strong sense of

duty, quite prepared to be bored, for you cannot go to Plymouth and leave out Devonport. I had no sooner driven my car within the grey gates than I became interested. I had expected a dockyard; I seemed to have entered an old public school or a cathedral close. His Majesty's dockyard at Devonport can give points to any model factory in the country. It is a beautiful sight. The buildings are grey and old, on either side an avenue of trees. The cobbled paths slope gently to the waters of the Hamoaze. At the dock gates is an old grey chapel. There is much green grass, the graveyard, it seems, of sloops and frigates, for from this greenness spring old figure-heads, their painted faces gazing into the sky, the grass shining upward on their chins.

'This,' remarked my guide, 'is our museum.'

He took me into a building full of wooden giants, figure-heads that dipped in many waters before the days of steam. Here these soldiers and sailors have retired; it is the most exclusive and, may I say, experienced service club in the kingdom. The members lean outwards from the walls, wearing old uniforms; dukes, generals, admirals, East Indiamen; a brave, stony-faced club of old giants. . . . What do they talk about when the dock gates are shut at night?

'Ah, sir,' sighs the Duke of Marlborough to George I, 'how would you like to feel the Bay of Bengal warm on your waistcoat again?'

'Or, sir, would it not be good and invigorating to feel a broadside shake you to the nose?' says the Duke of Wellington.

'Or,' whispers Nelson from his corner, 'the trade winds in the main-topgallant and the white spume on your cheek.'

'If you want to see the yard, we ought to get a move on!' said the guide.

He dragged me away.

In Devonport they were building a new cruiser.

Any girl who has made a coat and skirt can grasp the technical principle in a second. First the architects draw the plan. Then they paint it in sections on steel plates. Little engines with the Royal arms on them fuss over railway lines carrying the plates to high, noisy sheds. Men take the plates, put them on machines that cut steel as a knife cuts bread, and the patterns of the new cruiser emerges.

In one shed machines punch rivet-holes; in the next they bend inch steel-plate as easily as you bend a sheet of cardboard.

The engines puff over to the dockside with the sections.

At that moment the cruiser looked like a giant hen-coop. She rose above the dock, a rusty shell of a ship with men clambering over her and applying compressed air riveters to her flanks.

On the dock lay the pieces of a jig-saw puzzle, each one carefully numbered in white paint. When the builders required a few more yards of hull they sent down for section S310.

'Coming up!' said Bill on the dock, as the big crane lifted S310 in the air.

The men in the shell fixed S310 next to S309 and then sent down for S311.

High above the shouting and the clang of steel sections shot to earth sounded the piercing shriek of the compressed air riveters.

There was no slacking in the building of that cruiser. Now and again the men cast a glance towards a board on the dock which told them how many tons they had already built and how many they had added during the present working week.

'She's not being built against time for anything,' I asked suspiciously, 'for the Great War was the war that ended wars, wasn't it?'

'No, that's not it,' replied the guide. 'We are racing Portsmouth, where they are building a similar cruiser. We mean to win the race, too!'

Imagine with what emotion I discovered a queer little bit of steel with four holes punched in it lying ready on the dockside. An insignificant little angle of the hull, but, as I instinctively felt, my income-tax!

We were walking away from this complicated jig-saw puzzle when we came to a dry dock in which, queer sight in this nursery and hospital of the ironclad, lay a battered old warship of the Trafalgar era. She had square yawning portholes and a bow-windowed stern.

'That is the old H.M.S. *Implacable*,' explained the guide, 'which we captured from the French at the Battle of Trafalgar. She has been lying for years in Falmouth, and we are giving her a wash and brush up before sending her back as a training ship.'

Good old *Implacable*!

The painters and decorators were climbing over her, every sweep of their brushes making her look as game as a fighting cock. When she takes the water again in her new coat of paint, with her windows repaired and her hull patched, the new cruiser, if she is then ready, will instinctively salute her; or I hope so. . . .

A whistle blows, and the battleship-makers stop work.

They stream out in thousands from workshop and dockside.

Three policeman stand before the gates and touch men at random on the shoulder. Such men double off at once to a little office near the gates, where another policeman runs his hands over them to make quite sure, apparently, that they are not taking a battleship out to lunch with them. . . .

Over Devonport then falls an hour's intense silence, in which a lean grey destroyer steams into dock. She may have something wrong with her engine-room, with her guns, with her hull; or she may only have sprained her ankle somewhere at sea.

She struggles into the dock with the sure knowledge that Dr Devonport will feel her pulse and say:

'My dear lady, we'll have you right in no time!'

*

Devonport is doctor, nurse, and mother to the Fleet – chiefly mother. Devonport's work, like that of a mother, is never done, because all the year through her big grey children come limping in from sea to her; every year her new children leave her and go out to the ends of the earth.

CHAPTER FOUR

I fall in love with Cornwall and with a name. Describes a hidden Paradise and how wireless comes to Arcady. I meet rain at Land's End, and, late one evening, climb a hill, grasping the key of Tintagel

I

THERE is a strangeness about Cornwall. You feel it as soon as you cross Tor Ferry.

The first sight that pleased me was a girl with a shingled head driving a cow with a crumpled horn. I knew, of course, that I was in fairyland! And the next thing was a village that was trying to climb a hill. One whitewashed cottage had reached the top, but all the others had stuck half-way, with their gardens gazing in a rather surprised manner over their chimney-pots. In these lovely, disorderly gardens some of the oldest men I have ever seen had apparently taken root in the act of watching the bean-rows.

When I stopped to give the car a drink of water, a woman came to a cottage door with a jug. And she sang her words prettily, as the Welsh do. Like the Welsh, these people possess a fine Celtic fluency, so that their lies are more convincing than a Saxon truth.

And the names in Cornwall! Just take a map, as I did, and read them. Here the saints have taken root like white daisies in a field. Is there a saintlier country on earth? St Austell, St Anthony, St Mawes, and St Ives; St Agnes, St Neot, St Pinnock, and St Mellion; St Germans, St Breock, St Eval, and St Columb – they ring like a peal of bells over a meadow. And what strange Saints! Cornwall was converted by the Celtic Church, England by the Roman. These names preserved on the map of Cornwall are those of holy men from Wales and Ireland who, when the legions were recalled and England became a wild battle-ground of men and gods, guarded Christ in the mountains.

73

In a field I saw women digging potatoes, their skirts looped back, and beside each a little wooden tub in which they put the vegetables. They might have been in Brittany.

From a point of the hill road I looked down upon an estuary. The tide was running up among trees! See how the trees creep right down to the water's edge. There are white cottages, rather timid-looking, like fairies who have come unexpectedly to the edge of a wood, and everything about the place suggests how sweetly life runs to the old tune – fish in the nets and fruit on the trees, just as it was in the Golden Age. I wonder if people are happy down there, or is someone watching the tide run in through a screen of roses, longing for the splendid chance to earn forty-two shillings a week in a London office?

I had no idea where to make for in Cornwall. One road was as good as another. I took the map and one name curled itself round my heart. I do not think that in the whole length and breadth of England there is a more beautiful name. But to fall in love with a name is like falling in love with a voice heard over a telephone. A meeting might prove fatal. But not to risk the . . . impossible. I whispered it twice, and took the inevitable road to:

St Anthony-in-Roseland!

2

I am writing in the tiny bedroom of a cottage in St Anthony-in-Roseland. The thatch comes down so low that the upper part of the window-frame has a stubby beard. I can see when I look out of the window a clump of trees and a field shaped like a green dome; beyond is a vast emptiness of sky that means the sea. I cannot see the water, but I can hear a steady whisper of waves breaking in the little rocky bay below. That and the song of birds are the only sounds in St Anthony-in-Roseland.

I have said that I came here because I liked the name. I came prepared for the worst: for a mine shaft and a street of dreary shops. At Tregoney I left the main road and dived in a labyrinth of lanes so small that there was no clearance between the car and the hedge-banks. Green plants caught me by the arm and seemed to say: 'Don't go on; don't go on; a man who expects St Anthony-in-Roseland to look as it sounds is only gathering one more disappointment. . . .'

But I went on; and I came at length to the darkest tunnel of a lane I have ever seen. The hedges had grown up and formed arches the whole length of it; and the lane dipped down and down in green gloom and then rose steeply, in the manner of these Cornish lanes, bending suddenly to give a view of the sea, startlingly near, breaking on a rocky coast, the high hills lying back spread with neat, cultivated fields. Turning a corner I came to St Anthony-in-Roseland.

Now, if anything you have believed in has continued to be worth your faith, if anything you have wanted has not fallen below the expectation, you will realize my wonder when I saw St Anthony.

Twenty tiny whitewashed cottages stood dotted about among tall hedges. They were covered with flowers. The bees were busy in the gardens. In many gardens were those typical Cornish palm trees that rise twelve feet in the air and end in leaves like bunches of green bayonets. There was no inn, no post office, and the nearest shop, I learned, is at Gerrans, five miles down those luscious lanes. St Anthony-in-Roseland seemed lost, and happy to be lost, dreaming beside the sea.

There was no sign of life. The little white cottages covered with briar roses and ivy geraniums stood with doors open, yet no sign of man, woman, or child. No one seemed to have heard me drive up. Not a sound! I shut off the engine and walked on. I saw a footpath over a field; below was a tiny bay, nestling between two gaunt cliffs. Here was no sign of life. The waves came booming over the rocks; the sea-gulls were flying with wild, lonely cries. I stood there a long time. Dusk was falling. I shook free from the wild spell of this place, and asked myself where I would rest this night, for the map shows no way out of St Anthony but by ten miles of those bosky lanes and then a ferry, and another ten miles to Falmouth. I was tired. Would it be possible to stay the night in St Anthony and find out what kind of people live there? It would be good to stay in such silence, in such remoteness.

I went back to the cottages.

A rosy middle-aged woman, wearing a print apron, was standing at the door of a pink cottage, looking at my car as though it were an unnatural phenomenon.

'I wonder,' I said, 'if you could tell me where I could stay the night.'

A great bush of veronica was in bloom in the garden, the porch was smothered in geraniums, Canterbury bells stood beneath the windows, and the paths were lined with London pride.

'Well,' said the woman, 'I've got nothing for dinner, sir, but eggs and cream, because we have no shops, and everything is brought us from Gerrans in motor car – or else I'd gladly give you my spare room.'

I told her that eggs and cream were the only things I would dream of eating in St Anthony-in-Roseland.

'Well,' she said, 'come and see the room, and if it'll do Mr Tragonna will let you put the motor car in his cowshed up the road.'

There is a beautiful article to be written about cottage bedrooms; they are the least sophisticated sights on earth. Above a big white bed was the wording in silver type: 'Order my Steps in Thy Word'; to the left was 'The Entrance of Thy Word giveth Light'; to the right was 'Wait on Thy God Continually'. Beside the bed on a bamboo table was the Bible; above the bed was a shelf containing *Uncle Tom's Cabin*, *A Mother's Recompense*, *Straight Paths and Crooked Ways*, and *Owen's Hobby*.

It was small and white and virginal, this room: the kind of room the May Queen might have slept in. Gazing from the wall over the washstand was a saintly girl with long, flowing hair. It struck me that she would never look at me when I shaved in the morning, because her eyes were turned to higher things. She was called 'Resignation', and she had left a Christmas supplement in 1895. Near the bed was a touch of devilry in a wooden frame. A very different type of girl, in Turkish costume – but obviously the girl herself was from some nice road in Wimbledon – was standing in a harem accepting with eager coyness a love-letter thrust towards her through a barred window by a most suspicious hand. This must have given 'Resignation' some bad moments.

'I notice,' I said, looking through the window, 'that there is no one about. St Anthony seems asleep.'

'Well, you see, sir, there are no children here now. We are all old. We closed the school years ago. As children grow up here they have to go away and do for themselves. My boy, who was in the war, and my two girls are doing well. Some children come back to the farms when their fathers die.'

So that is the secret of St Anthony-in-Roseland. It has had its children, they have left the nest, and the old people stay on among the flowers. I looked outside and saw a tumble-down shack, half cowshed, half chapel, its wood rotting and its beams falling in.

'Oh, that's the schoolroom! I can remember when it was full every morning; and the noise and the chatter . . .'

Now the nettle and the foxglove seek to make a green pall for all that is left of youth in St Anthony-in-Roseland. . . .

It grows dark, the sun has gone down, the peace of open fields and open sky and the scent of warm flowers come in to me through the windows. The restless rhythm of the sea is like an endless wind blowing through a wood. One by one the sounds of day are stilled, until the robin is left alone to sing in his high-pitched elegy.

I know no sadder little song. Nature's Angelus bell. It has no beginning and no end. It ceases suddenly in the middle of a phrase as if waiting for an answer that never comes, or is perhaps inaudible to the ear of man. The light is drawn out of the sky minute by minute, and the little throatful of heartache goes on and on in the gathering darkness. . . .

'I've lit the lamp, sir, and supper's ready when you are!'
'I'll be there in one second.'
Down the darkening lane I hear the slow tramp of boots. An immense stillness seems to have closed its hand on the earth, and the words fade from this paper.

3

It rained before dark, and the wind sprang up, blowing in from the sea, bringing with it the deep boom of the waves. I was sitting with my host and his wife in their little kitchen, smoking and enjoying myself to my heart's content. Simple and sophisticated people meet in a delicious unselfconsciousness; they are at the opposite poles of congeniality. The light from a paraffin lamp fell in a yellow pool on the table, which was still littered with the broken bread of supper; and in this pool the big, brown hands of the labourer moved, teasing the coarse tobacco for his pipe; his wife's brown hands moved above her sewing.

Their eyes sought mine continually as they told me with smiles the little, untroubled drama of their lives; how they had come here forty years ago to this very cottage, how he had worked in the same fields for forty years, how forty crops had grown up under his great brown hands, how she had borne three children, and how this tiny cottage then became a nest in which a family was reared. Now old, and the young ones out in the world, these two still lived under that same thatch, he rising with the dawn, as he had done for forty years, going to the little well in the front garden, drawing ice-cold water, making a cup of tea for her before clumping heavily off to those eternal fields. . . .

The sweetest story in the world. In their beauty and simplicity they were like flowers, these two old people. None of the storms that break over men and women seemed to have touched them. In this deserted Eden they had not been hurt.

The dry leaf of a geranium ticked against the pane, and I could hear the steady pricking of the rain on leaves. Inside, the warmth and the light seemed to deepen the darkness beyond the window.

Suddenly we became alert. We looked at each other. Footsteps were coming down the road! Who could this be? In this village of old fathers and mothers there are seldom footsteps in the lane after dark; and the alarm clock on the mantelpiece said that it was almost ten.

The footsteps stopped before the garden gate, and they came on heavily up the path to the door.

'I won't come in,' said the voice of the farmer from up the hill; ''tes a rare wet night and my feet are muddied.' He looked towards me. 'I thought maybe that you might like to hear the wireless tonight!'

My host and his wife beamed rosily.

'You go and hear 'un, sor,' said my host; 'that be a rare thing that wireless, and there's no better wireless in these paarts than Mr T's, which is so laarge that 'tis possible to hear Lunnon, as clear the spakin' es as a bell, sor.'

So I put on a macintosh and waded up the hill with the farmer. My car was dry in the cowshed. The new litter of pigs were asleep. The cows were moving clumsily in the byre; and ahead the farmhouse windows shone yellow.

'This wireless has made a rare difference to us,' said the farmer, as he sat in his muddy boots and leggings, turning knobs and switching valves off and on.

There were three other people in the room sitting in the light of the table lamp, two old women and an old man. On the walls were framed pictures of the Relief of Mafeking, a large portrait of Lord Kitchener in a scarlet coat, and a picture of Queen Victoria wearing the crown, holding the sceptre and the orb.

'He's a beauty, he is!' said the old man, pointing with his pipe stem to the valve set. 'During that bit of a strike you had up in Lonnun we could heaar 'zactly all that wor passing as clear as I can see you, sor.'

'Aye,' said the old lady, 'we liked that Mr Baldwin, for he wor as plain as if he wor in this room, but Mr Churchill hemmed and hawed till you felt like wishing to get up behind him and give 'un a shove.'

They all laughed.

'Aye,' said the old man, 'if only, 'pon my word, they all spaake as good as the "nice man", it would be reaal graat, that it would.'

'And who is the "nice man"?' I asked.

'Oh,' said the young farmer, 'we call the chap who announces the "nice man", because we like his voice. It's a fine voice, sir, and I'm sure he's a nice chap, if you knew him. . . . Ah, here we are! Just listen to that, sir. "London calling the British Isles. . . ." Oh, Lor', there, it's gone, and we're getting Morse! I reckon this battery's run down! Now, listen! Now it's real good. . . .'

Into my ears, across miles of emptiness, came the sound of the Savoy. The door opened, and a cat walked in. I could hear people in London putting down their liqueur glasses, a tinkle of coffee cups, and a buzz of talk beneath the rhythmic thrumming of the dance band. . . .

'Listen!' cried the farmer, beating time. 'The "Blue Danube"! That's a real good tune, that is! It's clear tonight! That's the rain. . . .'

The tune ended. The buzz in the ball-room rose a tone. A stray voice said: 'Well, I can't do any better!' and a confused hum of other voices cut in. I could see that scene so plainly: the coloured gowns, the shirt fronts, the little gold chairs; the band on the other platform ready for the next dance. Kitchener was looking at me sternly. The cat was asleep. The old man was smoking; the two old women were sitting with their hands folded across their stomachs; and outside was the wildness of the night and the rain and the sea.

We talked about London. One of the old women was

curious to know what sort of a place the Savoy might be, how it looked, what people did there; all of which I tried to satisfy. They were genuinely thrilled when I described the inside of Broadcasting House, and proclaimed the fact that I had met the 'nice man'.

'Well, 'pon my soul, just fancy that, now!'

They all sat up.

I listened to a tango from the Strand and became sunk in a deep weariness. I said goodnight, and the old man took up my headphones. As I walked down the little path I turned and saw, framed in the yellow window, the new picture of rural England: old heads bent over the wireless set in the light of a paraffin light. London coming to them out of space: Queen Victoria and Lord Kitchener watching with a certain stern amazement. . . .

How sweet the air was after rain. The sky had cleared. The stars shone. The two collie dogs set up a great barking as I peeped at my car in the cowshed; and I went on down the dark, soggy lane towards the light of a candle that was waiting for me in a blue enamelled stick.

4

I have blundered into a Garden of Eden that cannot be described in pen or paint. There is a degree of beauty that flies so high that no net of words or no snare of colour can hope to capture it, and of this order is the beauty of St Just-in-Roseland, the companion village to St Anthony.

There are a few cottages lost in trees, a vicarage with two old cannon balls propping open the garden gate, and a church. The church is grey and small and, as a church, not worth notice; but it stands in a churchyard which is one of the little-known glories of Cornwall. I would like to know if there is in the whole of England a churchyard more beautiful than this. There is hardly a level yard in it. You stand at the lych-gate, and look down into a green cup filled with flowers and arched by great trees. In the dip is the little church, its tower level with you as you stand above. The white gravestones rise up from ferns and flowers.

Beyond the church a screen of trees forms a tracery of leaves through which, shining white in the sun, you see the ground sloping steeply towards the creek beyond which is that strong arm of the sea, Carrick Roads. Over the roof of the church blue water gleams; above it rise the distant fields of the opposite bank. This churchyard is drowsy with the bee and rich with a leafy pungency. There is also a tropic smell in it, a smell of palms and foreign trees.

An elderly clergyman was training a plant over a wall. He looked up and smiled.

'Yes, I am the vicar. Which do you prefer – those wine-dark rhododendrons or the pink? And do you notice that rather subtle shade in between? I like that, don't you?'

'Who was St Just, sir?' I asked.

'St Just was,' he replied, taking off his broad black hat and smoothing his silver hair, 'St Just was – I want you to admire those pansies! Now look at this. Isn't it beautiful?'

He bent down and, taking a deep velvet flower between two fingers, turned its head gently towards me.

'You were saying that St Just was –'

'Ah, yes, forgive me! St Just – oh, the trouble I've had with those japonicas.'

He shook his head.

'St Just?' I murmured hopefully.

'That tall tree over there came from Australia,' he remarked proudly. 'By the way, I have a tropical garden behind the church which you must see.'

I abandoned the saint.

'You have made this garden?'

'With my own hands I have made it,' he replied lovingly. 'It took a long time.' Here he straightened his spare figure and cast a look round over the indescribable tangle of loveliness. 'But it was worth it.'

He smiled at me, and quoted Isaiah:

' "Instead of the thorn shall come up the fig tree, and instead of the briar shall come up the myrtle tree; and it shall be to the Lord for a name, for an everlasting sign that shall not be cut off." '

I could say nothing. I watched the sunlight soaking through the leaves from above, moving in shadows over the tombstones; I listened to the song of the birds in the trees and the drone of the bees' wings. I looked into my companion's calm eyes and at his brown gardener's hands, and my first sense of irritation vanished; I understood that there was religion in this gardening; that to him every new touch of beauty which he brought to birth out of this rich earth was like a psalm of praise; that year after year he had added beauty to beauty round the House of God.

How many times we made a start for the church and were side-tracked by a clump of valerian, I cannot say. We walked round and round and up and down, climbing shady paths, coming out upon terraces, talking (with frequent horticultural interpolations) about local matters.

'The origin of Roseland – look at those brier roses – is a moot point. The legend is that it got its name when King Henry VIII spent his honeymoon here with Anne Boleyn. They are supposed to have stayed in the Castle at St Mawes. The story is – smell this leaf; it comes from New Zealand. I wonder if I did right to put that clump of rock plants so high. What do you think? Oh, the story? They say that when Anne Boleyn got here she asked the name of the place, and, receiving no answer, turned to the roses and said, " 'Tis Roseland, forsooth!" Now foxgloves in a shady spot . . .'

I tried desperately to hold him a moment, but he was off after some snapdragons. I managed to drag him back.

'Yes, it's a pretty story, but it probably isn't true! The antiquaries derive the word from Rosinis, meaning "the Moorland Isle". Do you hear that cuckoo? He's in a wood at the back of my house.'

We parted the trees and looked out on the peaceful

beauty of the creek; the tide coming up, the high, still woods, and, beyond, the deep waters of Carrick Roads.

'Incredible, unspoilt beauty!'

'There is a scheme, you know,' he informed me, 'I believe the Bill has passed through Parliament, to turn this place into a great harbour for Atlantic liners, to build ocean wharves and graving docks and a railway, for St Just Pool is a natural deep-water anchorage.'

A graving dock and a railway in Paradise!

'Nothing,' he went on, 'has been heard of this scheme for some time. It may have been dropped.'

We both cast a glance round the quiet churchyard. I imagined how it would look in the middle of Portsmouth. We walked on until we came to a grave in a lovely corner of the garden.

'My eldest boy,' he whispered, and we went on among the flowers.

'Forgive me,' I said, 'but you must be one of the most fortunate vicars on earth. Instead of sin, you have flowers.'

He looked surprised.

'My dear sir, you have no idea. There is sin, too.'

'But here?' I said. 'Among this? A mere handful of people living quiet lives. What sin can there be here?'

'My parish is a big one. My curate takes a boat on Sunday and visits my other churches. I have a large parish. I have care of nearly a thousand scattered souls; and – oh, yes, my dear sir – there is sin.'

I wanted to find out more about the sins of Eden, but he shook his head and smiled.

'Wasn't I telling you about St Just? Well, he, you know, was Jestyn, son of Geraint.'

I drew a deep breath.

'Geraint of the Round Table, who married Enid and "crowned a happy life with a fair death"?' I asked.

He nodded his head and smiled:

'And the legend is that when he died he was borne across the bay at Gerrans, just at the back there, in a golden boat

with silver oars, and buried beneath Carne Beacon. Just
before you go, do come and look at the fuchsias, won't
you?'

'Now and then,' I whispered as I went on out of Roseland,
'just now and then one seems to touch again the fringe of
romance: it's just a flying second that stays for a flash – and
never long enough to be grasped – before it flies on to
Eternity to join all the lovely dreams and all the foolishness
which one has, from time to time, lost.'

5

I left Roseland by way of King Harry's Ferry, where I heard
the legend that Bluff Hal (who obviously wished to show-off
before Anne Boleyn) swam his horse across the deep waters.

I came in time to the hilly town of Helston. The place
was full of bustle. Men were hanging up flags in the high-
street. Country carts were piled high with boughs of trees.
The inhabitants took boughs and placed them before the
doors of houses and shops so that they formed green arches.
It was, of course, the eve of the Helston Floral, or Furry
Dance.

Some archaeologists claim that this annual May-time
dance is the oldest custom in England. They say that it is
connected with the Roman Floralia, and that it has been
observed since remote times when Helston, now inland, was
a busy port and the chief place of export for Cornish tin.

'My opinion,' said a local antiquary, 'is that the dance
dates from the Plague of London. We were badly hit here.
The people flew in terror from the town and lived in huts
made from the boughs of trees. I think the Furry Dance is a
survival of the great rejoicing which must have taken place
when the town was once again habitable. It may be that the
dancing in and out of houses is a relic of the joy with which
people must have entered their homes again.'

But the whole thing is obscure. Apocalyptic old men will

tell you that 'years back' a fiery serpent flew over Helston, and in thankfulness because the serpent did not fall on the town the people went out, plucked branches from the trees, and danced in and out of each other's homes.

I was wandering round Helston in the evening when I heard the tune with which I was to become almost unhappily familiar within the next twenty-four hours: the town band was practising the 'Furry Tune' in the Corn Exchange. I looked in. Here were a number of Helston's foremost citizens, men and women, hand in hand, laughing rather shyly, as they practised the dance. All the time the band reiterated with maddening monotony that peculiar and historic tune with a great number of 'pom-poms' on the big drum.

It must have been just after six o'clock in the morning. I sat up in bed. The band again:

Pom, pom, pom, pom, pom, pom,
Pom, pom, pom, peromp, peromp-pom-pom.

Heavens! the Furry Dance had begun! I dressed quickly and hurried out into a sunny May morning. The little town looked as though decked for a heathen festival. The arches of sycamore and the bright oak branches had wilted a little in the night. The streets were full of people. The first dancers stood ready and the band was playing to awaken the town. The three main dances in Helston are the before-breakfast dance, the after-breakfast children's dance, and the noontide full-dress dance led by the leading citizens, their wives and daughters.

In the old days this before-breakfast dance was known as the 'Servants' Dance', because in former times every servant in the town started the day with a measure; but now the first dance is open to any one with the energy to join in. Perhaps forty or fifty young men and young maids stood two by two, hand in hand. The boys wore lilies of the valley in their

86

button-holes, the girls wore their Sunday voile or ninon flowered gowns, and very sweet they looked.

When the band struck up, the dancers stepped out two by two, hand in hand; then they would turn and exchange partners with the couple behind, execute a quick twirl, and, linking hands with their original partners, continue down the street.

I enjoyed this informal dance enormously. There was nothing self-conscious about it. The dancers laughed and joked with their friends and among themselves as they went tripping it in the early sunlight to that relentless tune. People came to the doors of houses to smile and wave to them.

The peculiarity of the Floral Dance is the tradition that the dancers must enter houses and shops by the front door and come out, if possible, by the back. Certain houses and shops are marked down beforehand, and it is into these that the band leads the dancers. I believe it is right to say that a householder or a shopkeeper regards it as a sign of good fortune when the Furry Dancers enter his premises.

I followed the crowd on the flank of the pretty, twirling, prancing line of couples, and the Furry Tune printed itself for ever on my memory. We went right round the town. I caught the eye of a good-looking girl, held out my hand, and she came, a little shyly, took hands and, after a moment's awful blundering on my part, we became quite good at it.

We descended steps still dancing, we brushed past the arches of green boughs at doors, entered houses, found ourselves unable to dance in narrow passages, so we just held hands and laughed until we found ourselves in a garden where the band, slightly disorganized by its ordeal, was valiantly pom-poming its way out by the garden gate.

It was all sweet and innocent and un-modern. My partner, who could blush, told me that I was a good dancer. I told her how pretty she was and how much I liked her green hat. She told me that she worked in a draper's shop;

and all the time we were tripping, turning, taking other partners, and meeting and resuming our conversation.

The dance ended in front of the Corn Exchange, where it had begun. We were all rather red in the face. My unknown fair one flashed me a glance, said goodbye, and went off to her breakfast and her drapery.

Before noon, when the main dance takes place, Helston looks like the Town of the Mad Hatter. Great crowds from all parts of the West Country fill the streets. They come by motor-bus from every part. And the local police form a lane in this crowd so that Helston's foremost citizens, in silk hats and morning-coats, their wives in garden-party gowns, may find their way into the Corn Exchange.

Sharp on the stroke of noon the band played the Floral Dance, and down the steps into the blinding sunlight came, two by two, solemn men in silk hats and morning coats, holding their ladies gently by the tips of their fingers. Mr Heath Robinson, who has immortalized tall hats, would have loved that glimpse of their glossiness jigging up and down in grave and respectable gaiety.

The solicitor was dancing. So were the doctor, the clergyman, the estate-agent, the bank manager and his wife – in fact, the hierarchy of Helston was stepping it out together two by two, then turning and changing partners with the couple behind to execute a smart but formal twirl.

They danced across the main street through the crowds and into a boot and shoe warehouse. The band became slightly incoherent as the door eliminated the bulkier instruments, notably the big drum, which dropped out of the festival for several bars, but the trombone survived.

Once inside, the sound of the Furry Dance seemed likely to lift off the roof. I expected to see the boots and shoes in the window jig on their perches.

The dancers emerged by another door and went down the street, rather solemn, self-conscious, and grave, as though performing a religious ceremony. They entered another shop, they went through a house dancing all the time, down steep lanes with that infectious monotonous Furry tune leading them on, into main streets, back streets, and round the Bowling Green, and so back to the Corn Exchange.

They did not stop dancing for an hour. They danced through a line of spectators. Thousands followed them, stumbling into the running water, which flows rust red from the tin-workings down the pretty streets of this 'quaint old Cornish town'.

Such was the climax of the day.

But, looking back on it, the best moment of all was the 'Servants' Dance' before breakfast. The visitors had not arrived in Helston. The eyes of the world were not fixed on the dancers. So for an hour or so the spirit of Merrie England lived again in Cornwall.

6

Land's End! From Roseland to Land's End: I could give you no greater contrast. I did not think that any place could look so much like Land's End. The wind was blowing in from the sea, bringing with it one of those white fogs that terrify the boldest sailors. Jagged rocks of granite polished by the waters jutted out into the steamy sea, the white spray breaking over them. Every two minutes the signal gun of the Longships Lighthouse went 'Boom, Boom!' through the fog; and it was very lonely save for three elderly women in spectacles, whom the wind was trying to blow inland, where, no doubt, in this magic part of the world they would have been turned into three spotted trout and absorbed by the stream of legend. They stood, resisting this persistent assault, with their backs to the wind, holding their flying tulle motor veils with hands full of postcards. A guide came up to them, and, sweeping a hand towards the eternal wildness of granite and waves, said, as if paying them a compliment:'

'You're the last three ladies in England!'

'Are we?' they said. 'Fancy that!'

'Boom, Boom!' went the gun in the white fog, and the waves dashed themselves against Land's End.

I rejoice that I did not see Land's End in sunlight, for then, no doubt, it would have looked just like any other stretch of rocky coast; but, with the white mist that turned to thin rain over the land, drenching the body and drenching the mind in melancholy, Land's End seemed like the end of all things. When I had shaken off the pirate from Penzance who desired to show me the two noted rocks – 'Dr Johnson's Head' and 'Dr Syntax' – I stood alone enjoying my sorrow so completely that if any one had come along and attempted to be cheerful I would have pushed him over the cliff.

This is just my idea of the Styx. I stood there wrapped in a shroud of sea fog, listening to the wailing of the gulls, watching a cormorant sitting on a wet rock looking just as miserable as I felt. Oh, the fascinating pathos of this place. I half expected a shadowy boat to form among the rocks with the inevitable boatman in the stern looking up towards me and beckoning . . . Land's End!

How on earth did the Phoenicians get here in their galleys from the sunny coasts of Tyre? No wonder the ancients thought it to be the very limit of the habitable world! . . .

'Boom, boom!' went the gun in the fog, and the seagulls set up a great crying.

There is competition to be the last house in England, the last shop in England, the last inn in England; and as every shop, inn, and house on this piece of rock advertises this fact, quite regardless that the next-door neighbour is equally convinced, the sentimental effect is ruined.

I have come to the careful conclusion that the last hotel in England stands on Land's End; the last inn in England is the white, cunning-looking 'First and Last' at Sennen; and the last church is Sennen Church. The Sennen inn has heard 'the gentlemen go by' many a time, and it still looks as if its eyes are shut! The innkeeper told me that he believes there may be some truth in the story that beneath this inn is a great vault in which the smugglers dumped their brandy, but he has never had time to go over the floors with a hammer. I believe this old story. I think this inn is sitting on a secret.

The thing that thrilled me is the last church in England, the little grey church of St Sennen, which every charabanc passes, which no motorist thinks worth a visit.

In the thin rain, and with the signal gun booming, all the melancholy of Land's End is gathered in Sennen Church-yard. I believe there is a legend that after a battle so terrible that a mill was worked with blood – a glorious Celtic touch that – King Arthur and his battered knights thanked God for victory in Sennen Church. That seemed far off and improbable as I wandered round reading the last epitaphs in England.

'Sacred to the memory,' I read, 'of Mary, the beloved wife of Captain S. Sanderson, and fourth daughter of the late Rev. Thomas Wood, of Newcastle-on-Tyne, who was shipwrecked on the Breson, and afterwards perished while being drawn through the waves to the boat, January 12, 185–' (the last figure was obliterated). 'In the midst of life we are in death.'

The Longships gun boomed its monotonous thunder.

I looked round the churchyard wondering if by any chance the last monuments in a country of monuments would reveal any merit.

I was disappointed. Over Thomas Smith, who died on September 29th, 1825, aged twenty-four, they had written:

Lo here he lies whose deeds deserved love,
His body here, his soul is far above,
But by the merits of the Prince of Peace
We hope he's gone to joys that never cease.

A naive farewell mounts guard above the remains of

Richard and Grace Pender, two young children who died in 1870:

> *My parents dear, don't weep for me,*
> *As we are now you soon will be.*
> *We leave the world and all its care,*
> *In heaven we hope to meet you there.*

The last touch of real poetry in England is written above the grave of Dionysius Williams, who departed this life, aged fifty, on May 15th, 1799:

> *Life speeds away*
> *From point to point, though seeming to stand still*
> *The cunning fugitive is swift by stealth;*
> *Too subtle is the movement to be seen,*
> *Yet soon man's hour is up and we are gone.*

I gained a cold thrill from that as I stood in the rain writing it down in a wet book. Is it a quotation? If so, who wrote it? Whenever in the future I think of Land's End I shall see not the jagged rocks and the sea, but that lichened stone lying above Dionysius (who would be 180 years old if he were still alive); that stone and that unlikely name with the rain falling over them, and in the distance the gun booming through the sea fog. . . .

> *Yet soon man's hour is up and we are gone. . . .*

I went back into Penzance, where people were, for no earthly reason, smiling.

7

I met him by the side of the road. He was a poor old man and near him was a heavy pack; so I asked if I might give him a lift. 'No,' he said, thanking me all the same. I could not give him a lift because the place to which he was going would be inaccessible to 'him' – here he pointed to the car.

'To her,' I corrected.

'To she,' he said, meeting me half-way.

This established contact, and we were soon talking like old friends. You cannot do this in England I mean in other parts of England! – for the Saxon is slow to accept you into his confidence, while the Celt loves words for their own sake. He brought out an empty pipe and just held it appealingly. An Essex man would have asked frankly for tobacco: my old friend was more artistic.

As we sat on the same stone, smoking the same navy cut, I realized that this old man was the Gordon Selfridge plus Northcliffe of the early world: he was the world's first trader and the world's first gossip column; he was one of the last of the Cornish packmen. The rich store of goods in his pack was only rivalled by the rich store of local scandal in his head.

'How long have you been a packman?' I asked him.

I felt the question to be absurd; and it would not have astonished me had he replied: 'Well, I began my round, working for Eli of Nablus, general merchant of Sidon, who came over to Britain once a year from 60 BC onwards with a cargo of seed pearls, which he swopped for tin. Then when the Romans left I did a rare trade in strops for sword blades.'

'These heere fifty years, sur,' he replied.

'Then you must be nearly seventy?'

'Well, I caan't tell 'zactly,' he replied; 'but putten one thing agen another, I b'lieve that's so, sure 'nuff, sur.'

'And you still carry that heavy pack?'

'Yes, sur, I carries him easy, though I do be an old man.'

Before the railway came to Cornwall and killed the fairies, and for some time after, the packman, trudging the weary hills on his round, linked lonely farmhouse to lonely farmhouse over miles of wild country. He was the one great thrill in the lives of the girls and women, whose eyes sparkled as he pulled out his trays and offered to their vanity cloths and trifles from the distant town. The motor-car and the charabanc dealt the profession its heaviest blow. Shops now canvass the wilderness with Ford vans; and the exiles on the farms, whose grandfathers lived within a twenty-mile radius, now take the omnibus into the nearest village and return with the shopping in brown-paper parcels.

One by one the old packmen have faded out of existence; instead of the eager doorstep welcome and the excitement as he spread out his goods he received a cold nothing-doing-today look, and the information that the misses left by the eleven o'clock charabanc to buy the new blouse length. Poor old Autolycus! He dragged his weary limbs out of commerce. A few still remain – notably round the Lizard – the last members of an ancient fraternity; and of these was my companion.

He pulled off the waterproof and opening his pack, displayed trays of assorted oddments: cheap shaving brushes, razors, pins, braces, corsets, studs, photograph frames, religious texts, black and white spotted aprons, combs, brushes, and ribbons. His prices were the same as in the small shops.

'I suppose you've had to alter your stock from year to year to keep up with fashion?'

'Yes, 'tis true, sur. When first I did taake un out on me back there waun't no saafety razors, and the faarm boys had no use for hair grease, and now they be all smurt and gay in town clothes.'

'What is the newest article you have been forced to stock?'

He pulled out a tray and showed, with, I thought, a smirk of distaste, clippers to crop shingled heads and many kinds of slides to hold back bobbed hair.

'In the old days,' he said, 'you never saw such hair, I 'sure ee, as you seed in Cornwall, and the girls bruushed it all day loong – that they did, I tell ee for sure, sur – and 'twas lovely to see; and now they've a-cut it arl off, and if you ax me what I think about un I tell ee they look like a row of flatpolled cabbages, that un do! Aye, sur, all the world must be in the fashion now. 'Tis different from t'ould days when I soold a packet of hairpins to every wumman I met.'

He smoked in silence as he mournfully packed up his aids to the shingled.

We fell to talking of the merits of the packman's profession. Like all professions it has – or had – its secrets.

'Well, sur, ef you bain't tired of listening to me, I could tell ee a lot about packmen. Ef you wants to maake money at this game you've need of a still tongue in your head, sure I tell ee. There was young Trevissey, when I was a chap, who had haaf the fellows from Penzance to Kynance Cove lookin' for him with sticks, for young Joe just sopped up stories like a spoonge sops up waater, but un couldn't hold it. Well, sur, that chap went from faarm to faarm over the length and breadth of the land tellin' Jennifer Penlee how young Jan Treloar was out courtin' Mary Taylor over at Mevagissey. Sur, that chap went through the land sellin' boot-laaces and spreadin' trouble like you never saw! Before that booy had been on his round more'n twice there warn't one maan or wumman who didn't knaw what every other maan and wumman was wearin' underneath their cloathes; and that's the truth, sur.'

'What happened to Joe?'

'Why, sur, they got to be too fearful to buy a shoestring from un! "Heere's young Joe comin'!" they'd holler. "Shut the doeer fast!" So un went away, and was never seen again in these paarts.'

We meditated solemnly on the tragedy of this novelist born out of his place. The old man knocked out his pipe and said he must be getting along. He refused assistance, and swung his great pack on his shoulders, waved his stock, and made off over a side-track among the scarred ruins of a dead tin mine. They say that this mine, which stretches beneath the Atlantic, was worked before the time of Christ.

The old figure disappeared among the craters, threading his way carefully, tapping with his stick; and I thought, as I watched him go, that he and the old mine were fellows, equally ancient – for the packman was probably here before the Romans – one outdated and dead: the other poor, old, and lonely, walking slowly along that same sad road.

8

I came to Tintagel as a man should, tired, fearful, and at evening. . . .

I have all my life thought of Tintagel as one of those places which no man should see. For eight hundred years the story of that king who rides down history on a harpstring has soaked itself into the imagination of the English people. Charlemagne for France; Arthur for England. The story grew here. On this grey rock above the sea, Uther Pendragon took that lovely queen, Igerne; and so began the story that ran through medieval Europe challenging the imagination of poet and writer, gathering strength and beauty, to break at last in the splendid climax of the 'Grail' music. . . .

Tin-tagel!

To thousands of English people those syllables go clothed in grandeur because there are two Tintagels: one is in Cornwall, the other in cloudland. One on the map; the other spun out of verse and music; and this is the real Tintagel, no dead rock in a grey sea, but a country of dream more real than reality, where there are still music, the breaking of lances, and the pain of love.

The sun was sinking seawards as I climbed a rocky gorge and came to the most desolate little valley, I think, in all the wild West Country. The sides of the cliff were scarred with grey splintered slate; half-way the rocks approach each other to form a kind of gate; at the end of the valley is a little bay, the sea foaming over a grey pebble beach and running through a cavern called 'Merlin's Cave'.

It seems as though a great sword has split this valley in two; on one side, perched high, is the tiny village of Tintagel; on the other side, covered in grass, wrecked by a landslide, are fragments of an ancient wall known to legend as King Arthur's Castle of Tintagel. The key is kept in a cottage among lemonade bottles.

'No, please, sir,' said a little old woman who uses the word 'please' unexpectedly. 'Please, it's too late for you to go up to the Castle tonight, please. But if you promise not to be long, please, I'll give you the key. . . .'

I began to climb steep, winding steps, cut in the face of the rock. The waves boomed below in 'Merlin's Cave', the seagulls flew below crying, and in my hand was the key of Tintagel.

Think of that. Wait a moment! In my hand was the key of Tintagel.

As a ruin Tintagel is the most disappointing castle in England. A wall that is several centuries later than King Arthur runs its crazy course on the cliff edge. It is indescribably remote, thrust up out of a grey sea towards the sky, with the jagged peaks of lesser rocks lifted like spears below it, and all around it the hiss and whisper of the sea. Birds rose from the grass before me as I walked; rabbits scuttled away to dive into burrows in which – who knows? – may lie some fragment of a sword.

A disappointing ruin, but a great experience. As I climbed the rocks and looked over the gaunt cliffs I seemed to come nearer, not to the gentlemanly knights of Tennyson or the paladins of Malory, but to the rough chieftains of history from whom the epic sprang. I saw Arthur stripped of the spell, with no Excalibur, but only a common spear, and the sun of Rome sinking into a sea of trouble on which the fortunes of England were to set their sails. How difficult it is to visualize King Arthur as a half-Roman kinglet. . . .

It grew dusk, and I saw the other picture. Do boys still read Malory? Do they lie on their stomachs in orchards with that book propped up before them in the grass? Do they forget to go home for food and lie on till the harvest bugs set about them and the dusk falls, reading that wild gallantry? Do they still go back through darkening woods, shamefully late, peopling the hush with the splintering crash

97

of steel point on jesseraunts of double mail, seeing in the waving of the trees the fluttering of banneroles and in the starkness of pines on a hill lances against the sky? I wonder. . . .

Tintagel is haunted. It is haunted not by Arthur and the Knights of the Round Table but by that moment in our lives when imagination caught fire and blazed. The ghosts on this rock are the great army of Englishmen and Englishwomen who in their youth believed in Excalibur and wept in sorrow beside that mere as the three hooded queens came in their barge with a crying that 'shivered to the tingling stars' to bear the dying king of Avilion.

When the wind blows from the sea at Tintagel a sudden grey veil is flung over this high ruin: a veil of damp mist that blots out the distant earth; it runs on into the valley like a cloud and is gone. No wonder that men believed strange things of this place and of the king who would come again.

I slithered down the rock steps and gave up the key of Tintagel to the little old lady, who said: 'Oh, please, thank you.' In her tea-room was an American girl from the south, who perpetuated the speech of some negro 'mammy' in her interesting accent: an attractive intonation impossible to convey in print.

'Tell me,' she said, as we walked through the valley, 'is it pronounced Tintagel, like that, or Tintadgel, for our literary society back home has deputed me to find out. If it's Tintadgel we're going to fine every one five cents who says it wrong. . . . My, I tell you I just can't say what I feel about this place!'

We agreed that it is difficult and that it did somehow bring one nearer the Round Table.

'And,' said the girl, 'what a lamb poor old Launcelot was, and what a shame that after all that fighting he never saw the Grail. My, but that was real hard! Galahad was sweet, too, but he was a dumb-bell! Merlin did a heap of silly things to show how smart he was, and Arthur himself was, now and then, a bit of a bore, I guess, to live with, but – oh, my! – I just love the whole bunch; I just love 'em, my lordy, almost to death. . . .'

We turned and looked down on the rock and saw the night mists creeping over it.

'To think I'm here,' whispered the girl from the far south, 'here . . . Tin-tadgel . . . Tin-tadgel!'

At night, with the moon, falling over the tumbled walls, Tintagel seems more dead than ever: the ruins of Egypt leap to life in moonlight, so do many of our castles and abbeys; but Tintagel is to be found only within the covers of a book.

And I thought, as I looked down on it from the other side of the valley, saw the thin line of light run along the walls, picking out a gateway here and a crumbled corner there, that most of us have belonged to that Round Table – so many of us, in fact, that if Arthur came back to give us youth again and called us out to joyous adventures he would have an army great enough to ride from Camelot to the conquest of the earth.

CHAPTER FIVE

I explore the Town of the Broad Arrow, am chilled by Dartmoor and cheered by Widecombe-in-the-Moor. Clovelly is 'quaint' and Barnstaple Market is hearty. An old man tries to tell me something in Zomerset, and on Porlock Hill I find a silk night-dress

I

A MAN cannot leave Cornwall without thinking a number of things. The men have been all over the world in ships. They come home on leave from mines in Canada and Australia, and from voyages of the Fleet. Half of them seem to be naval reservists. The girls, however, in small places, have never been to Truro. There can be no other part of this country in which so many brothers have been round the world while their sisters have sat at home.

I think that thousands of old people in Cornwall believe secretly in fairies while their grandchildren believe openly in the cinema.

A curious characteristic of English scenery is its ability to change itself in the space of a few miles. Towards Devon the rugged Cornish rocks gave way to a smoother, more comfortable countryside, a homelier, less disturbing vista of green and red fields.

'In England once again!' I whispered as I saw a man ploughing a real Devon field, the colour of red ochre where the earth was newly turned and of cocoa where the sun had dried it. A different country. I remembered the old man at Tregoney who told me that he was 'going up to England next week', and then corrected himself and said 'Plymouth'.

I ran through Tavistock and approached a smooth, open sweep of country, hill folded on hill to the sky.

Dartmoor! Just then I saw the grim broad arrow on the road, two men with rifles, heard the click of spades, and was conscious of swift scrutiny as I went past towards a grey prison on the open moor.

Princetown is surely one of the strangest towns in England: the Town of the Broad Arrow. A grey prison surrounded by a mighty wall built to defy the climber stands a little apart in a hollow with a warder holding a rifle at the gate. The main street is a row of grey houses which seems to have derived its architectural inspiration from the prison, as, no doubt it has, just as the occupants derive their livelihood from it. The grey prison is the parent of everything in Princetown.

Garden gates click and out walks a blue-clothed warder, his rifle under his arm, a key-chain dangling over his right hip. He turns and waves his hand to a woman who looks through the window after him; she holds up a baby and waves the small hand in his direction, and he goes on down towards the prison. All three, man, woman, and child, have been drawn to this gloomy town on the top of Dartmoor by the crimes of their fellows.

There is the sound of heavy boots on the road. A file of big, hulking men march along, carrying pick-axes. They are burned brown by wind and sun. They wear striped tunics and khaki trousers. Soft blue caps are set on their close-cropped, bullet heads. Before and behind march the blue-coated men with rifles.

All day long charabancs run into Princetown and pile up in the square. A morbid curiosity draws thousands of people to the melancholy Town of the Broad Arrow. Old women, small shopkeepers, young girls, troop down towards the nearest work-gang and stand, very solemn, and awed watching the men whom society has removed for its own safety.

'Who's that, and what did he do?' is the question they all ask.

The warders are not communicative. They stand at ease with their rifles, watching the men, seldom talking. What the convicts think as they see the herd of curious law-abiding folk gazing at them with a zoo expression is perhaps not all of it printable.

'It's a strange town to live in,' said a man who knows the prison. 'We get to know who's in. We've got A at the moment and B, and Y, who, you may remember, cut off his children's hands to spite his wife. Funny things go on here. Only the other day an old man over sixty was let out after twenty-two years. When the day came the old man was frightened to leave. He begged to be allowed to stay on. I believe someone agreed to take him on as a gardener.'

'I cannot imagine any living soul, no matter how old or out of touch with the world, wishing to stay inside those walls!'

'Can't you, sir? Well, I could tell you different. Some "old lags" are only happy when they're inside.'

' "Old lags"?'

'That's what we call them. Old hands or "old lags"; it's the same thing. . . . Are you fond of music? Well, you ought to hear some of the concerts they give inside there. The convicts are very proud of the choir. They're attached to it. The organist, who is a joiner by trade, is in love with his organ, and I believe has been let out on ticket-of-leave once or twice, but he's managed to get back to that organ of his. The bass has been out twice, and the alto, I believe, three times. No, sir, they can't break up that choir! They're all safe and settled in again for at least another two years, I believe.'

'You mean they commit an offence in order to get back?'

'Yes; something simple and not too dangerous, like sleeping in a church and pinching the offertory box. Then – back they come!'

I absorbed this new aspect in silence.

'A funny thing happened one Christmas,' he went on. 'They'd fixed up a big concert. In November the tenor was let out. Before the end of the month he was back, and the governor sent for him. "Jones," he said, but that wasn't his name, "Jones, I always thought you were a good sport. We give you a chance, and here you are again within a month!" What do you think Jones said to the governor? He said: "Well, sir, I thought I'd go straight, and then, sir, I knew you'd make a muck-up of that there concert, so I've come back, sir!" '

'I suppose the convicts have no contact with the outside world?'

'No; but they know everything that goes on. When an "old lag" comes back it's known all over the prison within an hour.'

'How?'

'By tapping on the hot-water pipes that run the length of the place. They sit in their cells and tap messages to each other in code. Why, bless me, when an "old lag" comes back he brings all the latest news from the outside world with him; messages from pals and relations, and he sits there tapping them out on the pipe and answering questions till he pretty near drops. . . .'

Princetown is, strangely enough, on the map of the American's pilgrimage. It was founded in 1808 as a prison for French and American prisoners of war. The church was built by French and American prisoners. In it hangs the Stars and Stripes, and the east window was presented by the United States Society of Daughters of 1812.

As a convict prison, Princetown dates from 1850. During the war it sheltered the consciences of objectors.

It was with relief that I turned away from the Town of the Broad Arrow. Some distance outside the town I slowed up to pass a working gang. High up on the hedge-bank stood a young convict, with a mild, simple face, and blue, frank eyes. I would have taken him for an honest fellow but for those terrible clothes. He looked at me with frank interest. (I wondered whether he was the man who had cut off his children's hands.)

Before him, as he sweated with his billhook, stretched the wide, rolling hills of Dartmoor, the free wind racing over them, the free clouds piling up over the edge of the downs. I wondered, as I shot away, whether he was conscious of this bitter contrast or whether he was in the choir.

2

So much has been written about Dartmoor that, dearly as I would love to paint its cloudscapes and the smooth sweep of hills, I feel that there is little left for a pen but a question: Has any Dartmoor novelist compared this eerie two hundred miles of Devonshire with the African desert?

Dartmoor is the green Sahara of England, a wilderness of hills and heather, hill folded on hill mile after mile, great clouds billowing, and over the moor the strange desert atmosphere as of Some One watching. Could any novelist tackle a more heart-breaking subject than the mystery which Dartmoor seems to hold? I doubt if any writer will ever wrest it from her. An untameable, aloof desert! Comfortable Dorset adores Thomas Hardy, friendly Exmoor loves Blackmore, Cumberland probably admires Wordsworth, but Dartmoor seems never to have given one stray thought to Eden Phillpotts.

To stand on a Dartmoor tor, with all the world, it seems, falling away to the distant horizon and the clouds moving just above your head, is to experience in some measure a kind of panic like the primitive fear felt by many people for thunder. A man in such surroundings seems so small and naked. All the pretence goes from him. He drops the mask of his civilization and is humbled and afraid. Afraid of what? He is rather like a rabbit moving in the open beneath the eye of an invisible hunter.

Now and then a cloud just skims the top of a hill, steaming a little at the edges and falling some way into the gullies in white mist, before curling up to join the main body and passing on as if it had delivered its message. In the heart of the moor are bogs, in whose soggy greenness are born the rivers of Devonshire. What a strange thing it is to stop with the flat of a hand the flow of a river which near the coast

104

bears great ships to sea! In the green valleys of Dartmoor
. . . but here I am falling into the trap! I have said too much
already.

In the shadow of Warren Tor, beside a road that cuts
straight over the moor like a stretched tape, stands an inn.

This inn is small, white, and built low, as if crouching in
defence from the wild winds which in winter must make its
chimneys scream. It has that air of sanctuary which most
inns possess in wild places. Even with the sunlight over the
porch and the fat tabby-cat asleep on the mat, the mind
turns inevitably to a thought of snow and wind and the
sound of a man hammering on that door with the spirit of
the wilderness at his heels.

All good inns should possess a boast, but the boast of
Warren Inn is the strangest I have heard: it boasts that the
fire in the bar has not been quenched for a hundred years.

I went in to have a look at this fire. A fox mask snarled on
a bracket over the bar. The room was dark, in the window
geraniums were brilliant red against the light, and the air
full of that comfortable tweedy smell of peat. The hundred-
year-old fire was the saddest fire I have seen in many a long
day. A thin spiral of blue smoke curled lazily from a huge
pile of peat, and there was not a hint of warmth.

'Who lit it and why has it always remained alight?' I
asked the innkeeper as we stood drinking beer together.

'I don't know,' he said, with the disappointing frankness
of the true Englishman (in Cornwall they would have had a
magnificent story about it!). 'It's the custom of this inn, and
has been for the last hundred years.'

I remembered the story of the American in Italy who was
told that a certain candle had been burning for centuries
and promptly quenched it with the remark: 'Well, I guess
it's time it was blown out!'

'Suppose,' I said, 'someone let it out?'

A sharp look of anger passed across my host's friendly
face.

'Not while I'm here!' he cried firmly, and brought his

hand down crash on the counter. That, I thought, is why England will never be a republic.

Over a second tankard he began to talk about the storm-bound travellers who have made their way to the inn lights during the winter.

'Long time ago,' said the innkeeper, 'long before my time, they say a man came here all snowed up in the dead of winter. In the night it was. And they gave him the front room. He went up to bed, being tired. Now, in his bedroom was a big old chest, and he must have been an inquisitive, interferin' fellow, for what did he do but fight with it till he opened it. And what do you think he saw?'

He took a drink, put down the tankard, and waited.

'I don't know.'

'He saw a lot of ice, and underneath a corpse.'

'How horrible.'

'That's what he thought, for he awakened the inn. "Oh," they said, "don't take on so! It's only feyther, who's being kept till we can take him to Widecombe Church!"'

I have verified this gruesome story, but believe that it happened, not in this inn, but in another inn of the same name which in old times stood on the opposite side of the road.

I watched the sun set over Dartmoor.

I have seen the sun sink below the Sahara, and this gave me a clue to that something in the sight of Dartmoor that chills the heart – its inhumanity! Here are no cosy acres, but miles that have never known the plough; miles that have never given food or shelter to man, woman, or child, miles that are as remote from humanity as the craters of the moon; that seem to say, 'I care not for man whether he lives or dies, and though you try to the end of time you shall not tame me.' The cruelty of desert and ocean is on Dartmoor. . . .

In the loneliness and in the stillness the sun sank toward the crest of the western hills, and a wind blew through the heather. I stood high on the moor in the centre of a stone hut circle, built before history began by some unknown race of men. What queer men they must have been, driven, perhaps from the cosy valleys and the shelter of trees, to live as exposed as flies on a wall in the frightening openness of a land bared to the sky.

The sun touched the rim of the moor in a troubled smoulder of cloud and slowly sank. There was no sound. No bird sang. No wheels creaked, no voice spoke; only the wind went with a faint whistle through the heather and the grass. In the silence and the vast solitude of sky and moor it seemed to me that the least religious man might well fear the opening of the clouds and the sound of a Voice. . . .

Overhead the first star shone, and in the dusk the rustle of the heather at my feet was like the movement of dark water.

3

I took one glance at the map, and sang in a loud but, I have often been told, distressing voice:

> *Tom Pearce, Tom Pearce, lend me thy grey mare,*
> *All along, down along, out along lee,*
> *For I want for to go to Widecombe Fair,*
> *With . . .*

There it was on the map! Widecombe-in-the-Moor! (Surely, in the song, they spell it Widdicombe?) It lay off my route; but lives there a man inured to convivial occasions who could resist going to Widecombe to see what it looks like? Not I? How many times, and in how many lands, I have assisted in the journey of Tom Pearce's grey mare to Widecombe I cannot say. I suppose that in every part of the world in which Englishmen retain their voices, and particularly wherever there is a Devonian, this old grey mare of Tom Pearce's has jogged along to the tinkle of wineglasses with Bill Brewer, Jan Stewer, Peter Gurney, Peter Davey,

Dan'l Whiddon, Harry Hawke, old Uncle Tom Cobleigh and all!

This song stands before the world as Devonshire's anthem and it is the kind of rich, full, mellow song that all men love.

The way to Widecombe lies due east across Dartmoor. I have already described Dartmoor as a desert. Moorland villages such as Widecombe are the oases in this desert. There are little clumps of green clustered in the hollow of the hills, sheltered, if shelter is possible, from the rougher blasts of the weather – little centres of humanity in the great wildness of the desert. I imagine that beer tastes better at Widecombe than on any other part of Dartmoor; fires are warmer here, and lit windows friendlier because of the grimness that stretches beyond. . . .

I sang the song all the way to Widecombe, and with such fervour that the hill (on which, you remember, Tom Pearce, 'seed his old mare down a-makin'' her will') took me by surprise, so that I nearly arrived in the blacksmith's.

Then I saw Widecombe! A line of tiny white, thatched cottages lying in luscious hedges, a hollow full of thick green trees, the tall grey tower of a church above them, a village green, an inn; and over the roofs, whichever way you look, the smooth, bald heads of the moors making a curve against the sky.

I never realized the power of song till I came to Widecombe!

Four charabancs were drawn up opposite the village green. Old Uncle Tom Cobleigh stood leaning on an ash-stick, his back bent, watching from the green the swift descent of the trippers with their cameras. Young men and young women roamed vaguely arm in arm through the lanes, languishingly or gaily, according to temperament. Elderly women swarmed over the church; men in holiday humour sampled the village inn. A hen crossed the road delicately, as if trying to avoid the cameras.

'So this,' I said to Old Uncle Tom Cobleigh, 'is Widecombe?'

'Oi zur,' said old Uncle Tom Cobleigh.

'From the look of it,' I said, 'I expect you wish the song had never been written.'

Uncle Cobleigh was quick in the uptake. He smiled.

'It be good vor trade,' he said.

'Do you ever sing the song in Widecombe?'

'Oi zur,' he said solemnly. 'We sings it after a zing-zong zometimes afore "God Save the King"! Oh, aye zur!'

I looked round and saw that one of the charabanc drivers was buying petrol from the village blacksmith, a man who looked to me rather like our dear old friend Bill Brewer.

A fiendish noise arose in Widecombe. Several spirited young men began to press the motor-horns of the charabancs with great vigour.

By twos and threes and fours the lingerers returned to their vehicles, seated themselves, and with a cheery wave of their hands to old Uncle Tom Cobleigh, thundered off towards the open moor between the hedges. On the wind was born the sound of song:

Old Uncle Tom Cobleigh and all!

Old Uncle Tom Cobleigh and all! . . .

An unnatural stillness reigned in Widecombe.

'The fair,' I said, 'seems to be over.'

Did you know that the devil is supposed to live at Widecombe?

This is so. In the church a delightful old ex-sailor, who was at the bombardment of Alexandria, told me the story of the most exciting thing that happened in Widecombe – before, of course, the invention of the motor-car.

It appears that one night years and years ago a horseman spurred into Widecombe and asked for a drink. It was a wild night. No one would have thought anything, perhaps, had the drink not sizzled as it went down his throat. He was, of course, the devil! The next thing the villagers knew was that this horseman had hitched his horse to the church steeple, which fell with a great crash. Then he rode away.

That is the legend: this is the history. On Sunday afternoon, October 21st, 1638, the tower of the church was struck by lightning, and fell, killing four people on the spot and injurying many, who afterwards died. This disaster is commemorated by surely the quaintest verses inscribed in any church. They were written by Richard Hill, the village schoolmaster at the time of the storm. He starts off as follows:

> *In token of our thanks to God these tablets are erected,*
> *Who, in a dreadful thunderstorm, our persons here protected*
> *Within this church of Widecombe, 'mongst many fearful signs*
> *The manner of it is declared in these ensuing lines.*

He goes on to describe how the people were singing a psalm when suddenly a terrific clap of thunder was heard:

> *Men so perplexed were, they knew not one another's faces;*
> *They all, or most, were stupefied that with so strange a smell*
> *Or other force, whate'er it was, which at that time befell,*
> *One man was struck dead, two wounded, so they died a few hours after;*
> *No father could think on his son, nor mother mind her daughter,*
> *One man was scorched so that he lived but fourteen days, and died,*
> *Whose clothes were very little burnt, but many there beside*
> *Were wounded, scorched, and stupefied in that so strange a storm.*

There is a lot more in the same graphic manner, and he ends up piously with:

> *We hope that they were well prepared, although we know now how*
> *'Twas then with them; it's well with you if you are ready now.*

When the last load from Ilfracombe has departed, Widecombe is as typical an English hamlet as you will find, with its village green, its church, its Satanic legend, its old lady of ninety-seven who has never seen the sea or a railway train (and is none the worse for it), and its philosophic calm in the face of publicity.

The smoking concert put it in the heart and the charabanc put it on the map.

4

I have always wished to see Clovelly, because for years I have been travelling in railway carriages which picture the charm of its curious High Street, the only high street in England too steep for wheels. The first thing I saw when I arrived was a grocer's boy delivering goods on a toboggan which banged loudly from terrace to terrace. I hope they take the eggs round by hand.

Clovelly is difficult to write about because it is the old-established beauty queen of England; and knows it. It cannot be left out of any tour because it is unique: an English Amalfi rising sheer from the bay. Beneath its apparent simplicity is a deal of artifice; it is a beauty spot that has been sternly told to keep beautiful. Its washing is displayed discreetly on a certain day. No signs disfigure its bowers: no motor-car may approach within half a mile of its sacrosanct charms, and when an old cottage dies it rises phoenix-like from its ashes exactly as it was, looking at least five hundred years old, but with 'C. H., 1923', inscribed on it.

Those two initials are the secret of Clovelly. Behind its beauty is an autocrat, the lady of the manor, Mrs Christine Hamlyn, who owns the town. At frequent intervals the native hear the tapping of her long cane on the cobbles, and they hurriedly hide Willie's second-best trousers, or any other blot on the landscape which might at that critical moment be defying the old-established 'quaintness'.

Clovelly's motto is, or should be: 'Every day and in every way, and, in spite of myself, I become quainter and quainter.'

And Clovelly is quaint! Clovelly is so beautiful, and has been beautiful for so long that it can well afford to take my knock at its self-consciousness and its postcard commerce with the contempt such remarks deserve.

Its steep, irregular High Street, with its little gabled houses bowered in flowers rising from the cobbles, their balconies nodding to each other across the narrow way, is a charming sight. The donkeys, with panniers on each side, which clip-clop up the cobbles with hooks on their hind shoes are 'quaint', and even the usual band of fishermen in blue jerseys who stand forever gazing out to sea seem instinctively to adopt 'quaint' poses as they sweep the horizon.

I have, in one day, seen more 'quaint' people than I ever hoped to see. Clovelly appears to attract them from soon after breakfast onwards. Immediately the morning's chara-banc arrived, a steady trickle of them passed beneath my window, very quaint visitors, and they all said, looking round and reaching for their cameras:

'Oh, isn't it *quaint?*'

There are girls in cycling knickers, young men with hairy legs dressed as Boy Scouts, thin young men with spectacles and open-necked shirts, who carry enormous rucksacks on their backs. It is disconcerting to look out of your window in Clovelly and observe three clergymen apparently taking your photograph. Then there are Americans. Six college girls from Alabama live exactly opposite. They think everything is just 'too cute for words'. When they have been in Clovelly another hour or so they will learn to use the word 'quaint' instead of 'cute'. Now and then a donkey climbs the hill with a girl who tries hard to hide her silk knees all the way up the High Street.

It is really very 'quaint'. We all agree about that.

When you get tired of buying postcards, or 'quaint' brass spoons with a Clovelly donkey as a handle, you can sail with the fishermen from the 'quaint' little harbour or you can go fishing in the bay. If you do either of these you will realize why Clovelly was built. The cliffs round the bay are all of soft red sandstone with the exception of that cliff on which

Clovelly stands. This is an unexpected spur of solid rock. Evidently in the old smuggling days this rock appealed to the first Clovellians as an admirable retreat, and, undeterred by the difficulty of constructing a village on an almost perpendicular slope, they set to work to make a harbour and a main street.

The view of Clovelly from the sea is one of the finest views in North Devon. The village looks like a bunch of white blossom in a green hedge. A row of white-balconied old houses stand at the water level and in the foreground rise the masts of fishing boats.

'What do you do here in the winter?' I asked a fisherman.

'We prepare for the herring fishing. The Clovelly herring is the best in the world.'

'And in the summer you fish for visitors?'

'Yes.'

'Is it true that the next village, Bucks Cross, is inhabited by descendants of shipwrecked Spaniards from the Armada?'

'I don't know, but they're a different kind of people from we!'

Early morning and late evening, when the High Street is not congested, are the best times in Clovelly.

In the morning you are awakened by a terrible clatter beneath the window. A herd of donkeys, you think, must have gone mad. You run to the curtains and see below one sedate animal walking down the street arm in arm, so to speak, with the village postman. On the donkey's back are the mail-bags.

In the evening the air becomes full of the scent of flowers, the white houses gleam sharply in the fading light, windows are lit, and you receive the strange impression that you are living on a stage. Clovelly seems too good to be true! From the little bastion overlooking the bay you can look out where, on the left, lonely Lundy Island lies like a whale out to sea. Girls with sunburned legs and sandals stand meditatively in the hush, drinking their evening draught of beauty; men suspiciously like artists prowl through the dusk; up the hill walk an affectionate couple – Clovelly is a great place for honeymoons – and the scene grows darker, more flower-scented, and more beautiful every minute. . . .

You fight with yourself. You struggle with the devil in you. You grit your teeth. You will be strong! You will not give way! No matter how beautiful it becomes you will not say . . . Resist, resist, keep a tight hold on yourself! You will not . . .

'Oh, isn't it *too* quaint?' says a voice.

Did you say it or – thank goodness! It was the girl with freckles who blushed when she signed the hotel register.

'That's the word I've been looking for,' whispers her husband sentimentally. 'You always say just the right thing, my darling!'

Somewhere a donkey brays; and you walk slowly up the hill.

5

Every Friday morning Mr and Mrs Bill Brewer, Mr and Mrs Harry Hawke, Mr and Mrs Jan Stewer, Mr and Mrs Peter Gurney, Mr and Mrs Peter Davey, Mr and Mrs Dan'l Whiddon, Mr and Mrs T. Cobleigh, and half the rural county, harness the old grey mare in the farm-cart and set out for Barnstaple.

The body of the cart is occupied by Sarah's brown calf under a net or by three protesting piglets. Beside the farmer's wife are two big wicker-work baskets, known by the old name 'panniers'. They are covered with butter muslin. In one basket are the biggest, reddest, and shiniest strawberries you ever saw in your life, a great jug of brown Devonshire cream, several pounds of bright gold butter, and a cheese; in the other lie two dead fowls and a duck, trussed and plucked, their intimate internals neatly pinned to their wings.

So the farmer and his wife, with a week's hard work in

byre and dairy ready for sale, jog stolidly along the country lanes; the crisp clippity-clop of the old grey mare an accompaniment to their thoughts, whatever these may be.

They draw rein in Barnstaple.

Here they part company. The wife arms her panniers and goes off in one direction; the farmer, after an exciting landing, makes off with the calf or the piglets in another. Husband and wife will not meet again till the end of the day, and then they will jog home together in an empty cart, talking finance.

The 'Pannier Market' to which Mrs Farmer takes her baskets is one of the most characteristic country sights you can see in Devon. Beneath a big roof supported by iron pillars about five hundred farmers' wives and daughters sit before their stalls on which they display their week's work. It is, generally speaking, a woman's market. For every dairy farmer who has a stall there are at least fifty women.

The contents of each stall are more or less uniform, because all these women are engaged week after week on much the same work. How people buy here puzzles me. One duck looked just as good as the other, one basket of strawberries as fresh and big as the next, and there seemed nothing at all to choose between one bowl of brown cream and all the other bowls of brown cream.

Yet all day long the aisles between the sitting stallholders are packed with connoisseurs, feeling ducks, sampling strawberries, choosing butter and cream. The air is sweet with a scent of herbs, fruit, and flowers.

The percentage of bobbed heads among the daughters of rural Devonshire is about one in two hundred. I gather that the use of powder and lip-salve is non-existent on the farm. The farmer's wife is a competent, business-like person and, like most west-country folk, a pleasant, ready-to-laugh-with-you type.

'This is poultry, zur, this is!' said one when I complimented her on a duckling. 'Not like tha gets up in London! The volk in London doan't know a chicken when they sees un, which isn't often. Oh, the ancient old fowl they give me and my husband to eat when we went up to Wembley year afore last! Them London volks . . .'

The shrill hubbub of conversation goes on all day long. 'Pannier Market', this stock exchange of the dairy, seems to be equally a social and a business occasion. If you listen carefully you can hear things like this:

'Oh, yes, and she's hopin' for a boy . . . one and nine a pound, ma'am, and fresh . . . but Nell tells me that Tom be a-courtin' that red-haired girl over at Challacombe . . . all fresh, ma'am, laid yesterday, ma'am . . . and Mrs Hawkins got her Jack to buy her one of them pianolas up at Crediton Show, that he did, a gurt thing that un plays wi' un's feeat . . . half-a-pound? Very good, ma'am!'

In the cattle market over the road is the other side of the picture. Here Bill Brewer, Harry Hawke, Jan Stewer, Peter Gurney, Peter Davey, Dan'l Whiddon, and Tom Cobleigh have met all their pals in a rich, ripe farmyard atmosphere.

They stand in crowds round the cattle-pens or crush up to wagons in which pigs protrude their snouts from nets almost into their faces. They lean watching a cow and a calf sometimes for half an hour.

'A vine cow!' says Bill Brewer reflectively, filling his pipe. Half an hour passes, in which the little blunt-nosed calves make mechanical mooings.

'Yes,' replies Harry Hawke, filling his pipe, 'she be a vine cow.'

They hold auctions in what I considered to be some foreign language round the doors of closed wagons. Inside the wagon fat sows stand restlessly waiting to be 'knocked down'. Such types I saw in this market. They can never happen again now that the safety-razor and modern dentistry have made such strides. An artist should go down to these country markets and make a record of the wonderful faces of the older generation. Such sudden, surprising tufts of white hair sprout from cheeks and from beneath chins, such mild blue eyes; such Falstaffian contours. The younger generation is different, less individual, already in line with the sad, modern tendency towards standardization.

Those ripe old Devonshire farmers are as fine a sight as the country will afford.

'Well, mother, hadst tha a good day?'

'Aye. Did 'ee zell the old zow?'

'That A did, and well! What hast tha in that parcel, mother?'

'A hat, George!'

'Aye, I might've known that. . . .'

The old grey mare jogs homeward through the lanes, over the hills, into the valley, and up to the farmhouse among the trees; and the end of one week's work has come hand-in-hand with the beginning of the next.

6

I was going to bed early, very tired, when I heard a gust of gargantuan laughter from the bar parlour of the inn. What was going on down there? . . . A yellow moon hung over Exmoor in a sky that was not yet dark. The hills, with their patchwork fields of sage and apple-green velvet, lay wrapped in a delicious duskiness; small clouds of flies hung, apparently motionless, in the air, and swifts cut across the sky like black darts, screaming as they flew. . . .

'Ha-ha-ha-ha-ha-ha! Ha!' burst again that sudden Homeric mirth from the bar. Through the open window came the sound of tankards banged down on wood. The smell of strong tobacco fought with, and conquered, the scent of night stock. Yes, I would go down and find out what they were so happy about. I would, I thought, talk to some old man. There must be good stories to be picked up over the tankards. . . .

I bent my head in the doorway and entered a smoky cavern of gloom. Clouds of tobacco smoke swirled in the light of a hanging paraffin lamp. The dark room smelt of beer, corduroys, dust, dogs, lamp-oil, and that indefinite whiskery smell of old men. Above the open fireplace sprouted a fine twelve-pointer; deer slots hung on the walls between grocers' Christmas almanacs. Behind the bar, the landlord, in shirt-sleeves, but wearing a felt hat as a badge of office, drank gin-and-water when he was not filling tankards with cider or beer. Facing him was a crowd of labourers, farm-hands, gamekeepers, young farmers, and others.

I edged my way towards an old man who sat in a corner of a wooden bench, smoking a pipe, as he took a bright-eyed interest in the noisy room. He was a marvellous old man, bent rheumatically forward, so that he will die, as he has lived, in the attitude of ploughing a field. Like so many old grandfers in this part of the world he had never wasted money on dentists. His teeth having left him long ago, his mouth had retreated to his jaw, giving to his face a singularly sweet and childlike expression.

'Here,' I thought, 'is the typical old man for whom I have been looking since I struck Exmoor!' He accepted a tankard of ale with a merry twinkle; and I settled down to hear the simple story of his life.

'Have you,' I asked casually, 'lived here all your life?'

He removed his pipe from his little cupid's bow and replied in a loud and incredible voice:

'Aay, zurey, tha goom a zowey apple-after killykoom.'

'Really?' I said.

'Aay,' he said, 'vur zeed ya sed es ee zai!'

He burst into a loud cackle of laughter and thumped his tankard on the table. I looked at him closely, wondering if a set of teeth would have made any difference. He apparently mistook my scrutiny for sympathy, and, edging a little nearer and pointing with his pipe, he began to utter a series of remarkable sounds. He would pause from time to time and say something interrogative, the clue for me to nod my head and say 'Yes' or 'No', which I did haphazardly; then off he would go again.

Anyone looking at us would have put us down as a couple of intimate friends.

After fifteen minutes I began to wish that I had never seen this old man. Mixed with my regret was annoyance, because I felt sure that he was telling me something of great interest. He seemed, despite his great age, a born raconteur; and as he warmed to me, he began to enjoy himself more and more. I knew it was no good listening to him, so I just looked at him till every tuft of hair and every deep criss-cross line on his old face was engraved on my memory forever.

He knocked out his pipe on the leg of the table and, turning his sunken blue eyes on me, said something which I knew to be by his tone of voice a question.

'Yes, most interesting! Indeed! Indeed!' I said foolishly.

But it was not confirmation he wanted but encouragement; and this remark seemed to satisfy him.

He leapt into conversation again and I could do nothing but marvel at the wonderful noises he made. He was a humorist (anyhow to himself), for he would stop and chuckle – signal for me to laugh – and then he would go ahead with the rest of the story. He was absolutely tireless. I thought that if he could be persuaded to do this on a stage in London he would be the talk of the town. Suddenly he was silent. I was so deeply relieved to find the flood over, that I said foolishly:

'I suppose nothing ever happens here?'

My previous remarks had apparently not quite touched him: this one did. It seemed to affect his local patriotism. He took me by the arm and whispered. Then he drew back to study the effect of his remark on me. Worn out by deceit, I had no spare expressions left. My face must have been a blank. He edged up and whispered again. It was no better. I could not understand one word. It was a trying situation.

I think he must have said something terrible, for evidently mistaking my look of dulled ignorance for one of chilled horror, he nodded his head quickly and reassured me that his previous remark was, in actual fact, true. Then he whispered again! I felt that there was no logical conclusion to our deadlock. We could go on like this for ever.

'I can't quite catch what he says,' I remarked to a man sitting near.

The old man turned to the interpreter eagerly and whispered that unaccountable sentence.

'Oh, zur,' said the other man, 'ee zays you zay nothin' ever happen 'ere, and you be wrong, zur! Why, ee zays, we 'ad a murder 'ere vive years back, that we did!'

'Time, gentlemen!' sang the innkeeper.

There was a hasty gulping down of drink, a confused mutter of farewells from which emerged the final stage of an argument, apparently hotly proceeding for some time.

'Keep thy London!' said an angry man in corduroy breeches. 'I've zeed 'un and I doan't like 'un! Keep 'un and gie me a stag comin' down Pollok Hill. . . .'

The big yellow moon saw a slow, heavy-footed company clump out into the road opposite the 'White Hart', stand a moment, and then scatter towards the village.

As I went to draw the curtain across my window, I saw grandfer standing on his stick below as if loath to go home. I wondered what on earth we had been talking about during that incomprehensible half-hour. I felt certain that I had listened to an interesting conversation which any man of the period of Simon de Montfort would have understood with ease. A philologist would, I think, have walked miles to have heard it. Dialect it may have been, but I believe it bubbled up from the well of English undefiled.

'Goodnight!' I sang out, but before he could get in the last word I drew the curtain.

7

Whenever I hear men boast of hills I will rise up in praise of the hills of North Somerset. The Devon hills are fair and woody, the Cornish hills are wild and craggy, but the hills of

Somerset rise up to the sky clothed in the cloths of heaven. How they lie in wait for you round corners, how they hold something back for the last quarter of a mile, how they stand up in clusters, six or seven together, like the domes of six or seven sunken St Pauls.

Somerset hills lift up to the sky fields which are among the loveliest in England. Seen from a distance they are a squared patchwork of gold, sage-green, apple-green, and red; the gold is mustard, the apple-green is wheat, the sage is barley, and the rich red-brown is ploughed soil. When the sun is over them, the cloud shadows moving like smoke, the scent of warm hay in the air, and larks holding up the blue sky with their little wings, the hills of North Somerset bring a man very near to prayer and make him thank God for life. . . .

Now the car took Countisbury Hill in a stride, as it were, and I sped on, admiring far below the deep blue-green of the sea, and to my right, the amazing sweep of Exmoor. I saw a stag leave the fern and go bounding into the valley; I saw the wild ponies, which look even tamer than the 'wild ponies' of the New Forest and of Dartmoor, browsing beside the road. So I came at length to the notorious Porlock Hill. Here I paused in doubt. Should I descend the old hill that slips away into the valley like a toboggan slide, or should I pay one-and-six and take the new toll road? Considering the average price for switchbacks at fairs and exhibitions, I thought one and sixpence almost a bargain.

I notice that they wisely collect it before you begin the descent, and not at the other end.

I went on steadily down the one-in-four gradient, the hind wheel in the air and the bonnet to the earth. As I was taking a bend in a most workman-like manner, and wondering about the humorist who had put up at a corner a red 'Dangerous', a motorcycle and a sidecar came warily towards me round a bend, making a noise like a machine-gun corps showing off to a general. On the motorcycle was an earnest young man: in the sidecar was a girl.

'Love,' I thought, 'conquereth all things.'

I proceeded sentimentally for the next half-mile, admiring the red gravel of the road, the rich red sandstone banks, the yellow cubes of sunlight falling through the lace of leaves, when suddenly . . .

I pulled up on the edge of a suitcase that lay, looking most out of place, in the centre of the road.

I imagine that Porlock Hill shakes off more luggage than any hill in England. There lay the suitcase upside down. When I picked it up, the clasps sprang back and the contents lurched heavily into the lid. I clumsily patted them back, and as I did so it was not possible to be unaware of a pink silk nightdress nestling in a most affectionate manner between a man's tweed waistcoat and his jacket. One other thing I saw – a small blue crescent of confetti clung like a burr in the tweed.

Well, what was a man to do?

I stood midway on Porlock Hill. The birds sang as, I suppose, they sang in Eden, the leaves moved and flittered as they moved in the first garden, and somewhere along that steep road Adam and Eve were exploding towards their honeymoon; and in my arms their trousseaux.

I sat down, hoping that they would return.

It was evident that these unfortunate souls had just that very day been married, because the first thing all newly-wed people do is to shake out every sock, shirt, pyjama, sponge bag and boot, in an attempt to eliminate these small red, pink, white, and blue pieces of evidence.

And it is a strange fact that all just-married people – of whom in July the world is over-full – believe that if they gather together every speck of confetti and burn it, no one will ever guess; whereas to the undeceivable eyes of hotel clerks, landladies, and chambermaids, honeymoon couples are an, so to speak, open book. . . . Just fancy starting married life with a motorcycle combination, a wife, and no toothbrush. That poor fellow!

No doubt, I meditated, he has dragged her from a family

which has just begun to appreciate her. No member of it believes that he can look after her, and the first thing the poor fool does is to lose all her clothes. . . . Here they come!

But I was wrong. A fat, red man and a fat, red woman slid down Porlock Hill in an Italian car, casting as they went a curious glance at the apparently insane person sitting under the hedge, nursing a large and unpleasant suitcase.

Down in the delicious Vale of Porlock I found the cottage of the police sergeant. He did not seem surprised when I handed him the bag.

'Honeymooners, most like!' he said psychically, and we both smiled. 'I'll ring up Lynton,' he added kindly.

If only newly-married people were mentally normal, they would realize, perhaps, how all the world loves a honeymoon, and they might do worse than wear a little confetti every day. . . .

After dinner in the Old Ship Inn I told this tragic story to a man and a woman, and it caused one of those sudden hushes in conversation at the end of which the man whispered:

'Well, thank goodness it wasn't ours!'

The woman blushed and looked prettily at her toes. (Really, in July honeymooners are thicker than blackberries in September.) So, all three of us having a sentimental interest in that bag, we trooped to the police cottage and knocked.

'Oh, yes, half an hour after you left it they came,' said the sergeant. 'On their honeymoon, all right!'

We all laughed. I walked back with the new Mr and Mrs through the darkening lane and into the little church of St Dubritius, to see something which all honeymooners should see, as they stand quietly hand in hand. It was very dark. I lit a match and the light flickered a moment on a marble man in armour and a marble woman sleeping together side by side: Baron Harington, who died in 1417, and his lady. Over these two is a gracious peace that confounds the cynic:

'Till death us do part,' I whispered as the match went out.

But in the last flicker of it I saw that Mr and Mrs were standing close together, their little fingers crooked, looking not at the baron and his lady but at one another; and in a most self-confident way.

So, feeling a thousand years old, rather sad, and very lonely, I said goodnight, and walked back to the inn, where I drank a large tankard of beer while a retriever came slowly out of the shadow and placed a black satin head on my knee.

CHAPTER SIX

Describes Glastonbury and the Holy Thorn. I sink into Bath, take the waters, hunt for Mr Pickwick, and see ships riding at anchor in the streets of Bristol

I

THE most conspicuous object in the Vale of Avalon is a high, rounded hill, crowned with a lonely tower, rising beyond the ruins of Glastonbury. This hill is known as Glastonbury Tor, and the building is all that remains of the old pilgrimage chapel of St Michael.

In the early morning before the sun is strong, a man standing on this hill looks down, not upon the neat flat pasture lands of the Vale of Avalon, but upon Avalon, an island again, rising from a steaming sea of mist. In summer the mist rises from the fields as if it were the ghost of that sea which covered the valley in the age of legend. In the cold wind that runs before the dawn a man looks down upon this faint, moving veil, watches it writhe in spectral billows over the land, steaming upward in faint lines in the high places and so exposing the darker objects beneath which, in this hushed hour, seem almost like the bones of heroes, or the hulls of legendary barges sunk in some old poem.

It was over this sea to Avalon there moved that 'dusky barge, dark as a funeral scarf from stem to stern', in which the hooded queens bore the dying Arthur, his scabbard empty of Excalibur. As the low mists move, curling upwards from the land, the lowing of cattle in the fields below rises starkly in the silence as though it might be the wailing that died upon this mere so long ago; as though in the first hour of a summer's day the Isle of Avalon remembers Arthur.

The sun shines, the mists go, and the green fields are smiling to the sky-line.

I am writing in the ruins of Glastonbury Abbey.

A hot afternoon is almost over. There is in the air that summer stillness like the peace of a cloister, in which – so they say in Glastonbury – the scent of mysterious incense sometimes drifts over walls to astonish men working in their gardens. I can, however, smell only the incense of new-cut grass.

An hour ago I stood on the summit of the Tor above Glastonbury in the shadow of the tower of the pilgrims' chapel of St Michael, now a patched ruin. When I looked east I gazed down at the Isle of Avalon; when I looked west I saw lying in a heat haze the isle of Athelney. These 'islands' are now hills rising from flat fields over which in the age of myth ran wide lagoons; and I thought that if a man were looking for the roots of England, this is the place to which he would come: in Avalon the roots of the Church; in Athelney the roots of the State.

Now I sit in the ruins of Glastonbury. Near me at the east end of St Mary's Chapel archaeologists are digging. They have just unearthed the yellow arm bone of a man which lies in the sunlight on a mound of soft brown soil. I wonder whether it is the arm of saint, abbot, or king; not that it matters much now. A man in spectacles is examining it expertly while the red face of the labourer who unearthed it gazes up earnestly over the parados of the trench, wondering if it is a treasure or a piece of rubbish.

It is so quiet here. The shadows of the yews lie in long pencils over the smooth grass, but – stay – it is not so smooth! There are grassy dips and terraces where once ran altar steps. From tree to tree is a chain of birdsong. Rising sheer from the grass, appalling in its appealing starkness, is the great arch of the central tower of Glastonbury Abbey, the two piers rising into the air, but not to meet; there is blue sky between, and on the high, cleft towers grass is growing. This with a few tumbled walls and the beautiful St Mary's Chapel represent all that remains of the once mighty

Abbey, the elder brother of Westminster and the birthplace of Christianity in England.

It is, perhaps, not strange that all places which have meant much to Man are filled with an uncanny atmosphere, as if something were still happening there secretly; as if filled with a hidden life. Glastonbury is like that. A band of tourists, who came in laughing and joking, move among the ruins, puzzled and ill at ease. Glastonbury has stilled their laughter. I hear the click and thrust of the labourer's spade in the earth, and it seems to me as each spadeful of Glastonbury soil falls on the mound that a spadeful of English history is stirred; in the brown dust that flies over the trench I seem to see the faces of anchorites, saints, priests, and kings; and in this pregnant dust of Avalon is drawn two of the greatest epics that have come from the English mind: one is of the Holy Grail and the other of a wounded king.

The Church of England has owned Glastonbury since 1907, and one must, at least, congratulate it on mowing the grass. But how is it possible that the Church has neglected for nineteen years to restore St Mary's Chapel, the site of the first church built by British Christians, and probably the first above-ground church in the world. This lovely ruin, whose four walls stand, whose magnificent Norman archways are almost perfect, could in a few months be made fit for public worship. What queer lack of imagination stands in the way?

And why, I wonder, is there no intelligent guide to satisfy the bewildered curiosity of the people from many countries who every day roam these ruins, drawn to them by the greatness of the name of Glastonbury? The Church could surely arrange that at least one guide should be available to tell people that this quiet field is the only spot in England linked by legend with a man who knew Jesus Christ. For centuries men believed that in A.D. 61 St Philip sent Joseph of Arimathaea, whose hands had laid Christ in the tomb, to preach the Gospel in England. He is said, according to the later legend, to have come with a band of missionaries bearing the Chalice of the Last Supper, which he had begged of Pilate. This Chalice had held the Sacred Blood from the Cross. Here in this English meadow Joseph of Arimathaea is said to have built England's first church of plaited oziers.

When the missionaries crossed Weary-all Hill ('weary-all' with the journey), Joseph, so the famous old story goes, planted his staff in the earth. It took root and grew into the famous Glastonbury Thorn.

That belief founded the international fame of Glaston-bury: for centuries it was an English Jerusalem, one of the holiest places on earth. Men came from the ends of the world to pluck a sprig of the Holy Thorn in order that it might be buried with them. Saints were gathered to Glastonbury to lie in its earth. The bones of Arthur and Guinevere are said to have been buried beneath the high altar. Behind the ruined abbey, at the foot of the Tor, is the mineral spring which was one of the wonders of the world. Its waters, heavily impregnated with iron, colour the earth, and everything they touch a rusty red; and this is the place to which the medieval pilgrim knelt trembling and crying – as I have seen pilgrims tremble and cry in Jerusalem – believing that here was buried the Holy Grail.

As I was walking over the grass of the choir, I came to a railed-off plot of turf which marks the high altar of Glastonbury. A man was walking across it behind a motor lawnmower! He told me that when automatic script was received in 1921, directing people to dig in a certain part of the ruins, he was one of the workers who found the hitherto unknown portions of the abbey indicated in the supposed spirit communication.

'Yes, sir,' he said, 'heaps of people say they see ghosts here, but I can't say that I have.'

He took a turn over the high altar and came back.

'See that bush? That's the Holy Thorn! The original one was hacked down by a Puritan who got a splinter in his eye from it and died. There are several offshoots round Glastonbury, and you'd be surprised at the number of slips we send away. One is going to a big church they are building in New York. We sent one to America not long ago for the tomb of President Wilson.'

The grass has come back to the altar of Glastonbury, but the Holy Thorn still lives!

Now the sun is setting, and the diggers are packing up. The arm bone has been taken away. . . .

'I have been to Glastonbury!'

Six hundred years ago a man writing this would remember the greatest experience of his life. He would remember the greatest church outside Rome, the sound of its bells, the smoke of its incense, the sound of perpetual prayer, the gilded shrine, the horde of pilgrims at the doors – saints in ecstasy, sinners in tears; and in every man's mind faith in the marvellous story that had grown up round a reed hut in the Isle of Avalon.

'I have been to Glastonbury!'

Now a man sitting on a carved stone in a meadow hears the robin chant evensong, watches the thrush hunt his supper in the grass of the nave. From the site of chantry and chapel the blackbird flies with a silver chink of alarm, and from the high altar of Glastonbury comes the sound of a man mowing grass. . . .

The labourer has climbed from the trench. He shoulders his spade and walks heavily away past the ruin that stands where England heard for the first time the greatest story in the world.

3

I entered Wells Cathedral just before noon. The cream-coloured church seemed empty. When I came to the north transept I saw a crowd whispering, standing about, sitting on stone seats, leaning against pillars and tombs, each member of it looking up anxiously at the west wall. There were charabanc parties, American families, market women, farmers and their wives, and young men and young women in cycling clothes.

'What are they doing?' I asked a verger.

'Waiting to see the clock strike twelve!' he replied.

Then I remembered that in Wells Cathedral is one of the most exciting clocks in England; in fact, with the exception of the clock in Strasburg Cathedral, probably one of the most exciting clocks in the world. It is six hundred years old, and it was invented by a monk of Glastonbury called Peter Lightfoot. At first sight Brother Lightfoot's clocks look like man's first attempt at an automatic calculating machine. The dial, which is six feet six inches in diameter, is a mass of lines and numbers. A large outer circle is divided into the twenty-four hours of the day: an inner circle shows the minutes. Round the hour circle moves a big slow star; round the inner circle a quick smaller star. Above the dial is a black cave in which things happen when the hour strikes – but I will tell you about that in its place.

In addition to telling the time, Brother Lightfoot's marvellous clock tells you the phases of the moon and the position of the planets. Beneath a gold moon is written in Latin, 'Phoebe ever wanders'; and as I tried to puzzle out all the information which Peter has crammed into his clock the silly thought came into my head that perhaps he referred to the moon, and – obliquely – to a woman. Who knows? Perhaps some unknown Phoebe wandering, sent him into a monastery, and gave the world this clock? (The influence of jilting on art and invention has yet to be written.) On the other hand, Peter may have been a solemn old medieval professor, poring over charts, drawing diagrams on the refectory table, the despair of the abbot and the butt of less congested minds. . . .

Ah; a rustle goes round the crowd! The minute star slides on to noon.

To the left of the clock dial, high up on the west wall, sits a smug little wooden man in the costume of Charles I's time. His name, is I believe, Jack Blandiver. He sits with his heels against two bells. . . .

Noon!

Jack Blandiver kicks out his wooden leg and brings his heel back against a bell; then the other one. He does this eight times. The clock dial, however, claims the attention of the crowd! From it comes a whirring sound. Out of the black cave above the dial appear four mounted knights: two gallop round to the left, two to the right; and at every revolution one of them is knocked back on his horse's crupper by the sword of an adversary. The tournament spins round to a standstill: the hourly fight in Wells Cathedral is over: the crowd is smiling with childish delight — the same smile that has gone round the north transept for something like six hundred years.

Just as the theatre was born in a church, the cabaret-show seems to have been born in a church clock. Bravo, Brother Lightfoot!

What a thrill there is in Wells. How can I describe to you the whisper of the water that runs in gutters, musically tinkling past the steps of old houses? In spite of the big charabancs that pile up in the square, it seems that the sound of coach-wheels has not quite died away on the London road. Wells is perfect. It is genuinely medieval, with no self-consciousness, and no abasement to the tourist. Behind the stout wall which runs round the cathedral is something you will see nowhere else in England: an inhabited medieval castle, complete with fortifications and moat. In this marvellous place lives the Bishop of Wells.

I sat on the grass beside the moat watching his lordship's ducks and swans. They have hatched the most delightful fluffy families. I saw a swan swim up and ring the bell of the gatehouse! I rubbed my eyes. Was this a fairy tale? I looked at the white bird, half expecting that he might turn into a prince in white satin breeches. He did it again! He took up a string that lay in the water and pulled it. A bell beneath the window of the gatehouse tinkled, the window opened, a crust of bread flew through the air and hit him on the head; he worried it under water, summoned his family to him, rang the bell again, and more food arrived!

I walked over the drawbridge and took the brass knocker in my hand. A small postern opened.

'Whenever the swans are hungry, they ring the bell!' explained a girl. 'We never disappoint them. We keep a tray of food always ready to throw out when they ask for it. They teach the cygnets to ring too! The ducks do it sometimes, but not so often as the swans. . . .'

I returned to the grass of the moat, watching the birds ring for their food. The cathedral bells chimed a quarter. The sun was mellow over old walls. I could see the fortifications of the Bishop's palace bending round to bastions fitted with sentry walks and slits for bowmen. What a place to live in.

'The mutton was tough,' said a voice. I looked up and saw a man.

'Yes,' replied a pretty girl, 'but the peas were simply delicious.'

They gazed at the moat, the drawbridge, and the swans; they turned and saw – perhaps – the central tower of Wells standing up above elm trees and the high wall, a big white cloud poised like a nimbus behind it.

'I never did think much of Cheddar cheese,' said the man.

'I adore Gruyère,' said the girl softly.

A piece of bread shot through the air and landed on the grey fluff of a cygnet's back.

What a place to dream in is Wells when the sun soaks down through the trees and the lichen on my lord's battlements shines like new gold. The chapter-house of Wells, that lovely round room, approached by the most alluring flight of steps I have ever seen, justifies a pilgrimage. . . .

'Those prunes,' said a departing voice, 'we had in Bath were the best I've ever tasted.'

Two more people came and stood above me, a man and a girl.

'Oh,' she said, 'how adorable! Just look at those little windows over the moat! Don't you wish you were Pelleas, dear, and that I was Melisande at the window, letting down my hair to you?'

'Don't be silly!' he said. 'How could you?'

She shook a cropped head.

'How unromantic you are,' she sighed.

They walked slowly under the trees arm in arm. . . .

The church clock struck the quarter, the half-hour, the three-quarters, the hour. It seemed to me, as I sat there wrapped in contentment, that the little mother moorhen who was taking four black chicks for their first swim was one of the most important people in the world.

4

I have decided that when I grow old, with or without gout, sciatica, rheumatism, or lumbago, I will retire on Bath with an ebony cane and a monocle. I like Bath: it has quality. I like Bath buns, Bath Olivers, Bath chaps, Bath brick, and Bath stone (which to my London eyes is the beautiful sister of Portland stone), and few sights are more stimulating to relaxed nerves than to sit on the hotel terrace opposite the Pump Room and watch the Bath chairs dash past.

We were often told in the Army that the speed of a squadron was the speed of its slowest horse; similarly the speed of Bath is that of its slowest chair. Some months ago the local paper reported that a woman was run over by a Bath chair. I am too tired and lazy to look up the files to find out details, but from my slight knowledge of Bath I imagine that the injured person and the pusher of the chair were probably sleep-walking at the time of the collision. That is the great danger here. As long as you can keep awake you may survive. When anybody yawns on the top of Combe Down the yawn goes right round Bath.

If you are a bad sleeper, as I am, you will know how gracious this place is. A delicious numbness drenches me; an adorable drowsiness sits on top of my head. I go to sleep at ten without counting one sheep, and I wake up at seven, feeling almost as tired, to swim for twenty minutes in a solution of warm pea-soup – only it tastes much nicer. Old men have told me that they attribute their agility, and their ability to drink half a bottle of port every night, to the fact that they, when young, did eagerly frequent these swimming baths so full of radium which generous Nature shoots piping hot into Bath through a deep rift in the surface of the earth. *Ohaaaah! Forgive my yawn! It is only five past nine!*

I once heard a bright young man say at a party that living in Bath was rather like sitting in the lap of a dear old lady. Nobody laughed, because it is true. Bath is the dear old lady of Somerset: grey-haired, mittened, smelling faintly of lavender; one of those old ladies who have outlived a much-discussed past, and are now as obviously respectable as only old ladies with crowded pasts can be. She nurses you with a shrewd twinkle in which you detect experience mellowed by age. You look at her lovingly, wondering how she could ever have been wicked; wishing that she could grow young again for one wild evening and show you! That might wake you up!

The crowds in Bath move slowly. Noises here are louder than anywhere else on earth. A motorcycle coming up Stall Street sounds like a giant rattling Cleopatra's Needle along area railings vast as oak trees. Bath was made for chairs. Sedan and the other kind. Anything else on wheels is a rude invasion. One of the most soothing sights in England is the vista through the black Georgian pillars in Stall Street – the Pump Room to the right, the lovely abbey in the background, the foreground occupied by the Bath chairmen in various peaceful attitudes.

On wet days the chairmen sleep inside their chairs with

the little doors closed, sitting up behind glass panels like mummies in their sarcophagi; on fine days they sleep outside them.

'Your profession is not an exciting one?' I suggested to a veteran chairman.

He considered for some time and replied:

'No.'

'I can't think how all you make a living out of Bath chairs.'

'We don't. We do a little carpet-beating now and then and odd jobs. It isn't much of a life. Inside the Pump Room you can see pictures of Bath in the old days. In those times people didn't mind paying for two men to carry them about in a Sedan chair, but now – Excuse me, sir! . . . Yes, mum, I'm free! Half-past four, mum, to go round Victoria Park? Oh, yes, the step's low and I go steady! Thank you, mum. . . . That, sir, is my first job today!'

O gracious Old Lady of Somerset, how I love to be nursed at your once-naughty knee! . . .

I just half close my eyes and . . . those two old men talking above the pale-green water of the great Roman bath! One is a general, the other a judge. Why are they wearing togas? Why are their feet in white-laced boots? It is, of course, because I have half-closed my eyes; and when you do this in Bath you see ghosts! Look how the tumbled pillars of the Roman bath build themselves up, how the dusty tesserae shine again with colour and form a pattern. The Roman bath is alive; old General X and Sir Archibald Y are standing on a polished pavement on which Diana runs with her hounds in leash. Do they know that they are wearing togas? Ought I to tell them?

But is it General X? No, he is General Caius Sciaticus of the Valens Victrix. Is it Sir Archibald Y? No; he is Marcus Rheumaticus of Londinium. (Funny nightmare place, Bath!)

'What a climate,' says General Sciaticus. 'By Jove, sir, what a damnable climate! It gets me in the knees. . . . By the

way, is it true that Boadicea's great-grandson has gone
Red?'

'He's a firebrand. It runs in the family, you know. I had
to crucify his uncle at Camulodunum last year. Perhaps you
heard about it?'

'A terrible country, but we're civilizing them by degrees.
How's your rheumatism this year? Has it ever struck you
that this hot water was placed here by Providence to hold
the Empire together? If there was no place in Britain in
which one could feel warm, what would one do? By Jove,
that's a pretty woman, the one with the yellow hair.'

'Yes, the wife of Dion Neurasthenes, the Greek financier.
Just travelling. Have you heard her speak? A pretty accent.
Listen. . . .'

'Say, now, don't tell me that all this hot water comes right
up out of the earth like this! Well, you certainly do surprise
me. It's the only centrally heated spot I've struck in this little
cold island. . . . Oh, I'd love to; I haven't been warm since I
left Athens. And the draughts! Aquae Sulis is sure the
draughtiest spot on earth. . . .'

I open my eyes and see that General X and Sir Archibald
are properly dressed again, and Mrs Boston certainly has
lovely yellow hair.

In the evening you can walk through the splendid streets
of Bath – magnificent streets lined with Georgian houses
standing stiff as lackeys behind pillared porticoes; elegant,
formal homes. There is the Circus, the Crescent; there is
Pulteney Bridge – England's Ponte Vecchio – there are
lovely Georgian gateways, and little queer streets round
whose corners it seems you just miss the flash of a red-
heeled shoe, the twinkle of feet beneath brocade, the sound
of a rather naughty little laugh.

It is very difficult, if you walk in Bath at night, not to find
yourself suddenly under the rather contemptuous scrutiny of
a man with a double chin and a heavy nose, whose three-
cornered hat shades eyes that lie in fleshy bags – Beau Nash!

'Sir,' says this ghost, 'I would inform you that a

gentleman of fashion carries a cane. I am glad to observe that you are not wearing a sword. Your hat is, sir, like a scullion's, and your legs are encased in two inelegant tubes of cloth for which, sir, I can find no name. You are, perhaps, a foreigner?'

'No, Beau, I come from London.'

Whereupon the ghost of Beau Nash, uttering an incredulous cry, vanishes; the two eyes go last, still fixed in a look of horror on your trousers.

So you return through haunted streets to the quiet hotel, where two old men, at war with lumbago, sit in the lounge, having loyally obeyed their doctors all day. The clock strikes ten. The devil enters into them. Their wives have retired to bed; no one will know. They call the waiter, and whisper wickedly:

'Two double whiskies!'

I think this is Bath's greatest sin! Outside, mercifully shrouded in darkness, is the Pindaric motto writ in Greek characters above the Pump Room: 'Water is the best policy.'

Aaaaaaah! How tired I am!

If I am awake tomorrow I am going to take the cure. I am going to have a mineral bath: I am going to sip the waters.

Aaah ! Forgive me. . . .

Goodnight!

5

I have been reading with avidity the medical pamphlets provided free in Bath, and I feel that my arteries become harder and harder every minute. I wonder whether the ache in my left eye is paraplegia. I have no idea what this is, but when I whisper the word something ominous seems in mid-air with bared claws. It is hardly possible that I shall escape from oxularia. (Obesity does not worry me.) Intestinal stasis? Well, perhaps! Chronic vesical catarrh? I wonder? As I glance down the long list of diseases cured at Bath – feeling a sharp twinge of fibrocitis, a swift jab of lithiasis, and an alarming touch of rhinitis – it is perfectly clear to me that the average human being's chance of seeing Bath more than once is about a hundred to one.

So early in the morning, wrapped in a dressing-gown, I gained the lift and was carried down to the baths to begin a day's treatment, just to see what is in store for most of us. I had decided against a mud pack, because I did not like the picture in the handbook, which shows a nurse building up a big black mud pie on a patient's foot. I considered the whirling bath, the hydro-electric bath, the heat bath, the hot-air bath, the vapour bath, the aeration bath, and came to the conclusion that probably the best bath for a man with no real honest symptoms is the deep bath; the characteristic bath of Bath; the bath with historic and literary associations, because it is simply the scientific version of the treatment as practised by the Romans and by those of our eighteenth-century forefathers who drew the first gout dividends before investing them for us at thirty per cent.

A man in a white coat took me into a tiled room. Sunk in the floor was a huge bath with six steps leading down to swirling green water. The water gushed in from the spring steaming hot at a temperature of 120 degrees as it comes up from the nether regions. Cold water was added till the temperature was 100 degrees.

I walked down the steps, was buffeted by the hot stream of radium, and the man in the white coat told me to sit down, which I did trustfully: for I could see no seat in the green water, but I met it just as my chin touched the flood. So I sat there, feeling hot and apprehensive. He told me to exercise myself gently: and I could tell that he considered me a genuine ptient, which made me feel quite ill.

'Which is the affected part?' he asked.

'Everywhere,' I said.

'General massage!' he cried briskly, taking up a big hose-pipe, placing the nozzle under water and shooting a strong stream of water several degrees hotter than the bath up and down my spine. This was a delicious experience. My spine purred.

In ten minutes the treatment was over.

The attendant stood at the top of the steps and received me into a hot towel. It was then that I felt my first real symptom – a sharp pain in the knee.

I went up and had a melancholy breakfast.

Now with us invalids the next event is the Pump Room.

At about eleven o'clock we drag our weary limbs to that stately Georgian building, which since 1796 has been the ever-open door to the gouty, the rheumaticky, and the sciaticky. This classic apartment is built above the three hot springs – the only natural hot springs in Britain – which shoot up half a million gallons of water a day into Bath.

A girl in a cap and apron stands at a fountain which bubbles with warm water. We limp on our sticks, and she hands us each a tumblerful of this water. We limp to a Chippendale chair and began to sip it. Now Sam Weller said that it had 'a wery strong flavour o' warm flat-irons'. Somebody must have dropped a dumb-bell in the source when Dickens tasted the water, for it does not taste strongly of warm flat-irons today. To be quite truthful, Bath water tastes just like any warm water. If you are imaginative, you can suspect a subtle after-taste of – is it warm flat-irons? It is not, however, 'wery strong'.

The water affects us differently. Some of us write letters, some go to sleep, some wander round as if recreated, looking at the Sedan chairs, at the statue of fat Beau Nash, at the calm bath of gently steaming pea-soup known as the King's Bath, now disused, but during the eighteenth century the place where, as Christopher Anstey noted: ' 'Twas a glorious sight to behold the fair sex all wading with gentlemen up to their necks.' Round the King's Bath are rings presented by grateful bathers in token of their recovery. One bears the name of lovely Barbara, Duchess of Cleveland; one given by Thomas Delves records that he was 'By God's mercy and pumping here formerly aided'.

139

Everybody drinks the Bath water. We invalids do it seriously; the casual tripper does it flippantly. We limp up and put our finger halfway up the glass and whisper: 'Only eight ounces this morning!' The tripper strides up heartily and says: 'A pint of the best, please, miss!' and the maiden of the healing spring gazes over the top of his head towards the sky, where, no doubt, she sees the great god Neuritis saving up his thunderbolts!

If our joints are equal to it, we can walk gently downstairs to see the 'source', the very heart of Bath.

An attendant in the nether regions unlocks a bronze door and we walk into a wall of white steam. Our eyes become accustomed to the gloom. It is very hot. The steam condenses on our hands and on our face in a clammy sweat. We see a Roman arch and Roman steps leading down to the springs. Hot water trickles, steaming down these steps. They are stained rust-red with minerals. Beneath the arch, just out of sight, bubble the hot springs which as long as there is any record have been pumping up their daily half-million gallons of water.

Why does this hot water bubble up to Bath? The latest theory is that there is a deep crack in the crust of the earth through which volcanic gases escape. They turn into hot water as they reach Bath. The old theory that the Bath springs are composed of sea water volcanically boiled and delivered in Bath is, I understand, being gently but firmly abandoned.

However that may be, the sight of the source is most convincing. We feel, as we stand in the dark Turkish bath looking into the steaming gloom, that here is something unaccountable, something unique, something rather terrifying. It looks as though it ought to do us a lot of good, and, of course, it does. There are nearly two thousand years of testimony behind Bath.

Then we limp back to luncheon, choosing those dishes marked with an asterisk on the menu: 'Recommended by the Bath Medical Council for visitors taking the cure.' Hors-d'œuvres are safe, soles Colbert are safe, veal is safe, roast duck is not, mutton cutlets are not, roast beef is not, Bath chaps are all right, lobster is not, stewed fruits and Devonshire junket are heartily asterisked, so we can let ourselves all out here.

If our doctor told us to sleep in the afternoon we go upstairs to sleep, which is never difficult in Bath; if he recommended exercise we limp down to the Sydney Gardens to listen while a military band plays Gilbert and Sullivan. It is so soothing in the sun under a tree. A pretty nursemaid in a canvas chair pushes the perambulator an inch forward and an inch backward as she sits watching the circle of scarlet coats raised above a circle of geraniums exactly the same colour.

The flowers that bloom in the spring, tra-la,
Have nothing to do with the case . . .

How delicious! How our old brittle bones desire to get up and dance to it. We tap a toe on the grass; and it replies promptly by stabbing us with a scarlet stiletto: 'Don't be an old fool!' it says. We look at the time. Four o'clock! Time to drink the waters again. So we rise heavily and limp off in the direction of the Pump Room. . . .

Then as dusk falls . . . but I cannot write any more. The pain in my knee is much worse. I was rather foolish to take that bath.

I wonder if the cure has given me rheumatism?

6

One of the greatest discoveries made by Charles Dickens was the name Pickwick. It is well known that he annexed this name in Bath. There is a village just over the Somerset-Wiltshire border called Pickwick. I went there to see it. It is a one-street hamlet on the Bath-London road, and all the houses in this hamlet are built of stone washed an attractive khaki colour at the expense, so I am led to believe, of the lord of the manor. At the entrance to the village street stands a big sign with the name written on it in tall green letters, so that every charabanc load that passes points suddenly and says: 'Ooh! Look – just fancy – Pickwick!'

That, so it seems is as far as anyone gets with Pickwick.

'Does a family named Pickwick live here?' I asked a native.

'No,' he said.

'Does the place take its name from a family that used to live here?'

'I don't know!'

'Did Charles Dickens take the name of Mr Pickwick from this village or from a man called Pickwick?'

'I don't know,' replied my negative friend, 'but he wrote his history in the "Hare and Hounds" down the road there.'

'What history?' I asked, mercilessly.

'Why, the history of Pickwick, of course,' replied the Pickwickian.

So that was that! (I should state that the rooms round Bath in which Dickens wrote are as numerous as the beds in other parts of England in which Queen Elizabeth slept.)

There is probably no name so well known, or so well loved, in English fiction as Pickwick; he and Falstaff will never die. So I set my shoulders to investigate the origin of the name, and I discovered at length how Pickwick entered English literature.

When Dickens visited Bath the White Hart Hotel which stood on the site of the present Grand Pump Room Hotel, was owned by a man called Moses Pickwick. This name – as Sam Weller noted with some suspicion – was written up over the doors of the coaches. Moses, in addition to his hotel, owned a profitable livery stable and ran a daily service from Bath. The name of Pickwick fell on Dickens like a ray of sunlight.

'What a name!' he thought, feeling for his notebook.

That was the beginning of the immortalization of

Pickwick! So well known is the name now that French students of English literature will talk freely to you about 'Monsieur Peekweck'.

But who was Moses Pickwick, and how did the name originate?

There is a curious story about him. He was, it is said, the great-grandson of a foundling. A woman driving through the village of Wick, near Bath, saw a bundle lying on the side of the road, which on investigation proved to contain the first Pickwick. She took him home, cared for him, and christened him Eleazer Pickwick, otherwise Eleazer picked up at Wick!

In the course of time the foundling founded a family in Bath, which grew rapidly prosperous. When Dickens arrived on the scene the great-grandson of Eleazer was a man of wealth and position. Dickens provided the fame. . . .

From this it was a step to the Bath Directory. Here I found that there are five Pickwicks living in Bath today. One is an organist, two are grocers and provision merchants, and the occupation of the remaining two is not given. I took up my hat and went out of the reference library in some excitement to meet the nearest Mr Pickwick!

'Is Mr Pickwick at home?'

'Yes; come in!'

A grave, middle-aged man looked at me with thoughtful grey eyes. I thought that I had never seen any man who looked so badly christened. I had expected a bald, bland, ripe old man with glasses, who would put his head on one side and twinkle at me, but the real Mr Pickwick might have been a professor of geology or a distinguished lawyer. I felt chilled.

'Are you – er – Mr Pickwick?' I asked.

'I am. What can I do for you?'

So we began. I discovered, as we made friends, that to bear the name Pickwick is not an unmixed blessing. It induces a horror of print. At hotels people look up at you when you give your name, and think that you are pulling their legs. Now and again hot Americans dash up to your door and cry: 'Say, put it there! I just wanted to say I've shaken hands with Mr Pickwick, for I ad-mire your ancestor more'n I can tell you. Yes, sir!'

'Thousands of people would be only too happy to be called Pickwick,' I said.

'Would they?' replied Mr Pickwick grimly. 'Through no fault of mine my name makes people smile. Pickwick was a silly old ass, you know. It is, of course, a remarkable name and a very notorious one, but it has the effect of causing notice wherever I go. No doubt I am too modest.'

As he was saying this it occurred to me in how many ways the name Pickwick might be of service to a man. In how many professions and trades is the ability to cause a smile before business begins the halfway house to success? Just think of a canvasser called Mr Pickwick! A client would, in spite of himself, see such a man. Who could help it? A Mr Pickwick could float almost any kind of a company, and people would, I have no doubt, follow him quite gaily anywhere.

'You are, of course, all one family?'

'I suppose so. I believe that a direct descendant of Moses Pickwick changed his name some years back for family reasons. They still live in the neighbourhood.'

'There are Pickwicks in America,' continued Mr Pickwick. 'My two brothers went over there. Americans show great interest in the name. To me, however, the name Pickwick has never done any good: it is a little too spectacular for my liking. When my son was invalided home from France the doctor saw his name and was so interested that he sat up with him all night across the Channel. I suppose that is the one occasion when the name really did something for us!'

But Mr Pickwick saved up the most interesting fact till I was going.

'It is rather a singular coincidence,' he said, 'that my

motor licence bears the names of Pickwick and Wardle! The Town Clerk of Bath is named Wardle!'

7

I crossed the Somerset border into Wiltshire and dipped into a little town that lies beside the ubiquitous Avon. It was, as Wiltshire towns go, quite a shock.

At first it looked Dutch; in other parts Italian. Holland on the flat and Italy on the hill.

The small, white stone houses clung close to the hillside; narrow flagged lanes twisted this way and that, with lamp-posts planted about, at the direction, it seemed, of distinguished artists. Wallflowers peeped over walls and trees leaned over the road, and one looked in vain for cypresses among the white houses. It was strange. An old man came towards me and I stopped him.

'Bradford-on-Avon!' he said.

'What do you do here besides looking like Perugia?'

'We make motor tyres,' he replied.

'Do many people know this place?'

'We get a few in and out quick to see the Saxon church. It's just round the corner.'

What a church! If you are ever asked in a general knowledge paper to give the name of the oldest unaltered church in England remember Bradford-on-Avon. Here is a church just as it was a thousand years ago: a tiny yellow stone building with three-foot thick walls and a nave only twenty-six feet long. It was preserved by accident. The legend of it never quite died away, but the church itself became in the course of centuries smothered in buildings till an antiquarian vicar in 1857 looking down from a hill noticed a stone roof in the form of a cross. He had the buildings pulled down, and discovered in the heart of them this lovely, unique building.

I met an architect in this church.

'One of the most remarkable buildings in England,' he

145

said, peering at the stones. 'I have a theory that when the Romans, who worked Bath stone for centuries, left England, the tradition of Roman quarrying and squaring stone was handed down from father to son in this tiny, then isolated, Saxon hamlet. The result is that this church is built on the Roman method – the squared blocks, the thin line of mortar – at a time when the rest of Europe had forgotten the art of it! Most singular!'

In the old inn of Bradford they give you tea in the room where Judge Jeffreys did his bloody work. The memory of Jeffreys will never die out in the West of England, where they still utter his name in a hushed voice. Hanging in the hall are caps and jackets made of Bradford-on-Avon broadcloth, which was famous long before the Yorkshire Bradford dealt in wool. They were found in an old oak chest in an attic.

'When I came here nineteen years ago,' said the innkeeper, 'I thought how foreign the place looked – like Spain.'

'Or Holland,' I said.

'Yes, or even Italy in parts,' he replied. 'I took an interest in local things, and I discovered that Bradford was rebuilt in the sixteenth and seventeenth centuries by Flemish immigrants, who came over to spin cloth. They still call a part of the town Dutch Barton. They brought with them an un-English idea of architecture; the hills make it look like Italy. I don't believe the story that this Bradford is the parent of the Yorkshire Bradford. That story grew because both towns were in the wool trade. The origin of the name is Broadford – the ford over the river. By the way, you must not leave without seeing our bridge. It has an old Mass chapel on it.'

'A Mass chapel on the bridge!' I cried. 'Give me my bill! That's one of the things I have wanted to see all my life.'

I saw it. Now I would like to know who owns it. Who is responsible for the repair of the Mass chapel of Bradford-on-Avon's bridge? Is it the town or the lord of the manor?

Bradford-on-Avon seems in doubt about it. In fact, none seems to care very much.

This little chapel, which stands leaning out over the water on a specially built pier of the bridge, dates from the Middle Ages. There are only four other chapels of the kind in the whole of England: at Wakefield, Rotherham, Derby, and St Ives, Huntingdon. I believe the building on a bridge just outside the village of Wick, near Bath, is a fifth. It seems incredible that a town which has given such care to its Saxon church can allow its next most distinguished possession to be in danger of collapse. Its stones are in need of preservation; the iron stays placed to keep them together have split; and the whole structure needs careful attention.

How slow someone must be in Bradford! If this chapel were restored, opened, and furnished, Bradford could collect shillings or sixpences all day long from people anxious to peep inside a building that is with four exceptions unique in England.

The recent history of Bradford's chapel is this; tool-house, ammunition store for Territorials, and lock-up. The weather-vane on top of the chapel is in the form of a fish, which gave rise to the local saying that a man going to prison was going over the river under the fish.

8

The first notable sight I saw in Bristol was a ship mixed up with the tramway system.

Ships come right into Bristol town. They nestle down with their cheeks against the Tramway Centre and go to sleep till the bananas are unloaded. Sometimes a full-rigged ship anchors with her bowsprit in the back of the nearest policeman and the shadow of her masts over the Clifton tramcars, and the men of Bristol think nothing of it! They have been accustomed to this disturbing sight for over nine centuries. It must occur to a man looking at Bristol for the first time that a city which welcomes ships to her bosom in this manner could not help carving a great future on the seas.

In the Middle Ages, when the masts of ships surrounded Bristol on three sides, thick as pine woods, and the spires of the churches rose up between them and behind, this city – this county – must have been one of the most inspiring sights in all England. . . .

One of those foolish travellers who cannot see the long procession of men and affairs behind an English city said, after boring me at some length on various subjects: 'Of course, you won't go to Bristol! It is a smoky hole of a place, and – there is nothing to see there.'

Nothing to see in Bristol! There is too much to see there! I could stay for a month and write you a different story every day. I could write about the bronze tables which sprout like toadstools from the pavement opposite the Exchange, the 'nails' on which the Bristol merchants formerly paid their accounts (hence the saying, 'to pay on the nail'). I could write about one of the finest modern universities in England; about the Dutch House, a half-timbered mansion that stands in a main street like a galleon in a modern port; I could describe at great length the sixteen almshouses of Bristol which include St Peter's Hospital – a marvel – and Foster's, with its chapel dedicated to the Three Kings of Cologne.

In a rather bitter vein I could describe the decaying north porch of St Mary Redcliffe – the church in which Chatterton claimed to have discovered the Rowley poems – a lovely carved thirteenth-century porch which, I imagine, must be unique in England. It is a delicate tracery of Bath stone, black with soot, and round it the medieval craftsman has let himself all out on grotesque carvings – men with the bodies of fishes and beasts; queer, half-human things creeping in niches or peeping round corners, and each carving a gem. This porch is decaying in a city which spends millions on good works.

My trouble in Bristol is that I cannot leave the byways. It

is a city as fascinating as London; and in the same unself-conscious way. Bristol hides itself up alleys just as London does. It gives nothing to him who does not search; but to the explorer Bristol is generous with the unexpected; with sudden glimpses of old things: queer old buildings; old steps; alluring doorways, and – always – the sight of a ship lying landlocked between two streets.

In Marsh Street, the centre of a maze of Georgian survivals, I came to the Merchant Venturers' Hall. No man who remembers the name of the two greatest venturers who trod an English quay – John Cabot and his son Sebastian – could stand for long outside this hall.

Inside, what did I find? Here one of the last medieval trade guilds is busier than it ever was; more vigorous; more important. As I was taken through spacious rooms hung with stately eighteenth-century portraits, through hall after hall into the banqueting chamber, where crystal candelabra hang from a high ceiling and a polished table gleams like a still pool, I could hardly realize that I was not in one of our own ancient livery company halls in the shadow of the Mansion House.

'We trace our history back to Henry II,' said the treasurer. 'Oh, yes; we are busy! We run the Merchant Venturers' Technical College. The almshouses round the corner for old seamen and seamen's widows was established by us in 1554. We look after the young and the old, you see.'

In the almshouses round the corner live nineteen old sailors and twelve sailors' widows. They live in a gracious old harbour of yellow cottages built round three sides of a paved courtyard. In the centre of the court rises a tall, white mast; on which the old men run up flags at emotional moments. When they limp to their doors and gaze up at the sky with eyes too dim now to cope with an approaching storm, these buildings take on the appearance of a becalmed vessel. They have sailed down nearly four centuries with an aged crew; a crew that changes every few years, yet always looks the same. Over the central building are these lines:

IN SEARCH OF ENGLAND

Freed from all storms, the tempest, and the rage
Of billows, here we spend our age;
Our weather-beaten vessels here repair –
And from the merchants' kind and generous care,
Find harbourage here; no more we put to sea
Until we launch into Eternity.

Over one door are the words – 'Elder Brother'; inside lives
Captain Andrews, skipper of this good old ship.

'Quarrels are our only trouble,' he said. 'I settle all
disputes if I can. Old men are often quarrelsome, especially
when they tell the same yarns to each other for years.'

An ancient mariner, with a beard sprouting from beneath
his chin in the real W. W. Jacobs manner, and a short pipe
apparently growing in his mouth, touched a peaked cap.

' 'Mornin', Cap'n! Fine day!'

'Aye, 'tis so!' said the skipper; and they both looked up at
the sky; and out towards the prow – or gate – of the good
ship, where a butcher's boy went whistling with mutton in
his basket.

What do these old sailors talk about? Here is a typical
conversation.

'The sea!' (contemptuous spit) 'The sea! When I signed
on in '59 the sea was the *sea*, but now it's just yachting!
Young fellows don't know what the sea is; they might as well
sign on in one of these here hotels. I crossed the Atlantic in
a sailing boat in '69, sir, with a cargo of salt for the
Newfoundland fisheries. The rats, mad with thirst – for they
got at the salt – gnawed through the lead pipes to the water
tanks. And when two days out we began shipping water,
and it was all hands to the pumps. Those were the days, sir!
Up in the rigging, with the sails froze hard as boards and
your nails torn off. Those were the days! Now you cross the
Atlantic in a hotel, and you only see the ocean by mistake
when you take a wrong turning, and meet it sudden
like. . . .'

'Who,' I asked, 'is that very old man?'

'That's the poet, sir. He can't write, but he can
remember; he recites his poems.'

'Would he recite them to me?'

'Of course he would; he hasn't had an audience for months! We know them all!'

The poet is nearly ninety. His name is Hook.

He sat at his bare little table, assumed a dramatic expression, turned to me a grey-bearded face, which might have been the face of a saint, and began his longest poem. What it lacked in metre and polish it gained in sincerity. It started on the dockside as the author was watching a ship unload, and it ended with the downfall of the Kaiser.

The old man's hand fell on the table, and his dramatic expression changed to a smile: the poem was over.

'I will now,' he said, 'recite you the one about the almshouse fire.'

'First tell me how you came to compose verse.'

He told me that the war had inspired him, and since then he had not been able to stop. He cannot write, but when he has saved up enough money he goes to a Bristol typist and recites his poems. He remembers twenty-five long epics.

I left old Seaman Homer sitting at his bare table and went out into Bristol, this thriving, thrusting modern city, with a crowded past, a busy present, and a great future, where so many kind deeds are hidden round a corner.

9

Among those inventions and devices which never fail to charm me, and, I suppose, all simple-minded persons, are cuckoo clocks, warming-pans, glass globes which, when shaken, deluge a subaqueous landscape in snow, and – camera obscuras.

I have found a really good camera obscura; a big one in which the figures are at least six inches high. It stands on the top of Clifton Downs not far from, and slightly higher than, the famous Suspension Bridge. Everyone in Bristol has, I gather, seen it and become weary of it, for I have twice paid down my sixpence and twice climbed the winding stairs to it, and each time the so-called Observatory has had to be unlocked for me. Yet every Bristolian knows it.

'The Observatory! Oh, yes; I haven't been there for years, but before we were married my wife and I used to go up there and look into the camera obscura!'

That is how they talk about it. Gazing into the camera obscura at Clifton seems a natural prelude to marriage in Bristol!

On Clifton Downs, the site of an early British camp, stands an innocent-looking tower, which is the eye of the hill. It is the remains of an ancient windmill, once known as the Snuff Mill, which was partially destroyed by fire in the year 1777. After lying derelict for half a century, a Mr West made his home in this lonely tower, in the year 1828 – ideal home for a star-gazer, an alchemist, or a camera obscurantist – and installed a telescope and the camera. The Snuff Mill then became known as the Observatory.

Today Mr West's telescopes have earned their repose, but the camera obscura, one of the largest in the country, is still doing its work well. . . .

I climbed to the top of the tower, and was shown into a small circular apartment. The door was shut to exclude all light save a thin beam filtered through lenses in the roof, which, falling downward so as to cover the surface of a large, round, convex table, reflected in sharp, coloured detail everything that was happening in the immediate locality.

Slowly the table revolved, exposing as it did so a new tract of country. . . .

How much more thrilling than a cinema is this ancient invention – at least to me. One is looking at life, not at actors. The colours in which the landscape is reproduced are perfect and the people who stroll calmly across the mysterious Merlin's table in the dark room, so deliciously unconscious that the hill has its eye on them, move without the jerkiness of the cinema, without the self-consciousness of the film actor. They are, in fact, so natural that one childishly follows them with a finger and pinches the empty air in a futile endeavour to pick them up. It seems that one should be able to capture one of them and hold him between the finger and thumb as Gulliver examined a Lilliputian.

An elderly woman walked slowly up to the downs, holding a parasol in a white-gloved hand. Two Clifton schoolboys strolled slowly along over green grass talking; a man sat on a wooden bench reading a newspaper, all of them unconscious that every movement made by them was reproduced on the slowly revolving table in the tower. As it moved I gained a glimpse of the thick woods on the opposite side of the gorge. I could see the wind moving the tree-tops and a thin puff of smoke ascending from a chimney. The view of Clifton Suspension Bridge seen in this way is more marvellous than the direct one. The thin, graceful thread flung from one side of the rocky gorge to the other is examined as a bird might see it in mid-air. One looks down on the towers and on that airy thread along which tiny motor-cars move, the footways over which go people, with, below them, two hundred and forty-five feet of a space ending in the river and the jagged rocks.

As I stood there in the dark I thought that a few hundred years ago any man who owned a camera obscura would have been burned at the stake or made Lord Chancellor.

The charm of looking into this reflection of life is the illusion it imparts of omnipotence. You are, as it were, enthroned anonymously in a position of unassailable safety, and free from detection, watching the little actions of little men. Nothing escapes you. A man blowing his nose in a scarlet handkerchief occupies the Universe for a second. There is also the charm of the unexpected. You never know what the next turn of the table will reveal, so that you stand in the dark like a second-class deity observing the working of a more powerful intelligence. Look! Under the trees a young father who has taken his family for a picnic is keeping the baby quiet with chocolate while his wife sleeps in the shade. . . .

Another move of the table . . . a fat man puffs slowly up the hill, desperately hot, mopping his head, supremely ridiculous. If you met him face to face he might be impressive; but here, with life just a shadow show, he is merely an amusing little clown in the circus of existence.

Another move of the table. . . . The scene shifts to a bosky dell. A young man is sitting on a seat with a girl. He looks carefully round to see that no one is looking. You know that he nervously premeditates kissing her. For the first time you feel that a camera obscura is rather a low-down invention. Why should you . . . not quite playing the . . . now he's done it; and made a frightful hash of it! Aiming an inexpert salute which landed on her ear, he has received a slap in the face, and . . . the table moves on!

You leave the dark room of this simple wizardry and look through the windows of the tower. How strange! There sit the man and the girl under a distant tree; there, in a shady hollow, the father feeds his young with chocolate; there stands the fat man puffing beside a fence; and in the remote distance walks the elderly woman whose parasol is like a little yellow mushroom on the grass.

Why, you wonder, has no writer of detective stories used the camera obscura? The eye of the hill lends itself to treatment.

You go down, and in your turn become a little painted shadow moving across the table beneath someone else's eye. You feel divine no longer! You wrestle with a gamin desire to turn round in the direction of the tower and put out your tongue, just to show some Peeping Tom that you know all about him.

CHAPTER SEVEN

I admire the three lovely sisters of England – Hereford, Worcester, and Gloucester. I cross the Border Marches and see a castle still watching Wales. In a field I come to the ruins of Uriconium and in Shrewsbury I have a nightmare

I

MY first impression of Gloucester was that of a city full of small, comely maidens between the fortunate ages of fifteen and twenty-five. In the evening they wear flowered voile – the material favoured by the taller maidens of Botticelli – and they walk up and down Northgate and Southgate Streets with the cathedral bells as a sweet accompaniment to their perambulations. Some of these small maidens are pretty; others, thanks to wise Nature's law of compensation, have beautiful legs.

Had I more time to investigate this appealing problem, I believe that I should discover that during the last twenty years or so six girls have been born to every boy in Gloucester. Local authorities to whom I have broached the subject attribute it to the match factory.

Most cathedral cities visited by me in the course of my search have been true to type: Winchester, Exeter, Wells: all sheltering beneath their historic cathedrals like dear old ladies under am umbrella. Gloucester is more difficult to discover. Unlike so many English cities through whose streets history has been flowing for centuries, Gloucester has not sought refuge on the retired list. This city, owing to geographical and other reasons outside the scope of this story, has not lacked the vitality of human endeavour since its right-angled streets were laid out by the Second Legion of the Roman Expeditionary Force in the forty-second year of our Lord. Here is something more than a great cathedral dreaming among elms: here is a Roman-Saxon-medieval city that has thrust its way into the industrial era without quite losing touch with an older time.

Gloucester is a cathedral city, a manufacturing city, a county town that knows what cartloads of cabbages look like, a spa – for you can drink the waters of Gloucester – and a port. How many people know that Gloucester is a thriving port – the most inland port in England?

This discovery is borne home to you in a sudden and rather surprising manner.

You are standing near the cathedral. A man wearing a blue jersey and a seaman's cap goes past. You think that he has been either shipwrecked in the Severn or is spending a holiday home from sea. Three or four more seamen meet him at the corner of the road! If you are new to Gloucester, and inquisitive, as all travellers should be, you follow them; and they lead you onward, away from the cathedral to the Port of Gloucester, where ships lie at anchor against the quays, between tall flour mills and grain elevators.

You realize with surprise that Gloucester is a little Liverpool of the Midlands. She has a graving dock, floating elevators, timber stores, and coal tips, all neatly hidden away in the broad estuary of the Severn.

Here the railway lines run beside the wharves; the sound of the steam cranes mingles strangely with the chime of the cathedral bells. . . .

What I, and all other casual visitors, love about Gloucester is the unusual experience of living in a medieval inn. When Edward II was murdered in 1327 and his shrine in the cathedral became a famous place of pilgrimage, the fortunes of many inns were founded; and of these some still remain to shelter the traveller.

The inn in which I am writing is entered through a huge archway constructed to admit a cavalcade, a pious lady in a horse litter, or a coach. The inn is built round a paved courtyard. A flight of stone steps in this courtyard leads up to an oak gallery running the four sides of the yard from which are the bedrooms, so that I can open my bedroom door, lean over the gallery, and keep in touch with everything happening down below. It is all so interesting and intimate.

I see, as I lean outside my bedroom door, the new arrivals drive into the courtyard and book their rooms. I see the chambermaids busy round the gallery; I see the boots down below in the courtyard 'booting'; I see the waiters crossing the yard bearing trays of food, because six hundred years have not been able to bring the kitchen, which is at one end of the yard, any nearer to the dining-room, which is at the other! In the depth of winter every egg and every breakfast rasher has to be carried through the snow to the table. Hail conservatism! I suppose travellers have been leaning over this balcony for six hundred years watching much the same scene – arrivals, departures, dusting, cleaning, food.

I would like to know when the proximity of cleanliness to godliness was defined. Certainly not during the Middle Ages, for there are only two baths in this inn, and in the morning the chambermaid summons me with the voice of a sergeant-major:

'Will you take your bath *at once?*'

And I have to dash out along the gallery to my place in the queue.

The thrill of Gloucester Cathedral is one that can never be forgotten. I stood dumb with admiration beneath the great drums of the nave built by men who knew how to design fortresses; the height, the proportion, the simple strength of these great columns is beyond description.

In the choir of Gloucester sleeps Edward II under a rich canopy. It was to this tomb that the pilgrims of the Middle Ages came with such profitable result that the monks rebuilt church and abbey from the proceeds of their piety. Then the cloisters of Gloucester! They stand alone among the cathedral cloisters of England. Their delicate fan-vaulting is a sheer miracle in stone.

As I was walking at night in Gloucester, admiring the

Roman layout of the city, at one moment lost in Glevum, at the next in medieval Gloucester, I heard, from beneath the ground it seemed, the sound of music. I went into an inn yard, and came to a flight of old stone steps leading downwards. Above them was the sign: 'The Monks' Retreat.' I descended and entered a cool, dusty cellar which would make the fortune of any man in Montmartre.

At first sight it appeared that the crypt of a church had been turned into a saloon bar. In a long, dim, vaulted cavern men sat drinking beside beer barrels. A bar ran the length of the vault, and a tireless electric organ occupied a remote corner. It was a weird, slightly sacrilegious sight. Had the occupants been Frenchmen and not solid Gloucestershire farmers I would have been prepared for some kind of shameless cabaret!

As I sat down beside a barrel and cast a curious glance round the dusty vault I noticed in one corner a confessional box and in another a stone stoup for holy water! I imagine this to be the most remarkable bar in England.

'Some think this place was an underground passage built in the old days, so that the pilgrims could get from their inn to the cathedral,' said the barman, 'but others think that centuries ago it was on the street level. . . .'

'Half a pint,' said an inhabitant.

The electric organ whirred and gathered itself together before plunging into a new tune.

The old inn courtyard was dark. A light shone in the gallery, casting shadows over the flagstones, flinging the shape of a great beam over the stone steps. I climbed up and leaned over the balustrade to stand a moment looking down into the yard that has seen six hundred years of wayfaring.

Modern Gloucester was hushed, and in this place seemed a memory of things old. Over the city passed a peal of bells, and in the square of sky above the little courtyard shone a few faint stars.

In Herefordshire the fruit trees stand with their lime-washed trunks in long grass. The air is drowsy with the pungency of summer fields; and over hedges the traveller sees men and women tossing up the yellow hay and tossing down the yellow beer and the pale gold cider; for this is the thirstiest job on earth. The pickers are busy in the fruit trees; in the lovely Wye Valley is a rich greenness of scenery that is unforgettably England; black satin cows stand at the edge of streams and rivers, swishing their tails in a patch of shade. . . .

Herefordshire, Gloucestershire, and Worcestershire are the three lovely sisters of England. I do not know which I admire most. . . .

In the early afternoon I stopped at Ross.

I climbed beneath those elms planted by 'the Man of Ross', and I looked down at the bend of the river and out over the green country that lies in calm beauty to the mountains of Wales. This is, I think, one of the most magnificent panoramas I have yet seen. In the River Wye small, shrimp-pink children were bathing, and in every dark patch of willows stood cows chewing the cud and letting the water ripple past their legs.

Hereford. . . .

A sweet, neat, smokeless, fruit-smelling town with some splendid half-timbered houses. I came to it over the Wye Bridge and saw the red sandstone cathedral standing with a gold cloud over the central tower. Gloucester Cathedral has grandeur; Hereford, with its richly ornate Norman nave, has a solemn sweetness. The nave of Gloucester creates wonder; the nave of Hereford leads the eye to the east window, where it stays content.

They were singing an anthem. The great church contained only nineteen people. They sing an anthem every afternoon in this empty church. I forgot the urgency of my day; I forgot everything but the high, sexless voices of the choir, echoing, it seemed, from above the high altar; I saw nothing but the little flushes of pink and blue falling on the stone through stained windows. The organ of Hereford is, with the exception perhaps of that in Westminster Abbey, the most beautiful I have heard: it is, as it should be, the voice of the cathedral; its calm sweetness places a hand over the spirit; and in this church, with the organ whispering through the aisles, the world and its problems seem over the hills of reality.

The anthem ended. A gold cross shone a moment in a ray of sunlight; and the white choir left the church. . . .

The treasure of Hereford is the Mappa Mundi – the map of the world – drawn on one huge sheet of vellum by a thirteenth-century monk. It is kept in the south transept shut in by oak doors. I opened these doors and looked at this queer version of the world, one of the earliest attempts at a map known to us. It is an education in medieval geography. The earth is drawn as a round, flat object, with Jerusalem in the centre, as the Greeks visualized the position of Delphi, the Persians Kangdiz, and the Arabs Aryne. 'This is Jerusalem: I have set it in the midst of the nations round about her,' says Ezekiel. In the Vulgate the twelfth verse of the seventy-fourth Psalm runs: 'Operatus est salutem in medio terrae.' England is drawn in the bottom left-hand corner: a little country full of cathedrals. What a wide, wonder-struck fairyland was the world of the Middle Ages! I have never forgotten a sentence which G. K. Chesterton wrote in, I think, *A Short History of England*, a history, by the way, without one date in it. 'The Middle Ages,' he wrote 'were full of all the world worships in children, because it has crushed it out of men. They were full, as the modest remains of the vulgarest arts are full, of something that we saw out of the nursery window.'

The sun was sinking when I entered Worcester Cathedral.

In the choir, with his feet to the High Altar, lies King John – a man who has not left one good memory behind him. What queer tricks Fate plays with men, so often preserving the evil and obliterating the good! King John directed that his body should be buried between the tombs of Worcester's two saints, St Oswald and St Wulstan. The saints have disappeared, but the bones of the wicked king remain covered by a portrait effigy which in 1216 was the lid of his coffin. It is a splendid piece of work. It shows him crowned, wearing the royal robes, and when new it was coloured. During restorations in 1874, the Office of Works which has charge of all royal tombs, made the hideous mistake of gilding it.

An interesting fact about King John's tomb is the light cast on an ancient legend when it was opened in 1797. The story went that John, realizing his slender chances of attaining heaven, ordered that he should be buried in a monk's gown, with the idea, apparently, that he might hoodwink the doorkeeper of Paradise! When his tomb was opened it was seen that the rotted remnant of a cowl lay over his skull.

They show you an engraving of this grisly sight in the chapter-house.

Another tomb at Worcester pulled me up sharply – the chantry of Prince Arthur, the elder brother of Henry VIII. Here is one of history's best question marks in England. Suppose this prince had lived? Henry VIII, who was educated for the Church, would have been Archbishop of Canterbury. What course would the Reformation have taken?

I found my car in the shade of an elm-tree, and headed north towards Shropshire.

As I went I thought what a fine thing it might be if the deans and vergers of other cathedrals in England would take Worcester Cathedral in its treatment of the public as their model. Worcester Cathedral welcomes the visitor at the gate, and will give him a seat in the choir if he can be persuaded to stay for a service. Wherever he goes he is made to feel welcome. Each tomb and each monument is labelled.

Worcester Cathedral recognizes that our cathedrals, as I have noted with surprise and delight, attract enormous crowds of men and women of all classes who are seriously interested in them as the repositories of our history, or are conscious that in them lies the clue to knowledge.

With the shadows lengthening I crossed the border into Shropshire.

3

There was dust in my eyes, dust in my throat, and dust in great clouds behind me when I came up from the lowlands in the early evening. In an oak-panelled room, where pewter glimmered like moonlight on still water, I poured a pint of ale down my throat; and the rim of the tankard was like a bar of ice against my forehead. A neat, freckled maid, wearing a starched cap on a red head, brought yellow cheese on a plate, and with it a great paving-stone of white bread.

How, I wonder, have I refrained so long from praising bread, cheese, and beer, the most significant, romantic, delicious, satisfying food that can pass the parched gullet of a wayfarer! Fat men in saloon cars can nose the French menus for *Sole Colbert* or *Bordelaise*, and for the many dishonest hashes devised by otherwise honest English cooks, but when I am hungry and the white road lies behind me mile on mile, give me bread, cheese, and beer.

The beer was of a deep mahogany brew, and sufficiently potent – for I was weary and susceptible to it – to lift me a little above the earth, so that sitting in the cool room, with a great blaze of late sunlight beyond the window, I was conscious of a romantic desire to fight or to pray, which is the essence of medievalism.

I put on my dusty hat as if it had been a helm with a *panache* towering above it, and I strode out into the hilly streets of Ludlow to admire those raiding, fighting border-men, those Welsh-beating sturdy Salop knaves, still driving before them, between rows of half-timbered houses, big brown cows and fatted sheep. (I imagine, however, that today the cattle really do belong to them; which just shows you how time alters all things!)

There was a smell of wood smoke.

England – as I noticed between Cornwall and Devon – has the knack of changing her expression in a mile. Gone now are the green Worcester valleys; the neat, pretty Hereford orchards; the trim Gloucester fields; here we stand on the wild borders of Wales. This town of Ludlow sits on a fair hill at the junction of the Teme with the Corve. They still practise archery in this town. They call themselves the 'Archers of the Teme'. Where the Teme bends beneath a high headland stands the majestic ruin of Ludlow Castle, the most famous castle from Chester to Hereford, and the most extensive border stronghold spared by time.

I went in over a dry moat and talked to the gatekeeper.

'Yes,' he said, 'it does look as though you'd find things under the grass here, but the only things I found when I dug out this bit of the moat were three ha'pennies.'

We mourned together for a while and I went on to the inner ward; so silent, so drowsy with afternoon sun, the shadows of turrets over ruined walls. Grass grows in the great hall, little pink flowers sprout from the 'Lions' Den', ferns raise their green heads in the Armoury. I found the rooms once occupied by young Edward V and his brother before they were removed to the Tower of London never to be seen again. In a watch-tower, I looked through a thin arrow-slit and saw, far below, the river, and, far to the west, the blue hills of Wales.

For hundreds of years men dined in Ludlow Castle with swords easy in the scabbards, ready to come out at the first shout from the ramparts. Here lived those turbulent Lord Wardens of the Marches who sat for centuries with their hands on their sword-hilts and their eyes on Wales. When the whistle of an angry sword had become almost a novelty

163

in other parts of England, it was one of the ordinary rural sounds in the Marches; when the sight of a man lying in the grass with a red throat shocked London, they held no inquests in Shropshire; and while in less troublesome counties men were building cosy manor-houses the marcher barons were still reinforcing their keeps and deepening their moats – the first die-hards.

Feudalism indeed died hard in that chain of castles from Chester to Hereford – the old Norman first line against the Welsh – each castle a violent little garrison, ready always to sally forth at a warning shout, watching always for the beacon light, listening always for the sound of a horn from the hills, a tell-tale movement of long grass, or the flash of the moon on a sword. . . .

It was with a feeling almost of reverence that I realized here in the Marches of Shropshire, with Welshmen always at hand, Englishmen were once too busy to kill foxes.

Life was a game of chess here in the old days, the castles now lost to one side, now to the other. Unless a man kept himself quite up-to-date in affairs he might visit his friend and find his enemy. There was Maud de St Valery, who for a whole year – her husband being away after someone's blood – defended her castle against the Welsh. It fell in the end, and she survived only to be starved to death in Corfe Castle by King John.

In the middle of the inner ward of Ludlow rises one of the four round churches in England. It is a beautiful Norman tower with the sky for its roof and the grass for its floor. Several ancient, indignant goats gazed up at me as I entered, and ceased cropping the grass.

I wondered whether Marion de la Bruyère prayed here! She must have done so. She is a lady in the only surviving medieval romance written round an English castle; it is the Geste of Fulk Fitzwarine, of which few people who visit Ludlow know anything. In this story is told how Marion, who was a ward of the baron of Ludlow during the reign of

Henry II, fell dangerously in love with a captive knight called Arnold de Lisle.

One night she contrived to give him a rope and he escaped. Life then became rather pointless to Marion. It is not difficult, as one walks the towers, to imagine, when surrounded by Welshmen with no one quite sure that the smell of burning was really the arras or someone trying to come in at the front door, that Ludlow Castle was hardly a cheerful place for a young girl. I imagine poor Marion de la Bruyère sitting at her turret, too miserable to get on with the tapestry or even to knit the dear baron a woolly, gazing over to the exasperating hills and sighing: 'Oh, if I could only see him again! That lovely straight nose of his! Oh, dear, I shall die! . . .'

One day the baron, things being dull at Ludlow apparently, decided to sally forth with his men at arms and kill somebody, just to keep things going in the Marches. Marion sought this opportunity to send a message to de Lisle, telling him that it would be quite safe for him to come to her, and he came to her one night when the moon was not too full. When she was in his arms a great tumult arose, for he had not come alone! He had brought a storming party with him, which was already in possession of Ludlow. When Marion realized his treachery she did the only thing open to a self-respecting girl: she took Arnold's sword and ran it right through him, and, opening the window, died on the rocks below!

Thus life in the age of chivalry.

The eyes of an angry old goat remained fixed on me in the chapel in which Marion must have prayed for her lover. An attractive theory, that of Pythagoras! Suppose this was Arnold, condemned to look so stupid, and to wander about those grounds eating the grass which he had trod as a captive, a lover, a traitor to love, and a conqueror!

'Arnold,' I said, 'you deserve everything that's come to you.'

He looked at me like an outraged elder and shook his

whiskers, whereupon a neat, slim she-goat of considerable attraction leapt nimbly from a window ledge and ran to him affectionately, nosing his whiskers with a white muzzle.

'Don't trust him,' I said, but woman-like, she tossed her head indignantly, and jumped through the window again.

High above the Teme, fronting the Welsh hills, Ludlow Castle stands, an air of gallantry about it still, and a certain truculence. It gazes with its little arrow-slits over to Wales as if not quite sure whether peace has been made with the hills or not.

4

Where the Severn flings a lazy arm round the fields south of Shrewbury, I came on men digging a trench within hailing distance of the by-road. Trench digging, as this generation knows well, can be one of man's most significant actions, and must therefore always attract the eyes of the thoughtful. I observed several wise-looking, spectacled men standing on the parapet of the trench gazing earnestly at each spadeful of earth as it came out of the mysterious depths.

'Ha, ha!' I said to myself, with a hand on the brake, 'here is a pretty story for a fine morning! Unless my map is all wrong, this is Wroxeter, or, as I prefer to call it, Uriconium or Viroconium and these men are, or I am no judge of men, professors and students of archaeology, tickling the tough old spine of Rome.'

This was magic earth. Those potatoes that grow insecurely beyond the trenches were trying to cover up one of Rome's bad bargains, a city built 1,856 years ago, that lived for about five hundred years and died violently, but, during its life, a little stage on which was played England's first historic drama.

It was, indeed Uriconium – 'the White Town in the Woodland'. On the edge of the trench lay bits of that sealing-wax red Samian pottery which they used to bring in great galley loads from Gaul; yellow handles of amphorae, thin red wafer tiles which the Legions knew how to bake as hard as steel. Radiating from the trench were other trenches and deep pits in which lay the heating rooms of Roman baths, the foundations of walls, and, most impressive of all, the roots of a row of stone pillars which once upheld the portico of Uriconium's public buildings.

Now when a man stands on the edge of a pit in which they are digging up Roman Britain the tiny fragments of red tile, the broken pots and the brown bones of men and beasts, the ruined walls should fly together and form a picture in his mind; a picture thousands of years old, but – *alive.*

'Uriconium was founded before the year A.D. 68,' said one of the diggers, 'by the 4th Legion, which was soon afterwards recalled to Rome.'

The year A.D. 68! Nero was lighting the Colosseum in Rome with the bodies of the first saints: men were still living who had heard the Sermon on the Mount. And these fields – Britain? The Britain of that day is a mist which blows aside a moment to show us vast forests and the wild tribes watching the Roman roads as they grew mile after mile under the picks of the Legions; when the mist parts, we see the white key towns of Roman Britain standing up behind their walls in pillar and portico – something new in Britain, little imitations of Rome, torches on the wild hillsides lit from that great flame of civilization which did not die on the sword of the Hun, but lived on in the Church and laid the foundations of the modern world. In the mist we hear the creak of galley oars in river and estuary; and in the mist we hear the war-horns of the Legions lowing like cows, telling the smallest wolf cub that something new and alarming had at last happened in Britain. . . .

'You see,' said the digger, 'it was a pretty big town. I traced the walls in the fields last year. There was a ditch beyond them!'

This Uriconium sat behind its wall on the edge of Wales

for five hundred years, a red-roofed town entered by red-brick gates and planned in blocks like a barracks. In the centre rose the white stone pillars of the forum. On market days its streets were full of goats and sheep and dogs and farm wagons, for it was not a military town like Chester or York, but an experiment in civilization: a town full of imitation Romans, ruled, no doubt, by Romans but inhabited by Britons dressed in togas. A young Roman official might have written to his mother in Rome:

'DEAREST MATER,

'We are making something of these natives. The wild ones we keep in the hills and the tame ones in towns. All the children here now speak Latin, and they all know the story of Romulus and Remus. You remember Marcus, who was at school with me in Rome? He is in Londinium, and I hear that he is going to marry one of these British girls. You must not call them painted savages, mater dear, for I may marry one myself! They are really lovely, and they get the latest fashion from Rome in ten days. We have a little Jew here who is making a fortune out of the new hair bands which all the girls of Uriconium are buying. Some of the wealthier natives live in really fine villas outside the walls, and talk like senators in the evening, when I often dine with them and show them how to mix Falernian. Life isn't too bad in spots. Thank the pater for the vine slips, which are not growing too well, for it is so cold here at times. . . .'

So for five hundred years the ordered life of Rome was lived within these walls; harvests sold, cattle sold, skins sold; and most men thought it was permanent perhaps. Only the hills knew differently as they brooded on the sky, only the grass knew differently, only the wind from the north, beating on Uriconium in the wild nights, may have whispered of the death of Rome and the coming of the wild men, who were afraid to sleep under a roof, with fire and with sword. . . .

168

'The end of it all?' echoed the archaeologist. 'See it for yourself.'

He bent down and pointed to a black stratum in the earth.

'Fire!' he said.

The mist blows aside again, and we see the galleys going back to Rome after five hundred years, returning to help the dying giant; and over England knowledge of the most pathetic message a Roman Caesar ever sent to a province – the message of Honorius: 'You must protect yourselves!' (which was the only thing that Rome had not taught Britain). Then the hill fires burned beyond the Wall, and the men who had waited more or less patiently for five hundred years came on in a ragged line.

'Look here!' said the digger. 'In this room we found the charred skeleton of a man and a woman. The man was clutching a hoard of coins. Over there we found two burned children. That is the end of Uriconium.'

And the last picture in the mist . . . 'the White Town in the Woodland' lies dead under the moon. The Saxons will not live there. They shun it as though it were haunted, as perhaps it is, by men in the white togas of Rome. In broad daylight they wander the ruins, stealing the Roman stones; and a few miles away, on virgin soil, they built Shrewsbury.

In a tin shed the excavators keep all the treasures dug from this dramatic field. There are piles of rich red Samian bowls, the stock of a hardware shop, because they were found bowl piled in bowl; on them in raised relief are Pan and Hercules and Diana; inside them are the names of the Gaulish makers.

There are dozens of Roman tiles which had been stepped on before they were hard by meddlesome children and animals. The foot-pads of dogs and the toe-marks of children, and the nails of Roman sandals, are preserved here as if they had been made just yesterday. So vivid are they that a man looks towards the ruins beyond the door, half expecting to see the child who was playing near the brickworks eighteen hundred years ago running home to tell his mother that he has hurt his foot.

The most important discovery at Uriconium is the huge inscription that was once above the public buildings. It records in beautifully formed letters that the local tribe erected it in honour of the Emperor Hadrian in A.D. 130.

Shrewsbury is a lucky town. All these objects are destined for her museum. In a short time it will be possible to see, labelled in glass cases, all that is left of 'the White Town in the Woodland'.

5

I blame it all on the moon and a lobster. . . .

When I drew back the bedroom curtains, the moonlight printed itself in green on the floor. It ran over the bed and lay slantways upon a grim wardrobe that stood in the shadow of the ancient oak-beamed room. A proper Puckish night, with the green wash over hill and field, a night for elfin horns and mushroom rings and strange scurryings in thicket and copse. Somewhere near, a dog, unable to sleep and not knowing why – poor little lost wolf – whimpered restlessly.

I lay in bed thinking of the many bloody things done in Shewsbury since Offa, King of the Mercians, sailed up the Severn in the eighth century and drove out the Prince of Powis. All the Saxon-Norman-Medieval shocks of the Welsh border reverberated in Shrewsbury. At the High Cross, not far away, they barbarously executed David of Wales in 1283. Here also the Duke of Worcester was killed in 1403, and in this same spot the body of Hotspur was exposed for three days between the millstones, so that all men might know that the king's enemy was dead. Falstaff, you remember, bragged that he killed Hotspur after a Homeric combat that lasted 'a long hour by Shrewsbury clock!' That made me smile. I thought of green fields . . . Mistress Ford and Mistress Page . . . the buck basket . . . Ellen Terry . . .

Stratford-on-Avon . . . how funny my slippers looked, so alone without me, standing in a pool of moonlight. Then, I suppose, I fell asleep.

Do you know what it is to awaken suddenly from deep sleep into instant wakefulness? I imagined that a cold hand had been passed over my face. It was so vivid that I dared not open my eyes because I felt that I would see the hand and – the thing to which it belonged. All this sounds so fatuous in daylight, but at times – rare times, fortunately – how childish, small, helpless and alone is man in the silence of the night. Outside the dog howled at the moon, that long, miserable whine known in Scotland as the 'death howl'.

If, I said to myself, I did not open my eyes and behave like a reasonable person, I would lose all self-respect. On the word 'three' I would look! One . . . *there was undoubtedly something horrible in the room* . . . two . . . *it might be leaning over the bed, for it seemed so cold and near* . . . th . . . *or perhaps the wardrobe door was slowly opening, or, much worse, slowly closing* – damn it! THREE! The moonlight lay across my face in a white bar, and the room was, of course, empty.

If you have ever experienced this waking nightmare, you will sympathize with my frantic attempt to sleep again. In the middle of the night a strange room can become filled with a horrible tenseness – a feeling as of something about to happen. If you open your eyes, the familiar objects take on a hellish intelligence; the furniture seems to have just stopped talking; if you close them, horrors creep towards you from every shadow, and you lie in a cowardly sweat, expecting at any second to be touched or to hear something. I lay there thinking of young Hotspur. I tried systematically to forget his stiff body between the two millstones; but back he came till I felt that he was sitting on the bed trying to tell me something.

I suppose that at such moments a man is not so wakeful as he imagines. He lies slightly drugged by sleep, unable to move, enduring the terror in the hope and belief that so long as he lies still the brooding climax to the atmospheric conspiracy may not, after all, arrive. To see a ghost would not, I think, be a very big shock, but to feel a ghost is horrible. Or are ghosts indigestion?

How supremely idiotic you feel in the morning when the sun shines and the postman is rapping down the street. . . .

No place could have looked less ghostly than Shrewsbury in the flush of morning. Feeling heartily ashamed, and vowing never to eat inland lobster when the moon is full, I set out to explore a town which for unaffected charm would be hard to beat in all England. Shrewsbury is delightful because here are more lovely half-timbered houses standing together than it has yet been my lot to see. And there are no tramcars. The streets of Shrewsbury are undeformed by lines or poles or wires. It takes you some time to realize what is, so happily, missing.

The situation of Shrewsbury is worth study. The men who chose the site knew their job, for here the Severn describes a circle in which, on rising ground, lies the town within a natural moat, surrounded on all sides by deep water save for three hundred yards on the north-east, where, of course, stands the castle. But the old houses of Shrewsbury are its chief glory. Every American should see them before leaving England.

I do not know whether there is a comprehensive book on the old houses of England; if not, it is the duty of some man with time and a camera to write it. Here in Shrewsbury, and, in fact, all over Shropshire, are rows of houses which were standing in Tudor times and even earlier, still inhabited, still young every half century or so under a new coat of whitewash and tar.

There is a charm about a busy, thriving country town like Shrewsbury, quite different from the more obvious charm of a cathedral city. A cathedral overshadows a town. Every town takes second place to its cathedral. Most visitors see the cathedral and nothing else. Your simple country town, which for centuries has been the little metropolis of a large agricultural county, teems with a wider life of great charm and interest to the casual observer. In ancient streets, where houses overhang the pavement, nodding forward in the sun like tired professors of history, the rich stream of English country life flows on unaltered in the main since Elizabethan times, and, in many essentials, since the days of the Saxon and the Norman.

I love Shrewsbury in the early evening, when the shops have shut and the girls who have been working all day come out in their best summer frocks. The local gallants stand at the street corners; the local warriors in khaki stamp or jingle on 'late pass' up and down the main street. You catch a glimpse of those three cornerstones of communal life: the country squire, the parson, and the country solicitor – the aristocracy, the law, and the church. Every omnibus stage holds a crowd of country people burdened with parcels. The baskets which they brought to market full of cheese or butter or eggs are now full of other things – gramophone records and ribbons, wireless valves, the best Sunday pair of lisle thread stockings, and a new knitted tie for dad. Shrewsbury to these people is a big place, her lovely, quiet streets are death-traps. They stand patiently waiting for the homeward charabanc that has done more than anything since the railway train to alter English country life, and has done it more effectually, by bringing the possibility of the town not to some distant station, but right to the end of a country lane.

I have seen more buxom country girls and more hale and hearty old farmers in Shrewsbury than I have seen since I left Devonshire.

The cows, also, are remarkably fine; so, I must add, are the sheep. Darwin, who was born here, occupies a place of honour on a plinth, his head the unthinking target of the birds of the air (which might have interested him), and his feet shod in the best pair of bronze shoes, complete with laces, it has been my luck to admire.

At night, especially under this witching moon, the streets of Shrewsbury take you back to Old England. Butcher Row at night is perfect. From one point of it there is nothing to be seen that can be later than the fifteenth or the early sixteenth century. Then, with the moonlight falling from oversailing stories, slanting from eaves, in the sharp black and whiteness of half-timbered houses silent in sleep, old memories come tiptoeing back to town; and it takes precious little imagination to see again the long procession of abbots and kings and bishops and mailed lords who have walked over this stage in their hour, leaving behind them both good and bad. . . .

Lobster is not essential for a Shrewsbury haunting.

CHAPTER EIGHT

I walk the walls of Chester, skirt Black England, tell the truth about Wigan, visit the 'Lakes', and make a dash at Gretna Green

I

WELL and truly was Chester called by the Britons Caer Lleon, the 'City of the Legions'. Chester is still the 'City of Legions', only they come from Louisville, and Oshkosh, New York, and Washington.

For years I have heard people describe the wonder of a walk round the walls of Chester. Naturally the first thing I did when I arrived here was to find the wall, which is not difficult. Chester, as you must know, is the only city in England which retains its medieval wall complete: a high red sandstone walk with towers at various strategic points along its course; on one side a handrail to prevent you from falling into back gardens, on the other a waist-high barrier from which in old times the Cestrians were in the habit of defying their enemies with boiling oil – and anything else that came handy. 'Blessed is he that expecteth little' is a wise maxim that has been drummed into me since I first sat up and wanted the moon; but I have never absorbed it. I realized this on the walls of Chester.

Any man might with justice, I think, expect that as he walked a medieval town wall something at least heroic would meet his eye, but the walls of Chester gave me only a much better idea of other people's washing, the gas-works, and the canal. You see Chester within the wall remains medieval, but Chester outside the wall is industrial. It has not been possible, with factory sites at one hundred and thirty pounds an acre, for Chester to retain a wide, open space outside the wall, and, consequently, the wall of Chester stands with its arms round beautiful old Chester, while ugly new Chester peeps over the parapet from the other side.

I had been walking for about ten minutes, admiring the small, reddy-brown cathedral through the trees, when I came to a turret approached by a flight of ancient steps, and on the wall was this dramatic inscription:

KING CHARLES

STOOD ON THIS TOWER

SEPTEMBER 24TH, 1645, AND SAW

HIS ARMY DEFEATED

ON ROWTON MOOR

Inside the tower a man was presiding over a little museum. He told me, just as though he was present at the time, that when the Royalist army was riding to reinforce the garrison at Chester, the Roundheads set upon them and routed them with poor King Charles standing on this tower watching every move of the game. There are various battlefield relics in the museum, also several Roman antiquities which take the mind back to the days when that magnificent Legion, the 20th, known as the 'Valeria Victrix', was the crack regiment of Deva.

I had been walking for miles, wondering if the wall of Chester ever completes its circle, when I came to that which any exhausted visitor must regard as a poor joke. Here, near Bridge Gate, is a long flight of steps arranged in sets of three and known as the 'Wishing Steps'.

'Why?' I asked a man who was standing on them, looking as though none of his wishes had ever come true.

'Well,' he said in the curiously blunt way they have here, 'you have to run up and down and up again without taking breath, and then they say you'll get your wish.'

I noticed a band of breathless Americans standing on the

176

other side, utterly vanquished. I decided to try no conclusions with the Wall of Chester and passed on in a superior way, mentally deciding to have a wish – for I can never resist these challenges of Fate – some morning when I could come fresh and vigorous to the steps. That, however, I learn is not playing the game; you must walk the wall first and then 'run up and down and up again', a feat which I shall leave to the natives – and to the Legions!

There is one feature of Chester which, to my mind, is worth ten walls. There is nothing like it in any English town – the Chester 'Rows'.

Chester is a town of balconies. The first impression I received of it was a town whose inhabitants spend a great portion of their lives leaning over old oak galleries, smoking and chatting and watching life go by below them in the streets.

'The Rows' are simply long, covered arcades formed by running a highway through the first stories of a street of old buildings. You mount from the roadway to 'the Rows' on frequent flights of stone steps and find yourself in the strangest shopping streets in England. Here are the best shops hidden away in the darkness of these ancient arcades, and it is possible to shop dry-shod in the worst weather. There is a peculiar charm about 'the Rows'. They are not typically medieval, because there is no record of any other street of this kind in the Middle Ages, yet they impart a singular impression of medievalism: through the oak beams which support the galleries you see black-and-white half-timbered houses on the opposite side of the street, with another 'Row' cut through their first floors, on whose balconies people are leaning and talking and regarding the flow of life.

The main streets of Chester give you the impression that a huge galleon has come to anchor there with easy, leisurely passengers leaning on the deck rails.

This peculiar feature of Chester has worried the antiquaries more than anything. Theories to explain how and why these peculiar streets grew up are numerous and none of them definite.

'Who knows why they are built?' said a local antiquary. 'One theory is that the ruins of the Roman buildings inspired the architects of later times. Another theory is that the arcades were formed during the Middle Ages to provide street defence against Welsh raiders; a third theory explains them on the ground that traders erected their buildings on the ruins of the Roman castrum, the most valuable ground, naturally, in the town, and, as other traders were attracted to the same profitable site, a further row of buildings rose up on the ruins behind the first, from which, of course, it is but a step to a covered arcade running the length of the street. But no one can say with certainty how they evolved. "The Rows" are one of the architectural mysteries of England. . . .'

Chester is as 'medieval' as Clovelly is 'quaint'. There is no getting away from it. At night a walk through 'the Rows' is eerie. These long tunnels are almost pitch dark. When the shops are closed they are deserted, for the Cestrians then take to the normal roadway, and you can walk on and on along this ancient highway, through colonnades upheld by vast oak beams, half-expecting to hear the scuffle of hired assassins and the gasp of a man with a dagger on his neck. I have yet to meet a more dramatic street.

Chester is so accustomed to ancient things that no one considered it strange to drink coffee in a twelfth-century crypt. There is a beautiful vaulted crypt which has been converted into a restaurant! I went there and sat utterly crushed by my surroundings. I looked round for the monks, but saw only young men and women, taking, so it seemed, sacrilegious sips of tea, and eating cream cakes.

One of the happiest memories of my search will be the recollection of the many times I have hung out of hotel and inn window before going to bed listening to the night sounds of towns and cities and villages. I must write a story about them some day. At night, when the tramcars have stopped running and the crowds have gone home, and the last American has drunk the last 'highball' in the smoke-room, ancient cities like Chester come most vividly to life. So you must leave me in Chester, under a big round moon, leaning out in the soft coolness of the night, watching the Valeria Victrix stack spears in the main street, and stand back waiting for orders to found one of the oldest cities in England.

And it was on the 'holy Dee', the broad, slow river that winds itself round Chester, that King Edgar in 973 gave away his character to posterity by being rowed in his barge by tributary princes. And it was in Chester . . . I could go on through history picking out little pictures of Chester; but it is so late, and the moon is riding high above this silent city, where old houses dream across old streets with their roots among the little red tiles of Rome.

2

The change of country at the Cheshire-Lancashire border is more startling than the change between Cornwall and Devon or between the sweet lowland counties and the wild marches of Wales. Here the traveller enters Industrial England.

I looked at the map. I was passing between Liverpool on the left and Manchester on the right, and about sixteen miles from both cities. Far off to the left I could see the Mersey estuary, with red smoke-stacks rising above the flat lands by the sandy shore. To the right there was an ominous grey haze in the sky which meant Manchester. For months I have motored through a green England which might never have known the Industrial Revolution. Round Bristol, it is true, I saw factories. I left Birmingham on my right, and saw no trace of that monster as I went on into Old England. Here was New England: an England of crowded towns, of tall chimneys, of great mill walls, of canals of slow, black water; an England of grey, hard-looking little houses in interminable rows; the England of coal and chemicals; of cotton, glass, and iron.

Yet how difficult it is to kill an English field, to stamp out the English grass, and to deform an English lane! Even here, within sixteen miles of the two great giants of the north, men were raking hay in a field within a gunshot of factory chimneys.

With the beautiful Old England that I love so fresh in mind, I stood ready to be horrified by the Black Belt; yet strangely, I stood impressed and thrilled by the grim power of these ugly chimneys rising in groups, by the black huddle of factories, and the still, silent wheels at pit-mouth and the drifting haze of smoke.

At Warrington I heard the clap-clop of clogs; at Warrington I saw mill girls with shawls over their heads; at Warrington I smelt for the first time the characteristic aroma which permeates the industrial towns and villages of Lancashire – fried fish and chips.

Mill towns look grandly impressive from a hill, but when you dive into their streets the stark ugliness of the long, barracky, prison-like houses, run up so quickly to serve the servants of the machines, gives you an ache. The only consolation is that these monster towns and cities of the north of England are a mere speck in the amazing greenness of England: their inhabitants can be lost in green fields and woodland within a few minutes. London is much more distant from a real wood than Warrington.

On Sundays, in all the grey villages of Lancashire, the miners sit on their haunches against the walls, their hands between their knees. They are the only Englishmen who squat like Arabs. In the centre of nearly every group is a white whippet on a lead. The men sit and smoke, regarding the highway with a certain bright expectation.

I saw with great interest a signpost marked 'Wigan'. Who could resist a glimpse of Wigan?

Wigan, were it not inhabited by a race of sturdy and rather tough Lancashire folk, would be the most self-conscious town in England. For years it has suffered from a joke. The words 'Wigan Pier' spoken by a comedian on a music-hall stage are sufficient to make an audience howl with laughter, and the ease with which the name works on the sensibilities of an audience is probably, in some measure, responsible for the great success of this joke.

Wigan, to millions of people who have never seen and never will see the town, represents the apex of the world's pyramid of gloom. So serious has the Wigan joke become that the go-ahead Corporation, who are full of local pride, take what steps they can to counteract it; but the silly old joke goes on! Certain Wigonians of high commercial standing believe that this joke delays the prosperity of Wigan, which not only affords rich sites for new factories, but also offers all the necessary conditions for manufacture, such as good transport, labour, and coal, so to speak, laid on in normal times.

Now, I had been in Wigan just ten minutes when I saw that there is no joke! Wigan is a spa compared with towns like Wednesbury, in the Black Country, and with certain of the Staffordshire pottery towns. I admit frankly that I, too, shared the common idea of Wigan. I admit that I came here to write an impression of unrelieved gloom – of dreary streets and stagnant canals and white-faced Wigonians dragging their weary steps along dull streets haunted by the horror of the place in which they are condemned to live.

This is nonsense. I would not mind spending a holiday in Wigan – a short one.

'This town has been badly libelled,' I said to a man who was standing in the main street.

'I'm reet glad to hear thee say that!' he cried warmly. 'I've lived in Wigan all my life, and wish for no better town.'

He beamed on me. He offered to show me the chief glories of Wigan. I told him that I wanted to find them for myself. Still he beamed on me! They all do this in Wigan if you go up and say frankly that the town has a certain attraction.

Wigan's swift reaction to praise is rather pathetic.

Now, when you enter Wigan expecting the worst, it is surprising to find a place which still bears all the signs of an old-fashioned country town. Its wide main street meanders down a hill in a casual, leisurely way. Along this street are many modern half-timbered buildings. The Corporation of Wigan has made a rule that buildings on the main streets must be rebuilt in the Tudor style, so that in twenty years or so there will not be a more original or better-looking manufacturing town in the north of England.

During an hour's walk round Wigan I discovered many things. Wigan was made by the Romans. They called it Coccium, which, I think, is a much funnier name. Perhaps the Legions went into fits of laughter when anyone said 'Coccium' in Roman Britain! All that remains of Coccium is a Roman altar, which I found built into the north window bay of the tower of the fine but much-restored fourteenth-century church.

King Arthur knew Wigan! It is famed as the scene of some of his most glorious exploits.

Beyond the Market Square I entered a park of about thirty acres. In it were Italian gardens and an ornamental lake. In slandered Wigan I found one of the few good war memorials I have seen in England, and also the largest open market-place outside Nottingham.

But no one could tell me the meaning of the word Wigan. So I went to the Town Clerk.

'The derivation is obscure,' he said. 'It is Saxon, of course, for we are very old. The Wigan motto is "Ancient and Loyal", you know. I believe that the word Wigan means "the rowan trees near the Church".'

'And this,' I said, 'is the name that rocks a thousand stalls!'

'Yes,' he replied, 'the Wigan joke has gone too far. It is

surprising what a joke can do to a town. It can spread an entirely false idea. Now just let me take you to the outskirts of Wigan, and you will agree that few manufacturing towns are surrounded by such rustic scenery. . . .'

We went round Wigan. Before we had left the town we smelt hay. Wigan is surrounded by fields which rise on the north towards Duxberry Hall, the only American pilgrim age in this part of the world, where the doughty Miles Standish was probably born. On the main road we came to the scene of Wigan's most cherished legend: a rough stone cross.

'That,' explained the Town Clerk, 'is Mabs Cross. It is mentioned in Walter Scott's *The Betrothed*. The story is that while Sir William Bradshaigh, a knight of Wigan, was away on the Crusades his wife Mabel, believing him to have been killed, married a Welsh knight. Sir William came home suddenly, discovered what had happened, and killed the Welsh knight, for which he was outlawed for one year. His wife Mabel was publicly shamed. Her confessor imposed this penalty: that once every week she must walk, barelegged and barefoot to Mabs Cross. I believe it all ended happily, and that husband and wife came together again!'

Within five minutes of notorious Wigan we were in the depth of the country. On either side were fields in which men were making hay; old bridges spanned streams; there were high hedges, delicious little woods, and valleys.

'This is all Wigan!' said the Town Clerk with a smile.

This town is interesting as a perfect example of a busy industrial town with a fine record in pre-industrial England. Wigan is not a mushroom town that grew up overnight on a coal-field. It has history, and behind it the tradition of centuries of loyalty to the Crown.

Henry I incorporated the town in 1100. A specimen of the twelfth-century seal is still in existence. During the Civil Wars Cromwell pursued the retreating Royalist army through the streets of Wigan, and in 1651 the Earl of Derby suffered a defeat at the 'Battle of Wigan Lane' which cost him his head. When the Mayor of Wigan goes out in state a sword is borne before him which was given to the town in 1660 by Charles II in special token of his favour for the loyalty of Wigan at the Restoration.

That was the closing event in Wigan's pre-industrial history. Then came King Coal in the nineteenth century, and Wigan began a new life.

4

I joined the Windermere queue at Lancaster, and hoped for the best. Everyone in the north of England seemed at this moment to have decided to visit what the guidebooks call so inanely, 'the land of the Lake Poets'.

In front of me was a heavy forty-five horse-power touring car containing a rigid old man in a young Stetson; in front of him was a dashing two-seater driven by a woman; in front of her was a closed limousine full of American tourists; in front of them was a family in a Ford; in front of that was a Rolls Royce, and leading the procession was a hatless young obstructionist lying full length in a fifteen horse-power scarlet bath with aluminium fittings and an exhaust pipe like a stove-pipe.

Behind me the queue lengthened car after car, my immediate neighbour a neat saloon in the fair but reckless hands of a beautiful maiden, who, by edging in and nosing my suitcases, seemed to be doing all she could to kill her father and mother. Had she been her brother I would have been rude to him!

So we sped lakewards. How sweet the solitudes will be tonight, I thought, as I kept my eye on the packed highway! Those lines written by Lakeland's chief historic character came most opportunely to mind:

> *These tourists, heavens preserve us! needs must live*
> *A profitable life: some glance along*
> *Rapid and gay, as if the earth were air,*
> *And they were butterflies to wheel about*
> *Long as the summer lasted....*

This is a remarkable prophecy. One might think that gentle Wordsworth, writing long before the first motor-car, had been granted a vision of the main Windermere road in 1926!

And now all the beauty of the day is gathered, as by the hand of God, in the west. The sun is setting behind the hills. Through my window I see a great sheet of water that within the last twenty minutes has lost all colour. The blue of Windermere has been drained away drop by drop as the blue has been drawn from the sky, it is now silver; the white swans are black against this glittering metallic sheet. The swallows fly high in wide circles; a jet-black boat moves on the placid surface of the lake, two silver lines widening from the stern. The sun, lost in a rich smouldering bank of cloud, drops minute by minute towards the crest of the hills. In the stillness sounds carry far . . . such sounds!

Two charabancs prepare to return to Kendal. A straggling band of Lancashire men in their Sunday clothes comes slowly along by the lakeside playing a concertina. Girls in summer dresses with blue string bags over their cropped hair, and young men whose bared necks rise from tennis shirts, pass down the hill singing; motor-cars hoot at the hairpin bend, and in the next room to mine a gramophone says that there will be tea for two and two for tea, a boy for you and a girl for me. . . .

With shattering indifference to man, the black and silver nocturne of evening is played to the end. The sun goes. Darkness spreads between the trees. A deep grape-blue mist hangs over the woods; a fish jumps in the lake, making a black pool for a second in the still, silver water.

'Oh, say,' a voice has just cried, beneath my window, 'if this isn't too poifect . . . why, it's just like one of his sonnuts!'

(Shall I throw a boot or just go on smiling? A grave temptation.)

Slowly – and so gradually that it is almost imperceptible –

comes that moment when a man watching the lovely pageant of light and half-light, can say that night has come. Over the dark hills and the pale waters is an unearthly radiance which is not that of either sun or moon, but something, it seems, like the cold light which washes the mountains of dead moons. Above the hills burns the first small star. . . .

No matter what opinion you may hold of Wordsworth as a poet, you must recognize him as a great, but unconscious, publicity agent. The solitudes which he loved are now well populated. Americans who come here in enthusiastic waves stand reverently before his cottage in Grasmere. The hunger for a pilgrimage of any kind appears to be a deep-seated spiritual necessity with them. (I found two of them paying homage to the house in which Harriet Martineau wrote her guide to the Lakes in 1855!)

One of England's great sights is that of a New York businessman, determined to get every cent's value from his tour, trying to work up enthusiasm for Wordsworth in the little churchyard at Grasmere:

> *A Rock there is whose homely front*
> *The passing traveller sights;*
> *Yet there the glow-worms hang their lamps,*
> *Like stars at various heights;*
> *And one coy primrose to the rock*
> *The vernal breeze invites . . .*

'Gee, that's great stuff! Say, listen, while I read it again. . . .'

The population of Lakeland may be divided into two groups – those who stay on the water level, sail in boats, seek suicide in their cars on the narrow roads and drink coffee in evening-dress after dinner on neat lawns at the lakeside; and those who, rising early, put on khaki shorts, grasp stout sticks, and leave the ground level before the first group have had their morning tea.

These picturesque ones are, to my mind, the only people who get the true value from the Lakes. Had I more time I would buy a Scout's outfit and join them; for the only way to enjoy this country is to climb away from the crowds and seek solitude in the bosky silence of woods or on the craggy heights of fells. I like to see the real Lakelanders returning covered in dust and victory as the shades of night are falling fast. Among them are men who would not say 'thank you' for Switzerland; and there are brown-faced, muscular girls in breeches and stockings who carry rucksacks on their backs and grasp stout ash-sticks. (I wish someone would design a pair of breeches which girls could wear without looking quaint or regrettable.) Then there are bug-hunters of all types. They chase the butterfly by day and the moth by night. There are geologists. There are, of course, ambitious maidens who steal off with camp-stool and drawing-board to transfer some part or portion of the landscape to drawing-room walls in Manchester, Liverpool, Birmingham, and even, so experience warns a man, Kensington.

I will not dare to compare the soft beauty of Windermere with the majesty of Derwentwater or the grand solitude of Ullswater, or the high serenity of Thirlmere and Coniston. If I have any preference it is for the smallest of them all: little Rydal Water, which is three-quarters of a mile long and, beside these watery giants, it is just a spoonful of blue in a cup of green hills. Rydal Water is a magic, satisfying lakelet – a little looking-glass in which the woody heights, by which it is hemmed, lie as in a mirror.

I saw it first at night. It was a clear, moonlit night, with no breath of wind among the trees. In the middle of the little lake, round and golden as a guinea, lay the moon. Sights such as this, hiding round a corner, lurking behind trees and suddenly revealed, pull a man up sharply and fling him on his knees. Had Rydal Water been in Cornwall or in Wales nothing could have disconnected it from the Excalibur legend; and most men would have believed it, for this is a mystic mere. . . .

As I looked, a water-fowl, surprised among the dark

reeds, flew noiselessly over the lake in the night, its little feet just tearing a thin silver line in the water. The moon danced up and down once or twice; then the lake composed itself, and went on dreaming.

5

This story has no right in this book, and I apologize for writing it. It happened like this.

I was finding my way out of Carlisle with the intention of crossing the Roman Wall that runs across England from Solway Firth to the Tyne, when I saw a signpost: 'To Gretna Green 10 miles.' I pulled up sharply:

'This,' I said, 'is where I go right off the rails. I *must* see Gretna Green! I'll take a holiday and – go to Scotland!'

How could I neglect to visit the scene of so much folly? In a few minutes I had left England behind me and was spinning along in a country which looked exactly like it, but was not. I had crossed the Border!

Scotland does not begin to get 'bonny' just here, but it was stimulating to realize that we were in the land of red whiskers and freckled maids, of brown trout streams, of purple moors, of great mountains, which, even in fair weather, wear white caps of cloud. At the cottage doors clustered brawny sandy-haired boys (who some day, of course, go south) and little girls who will grow up and speak the most delicious English in the world.

The road runs straight from Carlisle to Gretna, as if anxious to cut off all the corners and give a sporting finish to the race. At the end of this road – and in the heart of a great crowd – I found Gretna Green.

The blacksmith's shop stands facing the high road: a long, one-story building, half dwelling-house, half smithy. This is the building which rose to fame in 1754 when Lord Hardwicke's Act put a stop to the scandal of secret marriages in England. Before this Act became law secret weddings were held in many places in London, notably the

Fleet Prison, 'Parson Keith's Chapel' in Mayfair, now pulled down (the memory lives, however, in the names East and West Chapel Streets, west of Shepherd's Market, Piccadilly), and in the Savoy, where a notorious clergyman, Dr John Wilkinson, used to advertise boldly: 'Marriages performed with the utmost privacy, secrecy, decency, and regularity. There are five private ways by land to this chapel, and two by water'!

Scotland was not affected by the Act of 1754, with the result that Gretna, the first village over the Border, began to hear with financial satisfaction the clatter of a flying coach and four along the Carlisle road, and occasionally the report of a pistol as a defiant lover took a pot-shot at the pursuing coach horses. I seem to remember that one Archbishop of Canterbury, three Lord Chancellors, and one Privy Seal were married over the anvil at Gretna. . . .

A large crowd stood before the smithy. Half were Americans, the other half tourists from over the Border. The smithy looked to me the most practical proposition I have seen for many a day; its front was plastered with notices to the effect that within was a museum, that the famous 'marriage room' was on view, that postcards were obtainable! (I might have known that Gretna Green would by now be thoroughly sophisticated!) The air was sweet with the sound of a pleasant Scotswoman collecting the gate money. I banged down my saxpence and went in through the turnstile.

In the old and now disused smithy – who with an ounce of commercial acumen would waste this forge on horses? – I wandered round with the crowd, gazing at a rather dull little museum: the State coach used by Queen Caroline; anvils, the old marriage register, two rather appropriate 'repentance stools' from the 'auld kirk', and tall stove-pipe hats worn by various Gretna 'priests'.

I went out and talked to the caretaker, who was selling to a tourist a replica of a Gretna marriage certificate.

'You still have marriages here?' I asked.

'Oh, aye,' said the caretaker. 'Twenty-two this year!'

She pointed to a bundle of papers on a shelf. They were the certificates.

'Who performs the ceremony?'

'Weel, some bodies ask for the blacksmith, Mr Graham, but generally my husband is the "priest".'

I entered an inner room and had a chat with 'the priest'. This word means nothing. Marriage in Scotland is regular or irregular, both equally valid. If two people affirm their willingness to marry before witnesses, I imagine they can be married in the street.

'Will you marry me?' I asked the priest.

He looked interested:

'Aye,' he said solemnly, 'that I will if ye hae lived twanty-wan days in Sco'land.'

I appeared crestfallen. He told me that the ceremony is simple.

'I just say to the mon: "Dae ye tak' this wumman tae be your wedded wife?" and he says "I wull," and then I turrn to the gurrl and say: "Dae ye tak' this mon tae be your wedded husband?" and when she says "I wull" they sign the paper and I sign the paper and the twa witnesses sign the paper and they're lawfu' spouses according to the laws o' Scotland. That's a' there is tae it!'

'Is it really legal?'

'Oh, aye!'

I told him that I would consider it.

I learned that the old Gretna Green chase is not yet dead. Quite recently the priest was awakened in the middle of the night by an agitated mother (in the old days it was always the father), who demanded to know if her daughter had made a runaway marriage:

'Puir body, she was a wee bit previous, for they came the verra next day! . . .'

I found it difficult to feel romantic about Gretna. I suppose its chief atmosphere has always been commercial. Joseph Paisley, the old high priest of the Gretna marriage business, had a secret code with the postilions in order to find out what his clients were likely to be worth to him. They say he often made one hundred pounds a week.

The picture of a simple-minded old blacksmith joining two star-crossed lovers in wedlock is not historically correct!

I took the Carlisle road again, that road on which long ago Lord Westmorland, eloping with Miss Child, of Child's Bank, gained Gretna by shooting the leading horse of his father-in-law's team as its straining head drew level with the coach window.

There is, however, something about Gretna that makes one sympathize with the apoplectic fathers in the coach behind.

CHAPTER NINE

Tells of rain over Hadrian's Wall, of Durham and its saint, of the splendour and glory of York, ending with a glimpse into the ancient heart of this City

I

COULD I make a bargain with Time I would roll back sixteen centuries so that I might meet any Roman centurion who served on the Wall of Hadrian during the three hundred years of its military occupation. I would shake him warmly by the hand, stand him a drink, and say:

'I'm sorry, Marcus! I sympathize with you! I crossed the Wall from Carlisle – which you called Luguvallium – to Newcastle-on-Tyne – which you knew as Pons Aelii – and it rained, Marcus – how it rained! Seventy-three miles of rain over the Wall, and, by Jupiter, such rain!'

He would, I am sure, look interested.

'It still comes down like Hades, does it?' he would ask. 'Fancy that! We thought it was organized by the local gods against the Empire. It used to put out the cook-house fires, get into the wine-skins, give the Spanish cavalry frog, and when you stood on the parapet it would beat up against your face, blinding you and, oozing behind your chin strap, make your face smart like blazes. Jove's bolts! What a Wall!'

'I suppose you had duck-boards; and did they send you mouth-organs and woollies from Rome? I can imagine you all sitting up there on wet nights singing, "We are Fred Karno's Army; what ruddy good are we?"'

'Yes, we had a song like that to the hymn of the Vestal Virgins. The Picts and Scots used to sit out on the other side of the Wall, too wet to raid us, and join in. We had another song in the Centurions' Mess about the troops on the Wall. There was only one Roman to every mile, you know! The rest were Dacians and Thracians and Moors and Scythians; a kind of recruiting office poster: Types of the Roman

192

Army! The song went: "Oh, the Tungrians, the Austurians, the Batavians, and the Greeks!" It had a good chorus, and was very popular with the regulars in Deva and Eboracum . . .'

'We say Chester and York now.'

'Do you really? We had another song on the Wall: "Old soldiers never die, never die, never die; old soldiers never die, they only sneeze away-cc." Which was true. The Picts used to say that as long as a regular Legion kept its nose there was no need to sound the war-horn. We were a fine sight saluting the Governor of Britain or a visiting Caesar with the famous legionary sneeze – "the sneeze of the Faithful Thirtieth", we used to call it!'

'I suppose you got leave?'

'Leaf? Leaf? Not likely! The Wall was a life sentence. The first thing we did when we got up there was to marry and settle down. A British girl who couldn't marry on Hadrian's Wall . . . well, I can't imagine it! . . . I was Ballista Instructor to the 4th Cohort of Gauls at Vindolana. You should have seen the raw recruits from every part of the world who wandered up and down that Wall with half the gods of the earth hidden away in their vests. We spoke about twenty-five different languages, from Luguvallium to Pons Aelii. I had an old-timer in my cohort who used to be batman to Vespasian. He was always changing his religion. If a Moorish or an Egyptian god answered a prayer he would buy an image of it at once and pray to be transferred to Londinium; but the gods of the Wall knew him too well. . . .'

That rain from Carlisle to Newcastle! It swooped down from the north in great blown sheets, and it swept up from the south and met the northern sheets in mid-air above the Wall, where they fought in cross currents and fell together, lashing the earth. Every few miles I left the car by the wayside and plodded off over soggy fields to spot the Wall, which you can trace almost without a break for seventy-three miles.

193

At Housesteads I stood thrilled to the marrow. I have seen Pompeii, and I have seen Timgad in Africa, but to see this great Roman monument in our own cold northern lands! That wall was the north boundary wall of the Roman Empire. At this place it runs six feet high for over twenty-five miles: you can walk on it! How it scorns the lie of the land. It marches on straight as a Roman road where possible, then wherever there is a hill the Wall climbs it; it commands all the high ground from Newcastle to Carlisle. To the north is a deep trench, to the south another trench and a military road. The Roman Wall across England is the most marvellous engineering surprise in the country, and it is time that the Office of Works took charge of it and made it a guarded ancient monument.

The weather is rotting it slowly; miles of it should be cemented to stop decay. There are years of excavation along its course, for you can hardly dig anywhere without finding pottery or bones.

I stood wet through in Chesters, and went over the ruins of one of the largest forts on the Wall: Cilurnum it was called when the second ala of Austurian cavalry were stationed there. The foundations of the gates are to be seen; in the north gates the socket holes for the hinges are preserved; on either side are the guard-houses.

The prefect, or colonel, lived in superior quarters with a view of the Tyne. He had a bathroom and a heated sitting-room. In the centre of the fort stood a colonnaded forum. The stone gutter which took the rain drippings from the roof is still there; it was still full of rain! There are the ruts of chariot wheels in the stone pavements; three foot six inches from wheel to wheel, the same size as the chariot ruts at Pompeii. Underground is a vaulted chamber in which were found a rotted wooden chest and a pile of Roman coins; evidently the regimental pay chest. Round the central buildings are the barrack quarters for about three hundred troopers. Near the river are the regimental baths.

The Wall links up with Cilurnum on the east and leaves

the little fort on the west to run on over the hills. This fort has more gates than the other stations on the Wall; it has six, three of which open to the north of the Wall, or in enemy country. This has puzzled the antiquaries. Colling-wood Bruce says that he supposes these extra gates opening into No Man's Land were there simply 'because Cilurnum was larger than the other stations'. I suggest another theory. This was a cavalry depot. Any man who has done any cavalry training will realize that when the Picts attacked the Wall the first thought of this garrison would be to mount, draw swords, and get outside the Wall as quickly as possible. They could swing round through three gates upon the Picts, wheel into line, and deliver a charge in about three minutes. This, I think, is why Cilurnum has more gates than the infantry forts, and why they open to the north.

How little imagination it takes to see this Wall as it was: an eighteen-foot-high barrier from sea to sea, a tower or pill-box every mile and, dotted along the length, stone fortresses garrisoned by cohorts and alas. And behind each fort grew up villages where the married quarters were: villages with shops and workshops, and temples.

It is strange to think that for three hundred years the nations of Europe formed a defensive crust along the north of England. The Regular Army was at York and Chester, but the Wall was in the hands of the territorials, or auxiliary legions recruited wherever Rome had made conquests. Here, in the blinding rain and in the winter snows, were shivering Moors from Africa, men from Spain, from the forests of Germany, of France, of Belgium. All Europe and parts of Africa helped to defend England for three hundred years!

No doubt in time these foreign legions were alien in name only. When drafts did not come from distant lands I imagine that the villages behind the forts gave many half-British recruits to the Eagles.

The crumbling walls of Cilurnum are covered with a pretty crimson-purple rock plant, whose name is, I think,

Erinus alrinus. It is probably a South European plant. The legend, which I believe some learned man has contradicted, is that this tiny flower came over from Spain with the fodder for the chargers of the 2nd Ala of Austurians. . . .

I left the ruins of Chesters, and saw the Wall of Hadrian lying from sea to sea, firm and straight as a legion with linked shields. I lifted my voice and shouted, 'Ave, Caesar!' and there was no answer but the drip of the rain.

2

I am writing beside the River Wear, surrounded by flies, small winged dragons, and minute centipedes, which paddle drearily through the ink before route-marching all over the paper. It is a beautiful day. I went, with passionate sincerity, to do nothing except to lie back and continue to look at one of the finest sights in Europe.

High on a red sandstone hill, lifted like a challenge above the heads of the tallest trees, stands Durham Castle. Behind the battlemented walls, which are built sheer on the cliff's edge, rise the lovely, red-brown towers of Durham's Norman cathedral. Durham Castle crowns its hill like an armoured knight, and the city of Durham crowds round Durham Hill – a tight mass of houses and a main street no wider than a country lane – clustering round the fortified height as serfs might cling to the baron's keep for protection. Durham is in appearance as feudal as His Majesty's Tower of London.

What a site for a castle and a church. To sit beside this wide, slow river and to look up at this hill is to see Norman England.

How much romance, beauty and drama can be skipped over by a guide-book! As I was standing behind the high altar of Durham Cathedral earlier in the day I saw a large platform with one word carved in the stone: 'Cuthbertus.' The guide-book says: 'In the place of honour behind the high altar is the tomb of St Cuthbert, who died A.D. 687. The body still rests below. . . .'

Now as I read this bald truth my imagination went on a long journey. At the end of a tunnel of time, 1,239 years long, I saw a strange England, and I saw the hill of Durham before its great Norman church was built, before the stone Saxon church was built, before the first little reed chapel was built: just a woody hill of red sandstone, with perhaps a speckled fawn standing in the fern. The roots of Durham go back into an England difficult to see: an England wild, bloody, savage; an England which prayed to Wotan and Thor in the ruins of Roman temples; an England beautiful at this time beyond words, because, caring nothing for the clash of kingdom on kingdom, the sound of swords and the trail of fire, Christ was walking through English meadows humbly as He walked through Galilee. The legions of Rome had returned with shaven heads bearing not a sword, but a message.

Men have done deeds in the name of God which would have made Christ weep, but the story of the conversion of England to Christianity, with which Durham is so marvellously linked, is, I believe, one of the loveliest stories since the New Testament. Look back to a time long before the Council of Whitby, and you see the pilgrim monks tramping the weed-grown Roman roads to speak to men and women under an oak tree in a wood. These simple, holy men trudged the heather, traversed the mighty woods, and crossed the lonely hills to baptize the heathen Saxon beside wells and at the edge of streams. They were uplifted by a magnificent single-mindedness, inspired with a Christ-like humility, strengthened by a superb sincerity. How real a thing in those rough days was the brotherhood of the holy men. I have always loved the touchingly humble manner in which the Venerable Bede implored the monks of Lindisfarne to receive him as their 'little household slave'. What a picture this awakens in the mind!

You see the bearded, tawny kings of Saxon England

sitting, sword on knees, listening like children to the story of
Christ. (It was so often the queen and not the monk who
converted the king!) And slowly the wild old gods, Wotan
and Thor, left nothing behind them but the names
Wednesday and Thursday, as they crept into their twilight
before the coming of the Light.

The hermit monks rested together in lonely places; and
you see the first monastery.

When St Cuthbert died in the Holy Isle of Lindisfarne he
told his monks that if the pirates came again they must
promise to bear his body with them wherever they might
go. In 870 the long boats of the Danes were beached on the
north-east coast, and the monks of Lindisfarne, faithful to
their word, took flight, carrying with them the body of St
Cuthbert, and in the same coffin the head of St Oswald.
They journeyed through South Scotland and North England where the many old churches dedicated to St Cuthbert
mark, no doubt, their resting-places. After eight years'
wandering they settled near Durham at Chester-le-Street.
Here for over one hundred years the body of the saint was
undisturbed.

Then the Danes came again! Once more the faithful
monks bore their coffin away, and finally in 995 they came
to the high red cliff at Durham, and there they built over the
sacred body a little wattle church. They built a wooden
church and then a stone one. Into this stone church it is said
King Canute walked barefoot to the shrine of St Cuthbert. . . .

So Durham forms out of these far mists as a man stands
beside a tomb in the dim light behind the altar.

Durham Cathedral. . . .

I shall have no emotion greater than this in any
cathedral. This building is not magnificent: it is stupendous!
It is the most wonderful Norman church I have ever seen,
not excepting the great church of St Stephen at Caen. In
order to understand it you must realize how and when it
was built, and to understand Durham Cathedral is to

understand a number of other things which have nothing to do with religion.

In 1069, three years after the Conquest, William the Conqueror sent a Norman follower to be Earl of Northumbria. The men of Durham promptly slew him and his troops. This led to that appalling reign of terror in the north of England. William and his cavalry went through the north like a cyclone. They systematically stamped out life between Durham and York. They left behind them a country of charred ruins.

After this cruel display of authority Durham Cathedral rose up on its hill under Norman chisels. Its great nave, upheld by giant stone columns, was built by the notorious Flambard. It is, with the exception of the hypostyle hall in the great temple of Karnak in Egypt, the most awe-inspiring temple I have seen. It seemed to me, as I stood near the west door of Durham and looked at this vast dim church, whose pillars are like giant oaks, whose arches are austere, whose sanctuaries are built as if to withstand a siege, that this building is a declaration of Norman policy. I almost heard the voice of the Conqueror ringing down the nave:

'Look at this church! I have conquered England, and in England I intend to stay. When you pray here remember how I went with fire and sword through the north to punish you! I am very strong!'

That, so it seems to me, is the message of Durham Cathedral. It is a proof in stone of the strong new blood that had come into England.

I stood a long time on that tomb behind the high altar. . . . I must tell you that St Cuthbert, like many of the early saints, hated women. There is a line of dark Frosterey marble in the nave of Durham beyond which no woman was allowed to pass. Even after his death St Cuthbert hated women, because when in 1175 Bishop Pudsey began building the Lady Chapel at the east end of the church just behind the tomb of the saint, strange cracks appeared in the walls which the bishop took as an omen that the saint did not like a chapel even to the Virgin so near him. That is why Durham has its Lady Chapel (called the Galilee) at the west end.

I could write you another story about this beautiful building which is like an Eastern mosque: the men who built it had been to the Crusades. I could also write about the grotesque sanctuary knocker on the cathedral door below the north porch. When the sound of that knocker rang through the church two monks, who were always stationed in the north porch, used to run down and admit whoever knocked and lead him to the sanctuary from which, no matter how terrible his crime, no man might drag him.

But it grows late. I am much bothered by mosquitoes. I look up at that lovely rock with its church whose roots go back to the first English Christians. An odd little irrelevance creeps into my mind. As I stood beside the tomb of the saintly woman-hater earlier in the morning, I watched the pretty feet of three American girls walking over his grave. But they made practically no noise: they were wearing low-heeled shoes of plaited leather.

So Time takes revenge – even on saints!

3

If you are interested in old things, in beautiful things, and in the history of this country, there is one city which will exceed your expectation – York.

I entered York with a mind full of misconceived ideas, and at this moment I feel (rather fatuously) that I have discovered York. I am thrilled to the spine to find not a great bustling capital of the north, but a peaceful, astonishingly beautiful medieval town, whose over-sailing houses are encircled by white, turreted city walls, which are a hundred times more interesting than the walls of Chester. York is too good to be true.

It is, to me, incredible, that a great city which marches through English history to the sound of trumpets and cathedral bells and the beating of drums should not have disfigured itself with gasworks and factories. York is the lovely queen – as London is the powerful king – of English cities.

Why did I expect York to out-Newcastle Newcastle?

In the south of England we suffer from a false idea of the manufacturing north. It is almost within the times of our grandfathers that the coal-fields of the north became more important than the cornfields of the south, and we, having perhaps seen Sheffield from the train – one of England's saddest sights – imagine that a northern city must, in the nature of things, be an ugly one. The commercial prominence of those recent giants, Liverpool, Manchester, Leeds, Sheffield, Bradford, and Halifax, blinds us to the real north, which, apart from these areas of dense populations, remains, as it always has been, one of the most historically romantic and naturally beautiful divisions of England.

It is interesting to note that the industrial revolution has passed over such ancient aristocrats as Lancaster, Durham, and York. It is remarkable that Lancashire, which possesses Liverpool and Manchester, should own a delicious sleepy old county town like Lancaster, and this in itself is symbolic of the fact that the great industrial new-rich cities of northern England – vast and mighty as they are – fall into perspective as mere black specks against the mighty background of history and the great green expanse of fine country which is the real North of England.

As for Yorkshire, it is not a county: it is a country: it is the grand old Northumbria of Saxon England! I could find enough in Yorkshire to keep my hasty pen busy day by day for a year, and that is why I must fly from it as I flew from Cornwall.

Leeds, Sheffield, and Bradford are three small circles in a land of abbeys, churches, castles, wild moorland, and heavenly dales, unchanged in parts since that time when the first monks went through Northumbria with the first crucifix.

I walked round the wall of York – which really looks like a town wall – rejoicing in this peerless city. York is not conscious of its beauty like so many ancient towns; it is too old and too wise and too proud to trick itself out for the admiration of tourists. That is one of the many reasons why I love it and its little country-town streets and its country-town hotels, called after the name of the proprietor. Here are no 'Majestics' or 'Excelsiors', but plain 'Browns' and 'Joneses' and 'Robinsons'.

York, Rome, and London. . . . Those are, I think, the three most powerful place-names in Europe! They ring with authority. There is rock-like assurance and reliability in the sound of them which is woefully lacking in such names as Paris, Berlin, or Brussels.

The street names of York are so eloquent that no words of mine can better describe the flavour of this ancient city. Listen to them: Gillygate, Fossgate, Shambles, Spurriergate, Goodramgate, Coppergate, Swinegate, Ogle Forth, Tanners' Moat, Palmers' Lane, Aldwark. . . .

Do you need any further description of the old streets that run within the walls of York? I think not! (I was amused to find that York has a street called Piccadilly!)

From a distance York Minster dominates the city: it prints its magnificence on the eye and on the memory. Its exterior is magnificent: its interior is England's most triumphant anticlimax. No work of man could live up to the grandeur of those twin towers above the perfect west porch in which 'Great Peter', the biggest bell in England, takes hourly stock of Time.

I went round behind a guide with a crowd of Americans. Americans know more about York than we do: I wish more English people took the same anxious interest in our antiquities. There was only one fool in the party, an elderly and obviously too wealthy woman with a silver-headed cane, who asked more idiotic questions than I have ever heard in half an hour, culminating with:

'Say, guide, do you have an Archbishop of York these days?'

Her knowledge may have been naked, but it was unashamed.

The glory of York Minster is the glory of its glass. It is said to contain two-thirds of the fourteenth-century glass in England. The guide told us how many acres it would cover. I lost him and the Americans when I saw the 'Five Sisters' window. This window is a queen among windows, a tall, slender, mellow poem in glass for which I have no words. No words can describe it; it must be seen.

And, could I stand on the wall of York at sunset with all those men and women who have written to tell me that they love the beauty and the history of England. . . .

The sun sinks below a featureless plain right in the eye of the west porch of the minster. I stood on the white wall and saw it dip lower in great clouds and spirals of flame. Small pink clouds sailed above, and the little leaded panes of glass in the west windows shimmered like red-gold scales. This beautiful old city! How any Londoner must love it! London and York sprang from the same mother. Eboracum! Londinium! Twin cities of the Eagles.

The streets of York have seen so much – no wonder they doze with half-shut eyes! They have seen the Roman lictors clear the way for Hadrian. Two Caesars died at York. It was here that the Emperor Severus came in A.D. 210 after his campaign in the north: a poor, broken, miserable master of the world, hiding his swollen limbs in a silk litter. Among his generals rode his own son, who was waiting for him to die. They said that birds of ill-omen cried on the gates of York when the Caesar passed in, broken in mind but not in spirit, for he is said to have quelled a mutiny from his litter. When the miserable mutineers knelt before him he raised himself on the cushions and, pointing to his swollen limbs, said: 'It is the head and not the feet which commands!' I would like to have heard the dying master of the world say that. . . .

Trumpets blew and shields were beaten when Constantine the Great was proclaimed Emperor in York. How strange to think that Yorkshire sheep once gazed up from the grass to hear a great shout, 'Ave, Caesar!' from the walls as another master took the purple and went on to his destiny!

The clouds wheel in coloured splendour over York. . . .

In the crypt of the minster, hidden away in the dark, is a well. This well lay there before the great cathedral was built; the cathedral was, in fact, built to cover this well. The first cathedral of York was a wooden chapel erected over this well for the baptism on Easter Day, A.D. 627, of King Edwin of Northumbria and all his court. . . .

Now the sun sets. The face of the minster is washed by a pink flush from the west. In a few moments the quiet dusk will be stealing through the streets of York and 'Great Peter' will solemnly tick another hour from the slate of eternity.

4

Now and then if a man loves a city he is rewarded with a glimpse of her heart. . . .

I was standing by Stonegate, talking to an American (who is also in love with York), when down the dark street from the direction of the minster came, holding the centre of the narrow road, a procession of considerable splendour. First came the Chief Constable of York, booted and spurred, then came the Town Clerk in his robes, following him was a man wearing a fur-edged cap of the Richard II period, and holding aloft the great sword of the Emperor Sigismund, which always goes before the Lord Mayor of York. His Lordship followed, in a scarlet gown edged with brown fur. The Aldermen walked two by two in blue robes, chatting, and – strange and beautiful climax to such civic glory – there then came a long line of young orphans – little Blue Coat boys and little Grey Coat girls, very quiet, grave, impressed.

'Well,' whispered the American, 'what do you know about that?'

The Lord Mayor and the Corporation of York walking in state with the sword of the Emperor Sigismund before a regiment of poor little orphans! I gave it up and asked a policeman.

'It's like this,' he said. 'Every year the Lord Mayor and the Corporation attend a church service with the orphans, and when that's over he gives away prizes to the boys and girls in the Guildhall. That's all.'

'And it isn't advertised, officer?' asked the American. 'People aren't put wise to it?'

'No, sir, it just happens.'

'Well, what do you know about that?' said the American. 'Here's a great sight going on that hundreds of rubber-necking tourists would pay anything to see just quietly slipping through the streets as if it happened every day. Gosh, that's so darned English! I like that. The wonderful thing about England is that you have so much that doesn't need advertising. . . . Say, officer, will they let us in on this cery-mony?'

'I should just walk in, if I were you!'

So we walked into the Guildhall, unprepared for the sight that met us there. . . .

York Guildhall is one of the most picturesque halls in England. Its wooden roof is upheld by oak pillars, each one a great tree. The walls glitter with arms; the dim light falls through stained glass. . . .

Beneath a canopy on a dais at the far end of the hall sat the Lord Mayor in his scarlet robes; before him on the table lay the great sword of Sigismund and the silver mace of York. Grouped round the Lord Mayor were the civic dignitaries. Facing them, girls to the left and boys to the right, were the quiet, grave little orphans. The sun slanted through the west window behind the Lord Mayor's throne, and fell in a coloured pool on the stone floor. We stood rooted to the spot by the marvellous contrasts in this scene:

the grave old men in their robes, the lovely hall, the glint of swords and pistols on the walls, and the fresh faces of the children. Timidly, two little girls, in grey print dresses, walked out and began to dance in the pool of sunlight.

A piano played a simple morris dance, and the two small maids, with their neat little waists, their tight, braided hair, their slim little legs in coarse black woollen stockings, passed and repassed, advanced and retreated, smiling with parted lips, blushing at their ordeal, moving gracefully with many a twirl of rat-tail plaits.

And the Lord Mayor of York leaned his chin on his hand and looked down gravely over the sword of York, completing the sweetest picture I have seen in any city in England.

So it went on. The little girls danced two by two or in groups, and the bullet-headed little boy orphans gazed on solemnly and applauded wildly after each dance.

'There's something in this,' whispered the American, 'that gets me right in the throat; and I can't find words for it.'

'It's good,' I whispered back, 'to think that the Lord Mayor of one of the grandest and oldest cities in the world can give half a day to poor children, not fling them half a day, but devote half a day to them and bring out the city regalia for them!'

'Yes . . . and there's something more. I tell you it's one of the finest things I ever hope to see. This is my memory of England. Gee! look at that little ginger-headed girl . . . the way the light shines right through that mop of hair! I guess they couldn't tie that up in a plait. She's a picture!'

The piano became silent. The dancers left the floor, very pink, to flop down in their seats and smooth their print dresses over their knees and look prim and solemn. The Lord Mayor of York rose as a pile of books was carried in and he made a speech. He told them that York was proud of them, that York looked to them to become good men and women. They must not think that there was any bar to their progress. He turned to the little boys, and reminded them that a recent Lord Mayor of York was an orphan.

The children who had no fathers and mothers sat very still and wide-eyed, listening to the voice of the parent city.

The prizes were given.

'Jenny Jones, prize for kindness to her juniors!' (Great applause from the boys!)

Up walked Jenny, all blushes, curtsied low over the sword and mace of York, and retired clutching a book to her grey print chest.

'John Robins, prize for gardening!'

Up walked sturdy John, saluted, and retired clutching a book to his blue brass-buttoned frock coat. . . .

A great pile of oranges was planted down beside the sword – with two masers full of new-minted sixpences. In two long files the orphans of York marched through the pool of sunlight and took from the hands of the Lord Mayor an orange and a sixpence. As the last child walked away there was a rising up on the dais and the ring of the Chief Constable's spurs on the stone floor. Up went the old sword of the Emperor Sigismund, up went the big silver mace glittering in the shaft of light, and, with a rich gleam of scarlet, the Lord Mayor of York, the Town Clerk, the Aldermen, rose up and went slowly out into the late afternoon sunlight. . . .

The American and I walked out into the ancient glory of York with the feeling that this solemn, friendly old city had shown us great favour by admitting us to its annual children's party. Outside we encountered a band of busy tourists with their noses in guide-books.

'Say,' whispered the American, 'we know more about York now than a guy with a guide-book can know in a million years.'

And that, I think, is, to some extent, true.

CHAPTER TEN

Introduces Americans at Boston, Lincoln, and Peterborough, and discovers the smallest and happiest county in England, where men live by the death of foxes and collect horseshoes

I

CITIES have as many moods as men, or, I might add with reverence, women.

Some cities hide behind hills and show themselves to the traveller on the high road only at the last moment, as if unwilling to be discovered. You turn a corner, and there they are. Other cities prefer to surprise you: they spring out at you from an apparently innocent landscape, while a few – and these are perhaps rare – stand up nakedly against the white sky and call to you from far off. Lincoln is one of these.

The city of Lincoln is an inland St Michael's Mount. The flat, level fenlands stretch to the sky like a green and yellow sea – an ocean of grass and wheat. On clear days the towers of Lincoln Cathedral are visible for thirty miles, and the view of Lincoln on its hill, lying sharply cut against the distant horizon at the end of a Roman road, is one of the characteristic sights of England. It typifies Fen-land, it is one of those quick-change landscape acts for which England is so famous – a sign that you have left the north and have entered the flat lands of the east.

When I ran through Kirton in Lindsey, I saw Ermine Street running ahead for over sixteen miles, like a straight tape. At the end of the road, so small and clear, was Lincoln Hill. Every minute, almost with every second, the towers of the cathedral grew larger at the end of the road, till, at the last mile or so, they filled the sky. And I sang the legions' marching song about Lalage and Rimini. . . .

If ever you wish to imagine yourself in Roman Britain, go

to Kirton and walk these sixteen miles with half-shut eyes and you will see Lindum Colonia (I love the way the Ordnance Survey maps preserve these names in brackets) shining in white stone. Lincoln is a real limb of Rome, with Ermine Street lying like a sword to the north and the Fosse Way like a sword south-west.

I entered Lincoln at evening. From my bedroom window I have a fine view of the west front of the cathedral in splints. Tall scaffolding covers one of the towers, for this cathedral, like many another, feels its age.

When walking round the quiet close I met a middle-aged man, who turned out to be a Londoner on holiday. He had, so he told me, explored the great quartet of cathedrals – Ely, Norwich, Peterborough, and Lincoln, which is to the east what Hereford, Worcester, and Gloucester are to the south Midlands.

Every man, woman, and child in England should spend a holiday studying these two groups.

'I am going back to London with a new idea,' said this man after we had discussed the weather at great detail. 'I always thought that when I got on the pension list I'd live in a little place somewhere not too far from London – Surbiton perhaps, or even Guildford. Now I want to spend my last days in one of these cathedral cities where I can come in the evening, or on fine afternoons, to smoke a pipe in the close. Perhaps you don't know London like I do . . . the peace of these places makes you wonder . . .'

'Whether London is a dream?'

'You've hit it! Sitting here with the bells – which got on my nerves like blazes at first – playing a bit of a hymn every quarter of an hour, and the rooks cawing in the trees, and . . . you know?'

'The Dean's geraniums very red under a grey arch and the sound of an old man mowing the grass.'

'Yes, and a high wall round it all with gateways in it. It rests the nerves, doesn't it?'

'And stimulates the imagination?'

He tapped his pipe on the wall and smiled.

'Well,' he said, 'I've never been able to afford an imagination. That's a luxury. I'm a cashier, and cashiers with imagination go to jail. I suppose there are millions more like me who have plodded along on the same dreary old road of routine, at first wanting to stop and look over the hedges and then – just plodding along!'

He filled his pipe.

'You feel,' I suggested, 'that within these old walls there is something more important than the other people's money you have handled all your life?'

He laughed.

'How did you know? Anyhow, I'm going back in two days to strap-hang all the way from Ealing, and – I expect I'll forget!'

The cathedral chimes marked the half-hour, an ancient canon walked over the grass with a book. I thought the cashier – could one have removed his winged collar and his felt hat – would have made a good monk.

Lincoln lies on two levels. Old Lincoln on the hill has its feet in the past; new Lincoln below the hill made the tanks during the war.

One of the most interesting relics in Old Lincoln is the Newport Arch, the only Roman town gate still in use in England. I stood before this massive grey gate and watched motor-cars run in under the arch which has admitted the spears of the legions into Lindum. This arch has a little side arch, or 'Needle's Eye'. I believe many people think of a camel and the eye of a needle quite literally; if so, the Newport Arch will make this Biblical reference plain. The town gates in the east were shut at dusk, but the 'Needle's Eye' was open. A caravan arriving after the gates were shut had to camp outside the walls, but the master of the caravan could pass in through the small gate – a physical impossibility to his camels – and seek lodgings in the city. . . .

Lincoln Castle is one of the eight castles which it is

definitely known were built by William the Conqueror, but I arrived at closing time and they shut the door on my sorrowful visage.

On the level Lincoln is alive with crowds at night, but as you mount the steep hill, holding on to the hand-rail which is there to assist you, you mount up to quiet and peace. Between the eaves of old houses you see the massive screen of the west front and the twin towers of the great church lifted against the stars. You can think of Rome, if you like, or you can think of the last journey from Lincoln of the dead queen, Eleanor, which ended at the Cross at Charing; or you can think of nothing but the gracious beauty that lives in these stones.

2

A man who loves the rounded contour of the West Country is at first inclined to dislike the flat monotony of the Lincolnshire Fens. His eye looks round vainly for landmarks; there is nothing on which to focus. The flat land runs to the sky on all sides, and the presence of the sea is over the moving corn. Gradually, however, the peculiar atmosphere of the country grips the imagination. The slightest eminence becomes important; a windmill or a tall tree occupies the eyes, and the flight of birds is marvellous against the sky. As in all flat countries, the clouds billow splendidly over the rim of the earth, and you find the greatest beauty in the changing heavens.

The third 'part', or 'riding', of Lincolnshire is called Holland, and no district in England has been more justly named. I was heading for Holland when, standing up about ten miles away, I saw a curious tower among the fields.

'That's Boston Stump!' said a man in a cornfield.

'And what is Boston Stump?' I asked.

'It's Boston Stump!' he replied, and added 'Thickhead!' with his eyes.

So, feeling that there was no point in provoking him further, I slid off along the level way.

Boston in Holland. . . .

As I drew near, the 'Stump' proved to be the tower of a fine old Dutch church, standing on the brink of a slow, canal-like river. In a few moments I entered the cobbled streets of a town which, like Bradford-on-Avon, in Wiltshire, bears the stamp of a foreign trader. (If England contains any homesick Dutchmen, I recommend him to spend his weekends at Boston!)

Boston today is an interesting study. It is typical of the great town that has come down in the world. Like many an aristocrat, it manages to carry on bravely, so that, unless you knew of its past grandeur, there would be nothing remarkable about its present condition. In the Middle Ages Boston was the Bristol of the East Coast. There was no greater port in England, except London. The decline began with the Black Death, which decimated the eastern counties. The sea broke through the dikes, Boston Harbour silted, and the final blow was delivered by the gradual shifting of the commercial balance from east to west coast with the development of trade with the Americas. Boston at this time contributed to the very cause of her eclipse; her men helped to found Boston, New England, and now, by one of those queer tricks of time, the citizens of the famous Boston (Mass.) roam the quiet streets of the little-known English Boston commenting on its 'quaintness'.

When I wrote about Beaulieu Abbey in the New Forest I wondered whether an atmosphere of sanctuary could cling to an apparently dead ruin, and now, in Boston, I wonder whether an atmosphere of trade could cling to a town, rising superior to the buffeting of economic and geographical changes. Why not? Nothing dies harder than a street market.

Boston today, a town of 16,100 people, is not a sleepy old ruin. Its docks are still busy. They were unloading Continental coal when I walked round them; also fish, which they sell most appropriately by 'Dutch' auction. In the square I encountered one of the most melancholy markets I have ever seen. It is known locally as 'Bug Row', and the central aisle is, I understand, 'Flea Walk'.

Old iron bedsteads, bent and battered beneath the weight of heavy sleepers, rested on the cobbles, a woebegone sight. Ancient perambulators stood in a miserable row, bits of wood saved from the demolition of houses were stacked in little piles to be sold for firewood. There were a few books on stalls, piles of old iron, decayed bicycles. Purchasers sat on creaking bedsteads trying to work the shutters of doubtful cameras.

'All the small dealers try to raise a few shillings in "Bug Row" once a week,' explained a native Bostonian; 'but you ought to see the real market day, when the farmers and the corn merchants come in.'

A man tried to sell me a bag full of bed knobs. I have been wondering why ever since.

Three of those prim, sallow, enthusiastic, middle-aged lovers of England, in which Boston (Mass.) seems to specialize, were standing in the cells of the Guildhall, regarding moistly the bare rooms in which Brewster and other 'Pilgrim Fathers' were imprisoned after their attempted flight from England in 1607. . . .

Boston's greatest experience is, however, the long climb up the 'Stump', the tower of one of the largest parish churches in England. There are seven doors to the church, representing the days of the week; twelve pillars in the nave, representing the months of the year; twenty-four steps to the library, representing the hours of the day; fifty-two windows, representing the weeks in a year; sixty steps to the chancel roof, representing the seconds in a minute, and 365 steps to the 275-foot-high 'Stump', representing days in a year.

As you wind round and round in a narrow stone tube it seems that these steps have been much under estimated. On the way up two or three spirals are in pitch darkness. Now and then a voice with a nice Boston (Mass.) purr in it echoes from above.

'Say, are you coming up? Well, I'm resting round the corner!'

You wait, for there is no room to pass, till the sound of weary footsteps ascending warns you that the stone cork-screw is clear.

On top of Boston Stump I discover, of course, Gracie and mother and the professor from Boston (Mass.) gazing acutely over the Flemish landscape, trying to pick out the towers of Lincoln Cathedral, which on a good day you can see far off on the skyline.

Far below small boys playing by the slow green-brown river cup their hands to their mouths and shout:

'Throw down a penny, mister!'

Someone does this. The coin spins out in a great curve and falls with such a terrific phut! on the grass below that no one dares to repeat the act, in case it lands on the head of an urchin and kills him. . . .

'Boston!' whispers Gracie, looking down on the little town with its huddled roofs, its great square, and its river.

'I'm glad we've seen it,' says the professor.

'Isn't it time for tea?' suggests mother.

Boston . . . tea . . . a funny thing to hear on Boston Stump! I smile and pretend to find Lincoln.

'Say, daddy, I'll be right there in a minute!'

Click goes Gracie's camera. In a few minutes the feet of Boston (Mass.) awaken the echoes on the dark stairs of the church in which men prayed for – and received – a New England.

3

He was sitting in the hotel lounge with a guide-book, looking grim. I suppose a deceptive friendliness about me appealed to him, for he began almost at once.

'Say,' he said, 'would you have any objection to

answering a few questions? Bully, that's real good of you! Waiter, two dry Martinis. . . . Now, see here, I guess I've hit the wrong town! I've been through Lincoln-Shire and Gloucester-Shire, and Worcester-Shire, and – what the hell? oh yes, Hereford-Shire, and I've seen every darn cathedral in that bunch. Now, this Peterborough Cathedral! I kinda feel it's just a repetition of all the others, and that means that I've wasted a day. Maybe I should have gone right on to Ely?'

I tried to sum him up and failed.

'You didn't "get" the massive strength of the Norman nave here?'

'No, sir. I guess I saw it done better in Gloucester-Shire,' he replied dogmatically.

'Or the most unusual Norman apse, one of the glories of Peterborough, or the remarkable west front, which has been called "the finest portico in Europe"?' . . .

'Go slow!' he cried suddenly. 'The most unusual what?

He brought out a notebook and a gold pencil and began to write.

'I like to keep my diary up-to-date,' he said, with a friendly smile.

'Put in it, then,' I suggested, 'the story of these cathedrals. Men didn't just arrive with cartloads of stones and start to build a church. There is a story of faith and struggle behind every English cathedral. Behind Peterborough is a love story: an old story of a heathen Saxon prince called Peada who was in love with a princess called Atheleda . . .'

'Oh, gosh, these names put me right off!'

'Never mind, they were real honest to God people. This girl promised to marry the prince if he became a Christian. Many a time a woman of influence converted the early Saxon kingdoms. The prince consented, the conversion of Mercia followed, and eventually men built a church on the site of the present cathedral.'

He made a few rapid notes in his book.

'That was before William the Confessor?' he asked.

'Waiter,' I replied, 'two more very dry Martinis.'

I settled down to find out why this man had crossed the Atlantic.

Now and again there crops up in the vast army of cultured and intelligent American travellers – and no one respects the average American traveller more than I do – a man who drifts at great expense through Europe like a ship without a rudder. I have often wondered why; I ventured to ask him, and he was frankness itself.

'See here, I'll tell you!' he cried, pulling his chair up nearer. 'I've made a whale of a success back home. I'm vice-president of the Such-and-Such Corporation, and only six years since I was a junior in an engineering firm in a bum outfit in Kentucky. Well, I tell you, sir, things are different for me now. I gotta go to parties, dinners, and all that! I soon rumbled that if I was goin' to win out on my job I'd gotta be able to join in the conversation – *I'd gotta see Yurrup!* I just got sick of sitting around listening to a pack of fool women talk about Rome and Florence and Stratford-on-Avon and all that bunk. Believe me, sir, a guy who hasn't seen these places cuts no ice. . . .'

I began to like this man. His sturdy honesty of purpose was sublime.

'So,' I said, 'you came over?'

'Yeh! I took a five weeks' vacation. Two spent on the water and three to see Europe in. . . . And gee, I've busted around some: I've seen Rome, and Venice, and Florence, and Naples, and Paris, and Stratford-on-Avon, and all your darned cathedrals, and – I guess I'll be able to put it over on them when I get back. You bet I will!'

'But surely,' I suggested, 'it would have been better and cheaper to have bought some books and stayed at home?'

'No, sir, it ain't the same as travel! You gotta go right through with it. . . . Say, do you know London? Then you'd do me a real service if you'd tell me how I can see London in a day. . . .'

I took him to the cathedral. I tried to explain – leaving

216

out all architecture – that these great churches are the urns which hold the ashes of England's history. The dim aisles are sacred to a Past which is the splendid mother of the Present, for in them are gathered the men whose lives shaped, through stress and storm, through the dense drive of arrows and the smoke of conflict, through a war of words, and through victories, and defeats and losses more magnificent than gains, the destiny of the English people.

We stood beside the grave of a queen, one of the most unhappy women in history, whose dignified life and character must win more than admiration from all men – Katharine of Aragon, wife of Henry VIII. This tomb is passed by most visitors. It is covered by a marble stone, subscribed by the 'Katharines of England'. Every complex misery which can torture an unhappy wife befel this poor, lonely lady, a miserable pawn in a political game, a woman whose staunch life was broken on the diplomatic wheel, the humiliated member of that important triangle: Henry, Katharine, Anne Boleyn.

I love everything that history tells about her. She it was who, when Henry was abroad and James IV of Scotland decided to invade England, rallied the troops and addressed them before they marched north to win the battle of Flodden Field. Within a year Henry VIII was deep in the plot to divorce her. No matter how one realizes Henry's need for male issue, the insults and the humiliations piled on this loyal and able woman must always be one of the most shameful chapters in the domestic history of the English throne. When she died, worn out with sorrow and illness – to the unconcealed delight of Henry and Anne Boleyn – the King, in selecting Peterborough as her burial-place, said that he gave her 'the handsomest tomb in England'. If his bulky ghost haunts these aisles now, I hope it feels ashamed of that poor, quiet, forgotten grave. Unhappy Katharine deserves a more queenly tomb.

Peterborough is sacred also to the memory of another ill-starred woman – Mary, Queen of Scots. Her grave was

prepared by a man called 'Old Scarlet', who over half a
century before had prepared the grave of Katharine of
Aragon. When James I came to the throne he ordered the
removal of his mother's body from Peterborough to
Westminster Abbey. . . .

'Well,' said the American, 'no wonder you folks get so
much out of these cathedrals of yours. It's the family history,
skeletons and all. . . . Say, Henry the Eighth? Wasn't he the
fat guy with the ginger whiskers? Well, those poor wives . . .'

'Mary, Queen of Scots wasn't . . .'

'Oh, I guess I know that!' he cried. 'Those poor wives of
his certainly stood for a whole lot, and he was no beauty to
look at, but then women seem to like the ugly slobs, don't
they?'

'Have you,' I said, 'gathered anything this afternoon to
"put over on them" at home?'

'Sure!' he said, 'You bet I have.'

'Then this day has not been wasted.'

He caught a late train to London, and I can see him as
plainly as anything in a few weeks' time, shaving before
dressing for a dinner party, with his diary propped up on
the bathroom ledge, open at Peterborough.

'I guess I'll put that one over on them tonight – that'll
knock 'em for a row of cans. . . .'

I certainly hope it does.

4

I am the only person I have ever known who has been to
Rutland. I admit that I have known men who have passed
through Rutland in search of a fox, but I have never met a
man who has deliberately set out to go to Rutland; and I do
not suppose you have.

Rutland – which I believe most people think is in Wales –
is the smallest county in England, and the most remarkable.
It is only seventeen miles long and seventeen miles wide,
and it contains only two towns, Oakham and Uppingham,

neither large enough to be a municipal borough. The county of Rutland, nestling like a baby in arms between Lincolnshire, Leicestershire, and Northamptonshire, is included in 'The Shires'. Rutland is the only shire carved out of old Saxon Mercia not named after its county town, otherwise we would know it as Oakhamshire. On the other hand, no one would dream of calling it Rutlandshire! Tiny Rutland is the only example of an ancient Mercian division which has survived the West Saxon shire-ing of the district.

Throughout history Rutland seems to have been a kind of birthday present to queens or the favourites of kings. Ethelred gave it to his Queen Emma; Edward the Confessor gave it to his Queen Edith; John gave it to Isabella. If happiness is the absence of history, then Rutland is the happiest county in England, for the only bloody chapter in its annals is one battle, which, I suppose, just drifted untidily over the neat border into quiet but helpless Rutland. I suppose they tried to shoo it back over the border as they might a flock of geese! I am sorry about this: it is history's blunder. If this battle had not trespassed we might have called Rutland the Arcady of England.

I went on past fine fields of wheat and oats. A lovely rich gold county. No factory chimneys deform the rolling corn or break the gentle sweep of fields. Industries have sprung up in Rutland and have expired. There is something old-fashioned in the air here, I think, not congenial to the hurly-burly of modern life. Stone is quarried at Ketton, where about a hundred and fifty men are employed. St Dunstan's Church, in Fleet Street, is built of Ketton stone, and there is some, I seem to remember, in the Tower of London.

The villages of Rutland are delicious. Everything in this county is to scale. A Rutland village consists of church, vicarage, shoeing forge, The Saracen's Head, twenty white cottages, with neat pigsties behind them, and a village pump. I believe the last smock was seen in Rutland. . . .

'Where are we?' I asked.

'Tickencote,' said a shy little girl who was swinging on a gate.

If ever you are near Tickencote look at this pocket edition of a Norman church. I stood in the shady churchyard and thought that this solid little building, planted in this lovely soil soon after the Conquest, is one of the fairest things I have seen. The vaulted chancel is a marvel, but the most remarkable feature is a quintuple Norman chancel arch. There is nothing that I am aware of like it in all England. This arch resembles five huge decorated stone horseshoes placed one within the other. I compare it to horseshoes because horseshoes are somehow symbolic of Rutland. You hear them on the roads, you see the sparks from anvils spurting in dark forges, and the county town, Oakham, contains more distinguished horseshoes than any place on earth; but I am coming to that in a minute.

Oakham, the county town, looks like a village. The stocks are in position under the circular Butter Cross. There are thatched houses in the main street! I slowed down till my car ran silently over the road, for the 3,500 inhabitants of Oakham, were, I think, asleep! What two thousand years or so had failed to do I had no intention of doing!

A buxom wench, with a face like a ripe pippin and a waist made for the arm of an eighteenth-century gallant, gave me beef and beer in a room hung with fox masks.

'What do you do here?' I asked.

'Nothing till the hunting begins,' she said, blushing from the ears up. Fancy watching a girl blush! . . .

I looked round the room at pictures of horsemen taking fences, falling in ponds, hounds in full cry, hounds fresh, hounds weary. A retriever came in and placed a little black iced sponge of a nose on my hand. . . .

'Nothing ever happens here?'

'Oh, yes, sir; the Prince of Wales. He hunts here.'

I went out into the inn yard and through a great arch built to admit coaches.

The most interesting object in this sleepy, happy,

delicious county town is Oakham Castle, one of the finest examples of Norman domestic architecture left in England. Here they hold the assizes twice a year, and the judge is almost certain to receive a pair of white gloves, for no one commits crime in Rutland.

The Norman hall is hung with horseshoes, some of ordinary size and some beaten out of seven feet long strips of metal. Every time a peer passes through Oakham he has to give a horseshoe to the castle. If he refuses, the people of Oakham have the right to take one from his horse. (I suppose if a modern peer refused it would be legal for them to stick a nail in his tyres; and serve him right!) This custom is lost in the mists of antiquity. It is by some said to have originated in Norman times, when Walkelyn de Ferrier, Master of the Horse to the Conqueror, held Oakham Castle; others place the custom at a later date.

Many kings and queens have paid the horseshoe tax. The two latest come from the King and the Duke of York, who have passed through Oakham when hunting. Queen Victoria, Queen Alexandra, and King Edward VII are represented. One of the largest shoes was that given by Queen Elizabeth. The shoe given by George IV is of solid bronze, stands seven feet high, and is said to have cost fifty pounds.

The tragedy of Oakham Castle is that King George V never paid the tax.

'If only we could have got him!' said the caretaker to me. 'I believe he passed through on the railway once; but that doesn't count! When the King came here, as Prince of Wales, he looked round and said, "Where's Father!" '

It is curious that while kings have been giving shoes to Oakham, the little stone quarrying village of Ketton near by has for centuries been giving shoes to queens. This village still pays an annual rent of a few shillings to the Crown (*pro ocreis Reginae*) to provide the queen with leggings! This is, I imagine, a survival from remote Saxon times, when Rutland was generally assigned to the Queen. . . .

I smiled to myself as I ran towards the Rutland boundary. I have found England a hundred times since I started. Here it was again.

In all England is there anything quite so Old English as a county town where the fox is the chief industry, where they thatch the main street, tax peers, go to sleep in the afternoon, burn wood, never see charabancs or factory smoke, never, as far as I can find out, murder each other, and where the girls, when you ask them a question, look down at the floor and go red round the ears? Some day I will go to live in Rutland in a pink coat and drink a bottle of port every night.

And the subtle compliment they pay one in Oakham. After showing me the result of taxing peers for centuries, the caretaker looked up and said with a roguish smile: 'And may we expect another one – er, sir?'

I stopped at the boundary, where I stood up and took off a hat that was once new to the rich, gold fields of Rutland.

CHAPTER ELEVEN

The Land of the North Folk. I enter Norwich, prowl the sad sea marshes, and walk along a dead road. Describes the Isle of Ely and men who chip flint

I

IWAS lost in a Norfolk lane, so I stopped a man and I said to him:

'Good morning!'

He looked at me.

'Good morning,' I cried. 'Can you tell me if I am right for Norwich?'

He continued to look at me. Then, in an uneasy, suspicious way, he said:

'What d'ye want to know for?'

I might have been annoyed, but leaning out of the car and putting on an affable expression which I usually keep for tea-parties, I said:

'My dear old 'bor, I want to know because I want to get to Norwich.'

The ghost of a smile flitted over his rustic face, and he replied after some deep thought, rather reluctantly, and looking away from me:

'Well; you're right!'

I don't expect anyone to believe this unless he knows Norfolk.

Norfolk is the most suspicious county in England. In Devon and Somerset men hit you on the back cordially; in Norfolk they look as though they would like to hit you over the head – till they size you up. You see, for centuries the north folk of East Anglia were accustomed to meet stray Vikings on lonely roads who had just waded ashore from the long boats.

'Good morning, 'bor!' said the Vikings. 'Which is the way to the church?'

'What d'ye want to know for?' was the Norfolk retort.
'Well, we thought about setting fire to it!'

You will gather that Norfolk's suspicion of strangers, which is an ancient complex bitten into the East Anglian through centuries of bitter experience, is well grounded, and should never annoy the traveller. They mean well. Once they bring themselves to call you ' 'bor' (which, I conclude, is the short for 'neighbour' or, perhaps, 'boy'), you can consider yourself highly complimented. In East Anglia men are either neighbours or Vikings. If they promote you to 'bordom they will do any mortal thing for you except, perhaps, lend you money, for.one Norfolk farmer could beat any three Yorkshiremen at driving a bargain.

The word ' 'bor' is the most popular one in Norfolk dialect, except, perhaps, 'mauther', which means girl. Norfolk is full of sturdy, good-looking mauthers with magnificent necks and arms. Some wear flaxen hair in plaits round their ears and look like young Brünnhildes, reminding you that sometimes the Vikings settled down in Norfolk. Boadicea was a typical Norfolk 'mauther' before she took up politics.

I went on between hedges through a country mellow with the harvest. Is there a more magnificent sight in England than a large field of wheat ripe for the reaping? Such rich gold; such tall, majestic stalks like legions of gold arrows. I love the way you can trace the dips and falls of a field on the top of the tall wheat, and I love also the little stray winds that dust the corn stalks in small gusts, blowing them aside and passing on.

The churches of Norfolk are unique. The art of using flint for building is here developed as I have seen it in no other county. Hundreds of thousands of flints a few inches square are embedded in the mortar, forming a polished grey wall hard as steel and indestructible. The effect is most unusual, and if you have ever tried to chip flint – which is the most difficult, unreasonable, capricious stone in the world – you look at these churches with added reverence.

224

I must tell you that it was in these lanes that I met my first pig. I have encountered the cows of every county in England from Somerset to Cumberland, but this was, as I say, my first pig. She seemed, as I turned the corner rather quickly and headed right for her, to be reading her fortune in the middle of the road. She was a big, shrimp-coloured *prima donna*, with bloodshot eyes and she wore her tail in a small, neat knot. Awakened to realities by my swift arrival, for I had to jam on the brakes hard, she did a little leap and came running towards me under the impression, apparently, that she was going in the opposite direction. That was where I misread her. She had strong home instincts, and she knew that she had to get back past me. She gave this up, shook a couple of Bath chaps at me, and uttering a series of shrill feminine squeals, ran right ahead, calling on all her gods. As I observed her short, inadequate legs carrying all this bacon down the lane, I knew that in her disturbed mind she believed that she was doing about fifty miles an hour.

I tried kindly to edge past her, but she advanced a ham at an inappropriate moment and recoiled in horror from the bonnet. A ton of bacon in a narrow lane can be more stupid than the hen which belongs to the local suicide club. I hate to frighten animals so I stopped and dismounted, full of good intentions, with the idea of driving her back past the car. However, uttering reproaches in a most unreasonable manner, she dived into the hedge where – serve her right – she stuck fast.

2

I was sitting on a gate studying the map of Norfolk when there came towards me the first tramps I have seen – or rather the first obvious tramps I have seen – since Cheshire. The man was pushing a wooden box on perambulator wheels; the woman was walking a few paces behind him, carrying a small cardboard tray, and wearing the remains of a once fashionable long-waisted tailor-made costume. She came up to me, pulling the collar of the costume to her throat, which made me realize that she had nothing on beneath it, and asked me to buy a packet of lavender. Much to her surprise, I bought twelve.

The man was surprised; so was the mongrel pup who had one sharp ear cocked on the hedge and a rabbity look about his jaw. So we all stood smiling in a group.

'Well,' I said, 'It's an awful life, isn't it? But, thank goodness – catch – we have tobacco!'

Tramps sum you up quicker than a dog or a child. They decide in one second whether you are dangerous or harmless. So we got talking. . . .

'Steady job!' said the woman. 'You wouldn't be in no steady job, long, Joe, would you?'

Joe narrowed his eyes and looked down the road. He was a born tramp, a born walker, a born wanderer, half countryman, half townsman, quite young, but one of those people civilization will never break in. He had served during the war.

'Well,' he said in a tired drawl, 'well you don't pay no rent and you don't pay no rates, and no income tax, and you can get all you want to eat most times, and I like the country and I don't get on in towns.'

He told me that his 'people' were well-to-do village folk somewhere who wanted him to settle down. (He spat.)

'I won't 'ave no truck with them,' he said. 'They can keep their blinkin' money. I don't want it!'

'And you,' I said to the woman, 'how do you like it?'

She smiled. She also was a vagrant, I think; a much rarer type in a woman. Or she may have been just slipshod and lazy.

'I've seen better days,' she said, putting on a miserable face and drawing her coat collar up.

'Go on with you!' I laughed. 'Admit you'd hate to know where you'd sleep next week!'

She laughed.

226

'Perhaps I would . . . tho' it's cold sometimes and me stockings dry on me legs which gives me rheumatism something cruel at times.'

'I wonder how long either of you would stay in a house?'

'Not long,' said the man definitely. 'Here, boy, come away there! He's a sharp dog, sir, I've been offered quids for him. No, he's never caught a rabbit. . . .'

At this untruthful moment a stout ran across the road, and the dog was on it like a dart. We tactfully changed the subject.

They told me far more than they realized. The fun it is to tramp from town to town as members of a lazy, irresponsible brotherhood, meeting friends in doss-houses every night, swopping news, hearing how old So-and-So did such and such a thing; putting out all the eatables on the table and holding an auction, then wandering on and on again, listless, without ambition, unenvious of other men, just drifters. . . .

He whistled the dog, nodded to me; she smiled and showed teeth and they went off down the road; the man pushing the truck that held all their worldly goods; the woman a step or two behind; the mongrel questing ahead. You could not feel sorry for them. I believe they were happier than any millionaire; happier in fact, than most of us.

I struck the main road and made for Norwich.

3

The most surprising thing about Norwich is that it contains the only Norman cathedral in England unknown to Americans. Norwich is not on the pilgrimage map, and the reason is geographical. The tourist stream flows due south from Lincoln to Peterborough–Ely–Cambridge, leaving Norwich in the great eastward bulge of Norfolk fifty miles to the left. Some day, of course, the people who map tours will discover Norwich (and the fourteenth-century hotel which has hot and cold water laid on to the bedrooms), some day, maybe, Norwich may even discover itself.

Norwich is a confusing, characteristic city. It was tied up into hasty knots centuries ago and has never been unwound. It is characteristic of Norfolk. It is a monument to the north folk and it bears the marks of all their peculiarities – it has flint walls and is difficult to know at a glance! Norwich in Somerset would be unthinkable; it is an expression of sturdy East Anglia. I came here knowing nothing about the city except that it has always made money, that it once was the third city in England, that when its weaving trade went north after the coalfields, Norwich just put on a flinty face and learned how to make women's shoes. Trust Norwich to survive!

I saw a red-roofed city dominated by two landmarks: a slim cathedral spire second only to Salisbury and a great square Norman castle on a hill in the heart of which – so George Borrow said confidently – sits an old heathen king 'with his sword in his hand and his gold and silver treasures about him'. I went through queer medieval streets, many paved with cobble-stones, all distinguished by a picturesque dowdiness; some Flemish in appearance, full of houses with the big inverted V on the top story where the hand-looms were housed; and at night beside the river I might have been in the England or the Netherlands of the fourteenth century with the moon falling on huddled roofs, the lamplight moving in slow waters, the dark figures of men and women going through dark alleyways between the leaning eaves.

Norwich has been called the 'city of churches'. It struck me also as a city of public-houses and canaries. In hundreds of little homes the shoemakers of Norwich breed prize canaries and discuss points as keenly as Newmarket discusses a horse. If you wanted to stop the traffic in Norwich, the quickest way would be to walk through the city with a first-class Norwich Plain Head on your finger.

'Those are the boys that pay the rent!' said a shoemaker's wife to me, nodding to a cage full of little gold birds.

I met a man who keeps, in the season, more than five thousand canaries. He exports them to Australia, Canada, India, New Zealand.

'The ship's butcher, being used to livestock, looks after them on the voyage,' he told me.

I was offered a Plain Head cock for five pounds and a Crested hen for four pounds; but I managed to get away alone.

There comes a time in the life of all old cities when the city fathers should form a coalition government to decide whether their city is to preserve its ancient beauty or to become a second Leicester or a little Birmingham. Norwich it seems to me, has reached this point.

In fifty years' time Norwich will either not be worth looking at, or it will be one of the most beautiful old cities in England. Few cities possess so many complete streets of half-timbered houses, some medieval, some Tudor – most are disguised by ugly Georgian plaster, which, if scraped off, would reveal the old red-brick and oak. Under intelligent treatment Norwich would emerge like a restored oil painting. The local authorities should spend a weekend in Shrewsbury in order to realize the remarkable chance that lies immediately before them. Then, on their return, they might catch the architects responsible for putting up new banks like Georgian cinemas – if you can imagine that – and hang them in the iron cage which they will find ready in their castle dungeon; a cage obviously designed to hold a bank architect.

It is, of course, rather difficult to forecast the future of a city which pays hundreds of pounds for the work of a Norwich artist, yet allows water to drip on his grave in a Norwich church. I refer to John Crome, who is buried in St George-at-Colegate.

Strangers' Hall, which stands in a small courtyard in a busy street, is one of the most beautiful small medieval houses you will see in England. Norwich is packed with these unexpected places.

The cathedral is full of splendid Norman work, notably the nave. I imagine that this is the least-known cathedral in England. The clerestory, set back within a wall-passage, has Norman lights; the aisles also are Norman. There is a curious opening in the roof through which the monks used to let down a swinging censer. Norwich Cathedral has not the situation or the west front of Lincoln, but to me it was vastly more interesting than the more famous church. In a little plot of ground outside the cathedral rises a white cross:

TO THE PURE AND HOLY MEMORY OF

EDITH CAVELL

WHO GAVE HER LIFE FOR ENGLAND

OCTOBER 12TH, 1915

Every Saturday morning the City of Norwich becomes Norfolk. The whole county pours into town, the narrow streets fill . . . the squire and his good-looking daughters, the farmer and his buxom wife, scores of strong-limbed 'mauthers', drovers chewing straws and plodding along with their eyes on the back view of cows.

The cattle market, which Cobbett said was the 'best and most attractive' market in England, fills, pen by pen, with sheep and oxen and pigs. Flocks of sheep move in dust, the air is full of lowing and bleating, and hoarse cries, and the crack of sticks and the ring of hobnailed boots on the cobbles. Cheap-jacks who have tramped the roads open ancient Gladstone bags, and display strange goods to a ring of stolid Norfolk faces; faces not dull or simple but simply padlocked with caution and the determination not to be 'done'. It must be hard work to sell things in Norwich market.

'This solid-silver cigarette-case was left in a train. I'm a-tellin' you the truth! Surprising what people leave in trains, ain't it? It belonged to a lord. Look! There's what they call his monogram. Lord Blank! Come on now, who says . . .'

But no one says anything! It isn't done in Norfolk. You let the other fellow say it all first!

A man drives up in a mysterious motor-van. The sides fall down to reveal a little stage set with two chairs and a table, on which is an electric battery. The walls are plastered with tributes to an electric-current rheumatism cure and rather inconsequent X-ray photographs. Slowly, timidly, an old country woman mounts the platform and holds the terminals, white-lipped. Her relatives stand below waiting to see her killed or cured. The current is switched on, her eyes pop out of her head; she steps down.

'Do you feel better, ma?'

'I believe a' do!'

In the public bars the Norfolk farmers split farthings all day. Is there such acute bargaining anywhere else in England? A pig and fourpence will keep two Norfolk farmers busy all day long.

'A cigar,' said a fine, red farmer who came into a shop in which I happened to be buying tobacco. 'An' doan't yew give me none ov yar muck neither, 'bor. . . .'

(No one goes word-mincing in Norfolk!)

'Ninepence!' said the tobacconist, showing him some.

'Sevenpence . . .' said the farmer.

'No, ninepence is the price.'

'Well, yow can keep 'um! . . .'

'Eightpence,' said the tobacconist. 'Will you take it?'

'Ah, 'bor, that I'll dew, tho' it ain't worth it!'

When he had gone the tobacconist said:

'It was an eightpenny cigar, but it would never do to admit it.'

In moonlight Norwich from the castle walls lies with shining roofs, the green light rippling the length of the thin spire of the cathedral and falling into the dark, narrow streets. A drover behind his sheep crosses the empty market square in a pool of lamplight; and it seems that centuries have slipped back; that the Norwich looms are clacking once again; that along the deserted riverside are the ghosts of Flemish masts.

4

Beyond Cromer, from Cley-next-the-Sea – which Norfolk men pronounce Cly – the level salt marshes run for miles towards a thin ridge of yellow sand, beyond which is the ocean. The tide goes out for miles and returns at a canter. It is desolate. The wind whispers. The sea birds cry. No men but naturalists disturb the solitude of the salt marshes.

The wind blows through miles of sea lavender, great lakes of pink and purple, and the gold clouds pile up over the edge of the sea and roll landwards like great galleons. The light, falling on this flat land squarely, intensifies colour so that you cry out at sudden glories in the painful knowledge that nothing but watercolour can tell the story truly. The sea marshes are full of life. A blue-grey heron lifts noiselessly above the green reeds and sails away with a slow beat of great wings, his long legs held stiff behind him. He settles. With keen eyes you can see his head lifted to the level of the reeds watching you. White gulls sit in rows on the shells of wrecked fishing boats.

There is a sudden flurry of white and a great screaming. Up they go in the air, orange feet tucked into soft white undersides, wheeling, turning, poised in the air motionless, then down, down like white darts with a sudden outflinging of orange feet; for the tide is coming in, rushing in, swirling in up creeks and the twisty channels. One minute the oozy banks are dry; the next they are alive with a brown snake of water that writhes and bubbles, lapping the bright fringe of samphire at the edges.

And it is lonely, with the water lapping and the birds crying and the wind pressing the blue thrift backwards from the sea, for this is a strange No Man's Land: it is not land and it is not water, but a queer beautiful region half land, half water; and it seems to you that the sea fights for it daily and the grass defends it. When you turn your back to the salt marshes you see, far away, flat meadows and green land and villages, clear-etched, and grey flint church towers rising above the trees. To the left and to the right a thin line of woodland is the colour of the bloom on a purple grape.

All along the coast at the edge of the great salt marsh are curious little villages which were once seaports. Huge flint churches in desolate meadows tell you that yesterday this coast was alive with men and commerce. There is Blakeney, whose church has an extra tower, once a lighthouse, now eloquently ruined; there is Cley; there is Salthouse; there is Weybourne, in whose ancient bay the wild-fowl nest; there is Wells-next-the-Sea – all old seaports which the sea has deserted.

In a cosy vale is the village of Stiffkey. It is a curious little village noted for its cockle women. I went down to the long sea marsh. I crossed rotting timbers flung across creeks, and I went on for miles through mud and marsh till I came at length to the distant ridge of sand which has wrecked more ships than the Needles, and the incredible expanse of shore. Dotted about this gold plain were bent black figures raking up the famous 'Stewkey blues', as the cockles are called.

One cockle gatherer came towards me bent beneath the weight of an enormous sack. It was impossible to tell whether this strange figure was that of man or woman. She was wearing a black divided skirt. Thick worsted stockings, wet through with salt water, clung to her legs. She wore a black shawl over her shoulders and a sou'wester that buttoned like a Kate Greenaway bonnet beneath her chin. When I stopped her she lifted her face, and I saw that she was an ancient dame of at least seventy. Her toothless little mouth was pressed primly in below a smooth apple face etched with a million fine lines, and her eyes were blue and childish.

Like many people in this part of England, she was frightened of questions. I asked her if she was strong enough

233

to do such hard work, and she said that she had been doing it since she was a young woman.

A few years ago someone wrote up Stiffkey and its cockle women in a cruel light. It was alleged that intermarriage had so affected the inhabitants that the men did no work while the women slaved to keep things going.

'That's a pack of nonsense,' said the ancient cockle gatherer. 'Our men work on the land, and we women have long before living memory gone down to the sea to get the cockles. I started when I was married, when I wanted extra money to bring up the children; and that's why most of us do it.'

She turned towards the sea and said:

'Those are the last cockle gatherers you'll see in Stiffkey. Girls today want to be ladies. They don't like to get themselves up in such ugly clothes and go down to the sea as their mothers and their grandmothers and – yes – and their great-grandmothers did; and they don't like hard work, either. . . . Yes, we're the last cockle women, we old ones. . . .'

A look of absolute horror came into the face of this old woman when I asked her if I might take a photograph of her. She put her hands to her eyes as I have seen Arabs do when faced by a camera.

'No, no,' she said, and looked round for cover. I soothed her with great difficulty.

It was not modesty, I think, or the thought of being photographed in such queer garments. Here and there in remote parts of England there exists still a curious belief that to be photographed brings bad luck.

There are few stranger sights in England than the return of these cockle women before the galloping tide. Slowly, heavily, they come with dripping sacks of 'Stewkey blues' on their backs. Most of them are old women, who belong to a tougher generation. Some are middle-aged. Now and again a girl goes down 'for fun', to see how her mother earned extra money to bring her up. The salt spray drenches their short skirts, the wind lashes their bare legs, as they come plodding in over the salt marshes.

This is a curious part of the world. A region barely touched by tourists. A region rich in history and packed full of atmosphere. You can stand on the salt marshes towards the end of the day, with the sun mellow over the windy fields of sea lavender, and it takes little to imagine the Viking ships beaching on the distant strand – the big, red, bearded men wading to the shore, dragging their great double-bladed swords through the purple marshes, shading their eyes to the distant land.

There is a melancholy over the sea marshes quite impossible to describe. You feel that it is good to be alone here, good to wander over the featureless land, listening to the shrill crying of the birds and to the sound of the wind in the grass.

5

The silence of death lies over the Peddars Way.

A man can walk for many a mile in solitude on this ghost of a mighty road. From Thetford it runs six miles to Hockham, then, straight as an arrow, it lies for thirty miles, sometimes hidden beneath the fields, through Castle Acre and Great Bircham to the coast at Brancaster. Long before men knew the name of England they knew the Peddars Way. How old it is no man can say. When the Romans came it was an antiquity, trodden hard by countless generations and the Romans were glad, because it was straight and to the point, and saved them trouble. In the Middle Ages the Peddars Way served a new England, and led to one of the saintliest spots in the land – to Our Lady of Walsingham. . . .

Now the Peddars Way is dead.

The little cottontail plays upon it; the weasel and the blackbird own it; for the feet of the men who made the

Peddars Way went into silence many centuries ago along the road to Eternity.

I am writing this beside the old road. Where I sit I can see the ghost of it under the grass, broad and embanked, slipping into the distance over the fields. Here it is drenched in green gloom. The thick trees which hedge it arch themselves above it, and in the hush of this still afternoon I fancy that the leaves have just stopped whispering together of the things that once went by along the Peddars Way.

I am conscious that this is a ghostly spot. Every time a leaf falls, every time there is a sudden rustle in the undergrowth I look up, half-expecting to see a figure not of this age coming towards me along the dead road. Once I looked quickly behind me ... there was nothing but an unnatural stillness. Even the birds seem hushed along the Peddars Way. They say that Black Shuck haunts this road, as he haunts the coast near Cromer. He is a jet-black hound, big as a calf. Between ourselves, he is the Hound of Thor. He still haunts Norfolk on nights as black as himself.

An empty house can be ghostly, but ghostlier far is an empty road which no men use. The beauty and the magic of a road are something this age does not know: our roads are too good and too many, and we never notice them except when they are bad or in the hands of the road mender. But there was a time – and the Peddars Way belongs to it – when a road, like fire and a roof, was one of the primitive blessings of life: and, more than that, a sign that men could combine in a common task and follow the same track to a journey's end.

The Peddars Way was planned long before history began. It has seen men use the flint mace-head; it has seen the stone weapon give way to metal; it has nursed the dawning civilization, century after century leading such traffic and such commerce as there was away from the wilderness: first a savage trail, then a road.

The legions came, perhaps straightened out a corner here and there; and it led them from Camulodunum (which we

236

call Colchester) to Branodunum on the Wash (which we call Brancaster).

So far the Peddars Way knew war and commerce; centuries were to pass, and it was to know religion.

In that remarkable collection of old houses called Walsingham, north of Fakenham, stands a scanty ruin of the mighty abbey which from the time of Henry III to the Dissolution drew king, queen, and commoner to the shrine of the Virgin. At first the shrine was a modest wooden chapel, but when Nazareth fell into the hands of the infidel the monks of Walsingham, by one of those perhaps not accidental strokes of fancy, for the fortunes of Glastonbury were once firmly financed by another such inspiration, said that the Mother of God, driven out of Palestine, had taken up her abode in Norfolk. They said subsequently that their shrine of Our Lady of Walsingham was actually the Sancta Casa from Nazareth.

Then the Peddars Way became the pilgrims' way. It heard the tapping of the pilgrim staff. It saw men and women from every part of Europe making their way to Walsingham. It saw pilgrim cavalcades like that which Chaucer took so gloriously to Canterbury, it saw the poor man hobbling by the roadside, it saw the King in all his majesty riding a tall charger surrounded by his Court. Henry III, Edward I, Edward II, Bruce of Scotland, Henry VII, and, before the religious revolution, Henry VIII, all took the pilgrims' way to Walsingham. When they reached little Houghton-in-the-Dale they removed their shoes (there is still a house here named Shoe House) and continued the rest of the way barefoot.

Unless you have seen a pilgrimage, it is difficult to imagine this scene. I have watched the pilgrims start for Mecca, and I have seen Syrian Christians on their knees in Bethlehem and in Jerusalem, tears rolling down their faces as they kissed the end of sticks which the priests push through marble pillars to touch some sacred relic. . . .

In the famous shrine stood the statue of the Virgin, and

Erasmus, who visited it in 1511, said of it: 'There is little or no light in it but what proceeds from wax-tapers yielding a most pleasant and odoriferous smell, but if you look up you will say that it is the seat of the gods, so bright and shining as it is all over with jewels, gold and silver.'

Strange relics were kept in the shrine, including a flask of the Virgin's milk and a joint of one of St Peter's fingers.

There came a day when the last pilgrim abased himself before the shrine, and soon the Peddars Way saw men come riding, and in the midst of them Our Lady of Walsingham, plucked from her candlelight, going on her way to be burned at Smithfield. Then the Peddars Way knew that some strange thing had happened to England; and the grass began to grow.

The sunlight slants down through the leaves on the old broad track. In moonlight it must look wonderful. Some day I will come back and walk the Peddars Way by moonlight, and it will not surprise me then to be spoken to in the stillness, perhaps in a tongue no man knows, perhaps in Latin, perhaps in Norman French, perhaps in Tudor English.

For all these tongues have wagged along the Peddars Way, but what they have said only the road knows and it is dead, or in a sleep like death, with the grass above it and only the song of birds to remind it that the world goes on.

6

For the last ten days I have been miserable. I have been prostrate in bed with a red-hot throat and a foul temper which turned into a fine pathos, and the dismal belief that I was about to commit the supreme sin against good manners and die in an hotel. You may do almost anything in an hotel but die there.

One night, under the influence of a cocaine pill and a raw egg, I sat up and wrote the most miserable essay that has ever been written about the country graveyards of

England, the fine old yew-trees, and the lichened head-
stones. The doctor read it and took away my pen, and so,
quite helpless, I sank into fever, my only pleasure the poor
one of watching my hand open and close against the light
from the window, wondering why it was my hand and who
on earth I was. (Perhaps if you have had millions of
streptococci in the throat you will understand!)

However, the evil dream is over, the germs are slain, the
boots, who has neuralgia, has the cocaine pills, the
chambermaid has the gargle, and I, at last, have the open
road, and an occasional glimpse of the sun.

Now in England there are many magic 'islands', the only
islands which refute the geography primers because they are
entirely surrounded by dry land. Centuries ago these
'islands', which today are merely hills rising from green
fields, were surrounded by marshy waters that have at
various dates been drained away in the interests of
agriculture. These isles are: the Isle of Avalon in Somerset
to which, says legend, the hooded queens took the dying
King Arthur; the Isle of Athelney, also in Somerset, where
King Alfred gathered his forces before he smashed the
Danes; and the Isle of Ely in Cambridgeshire, from whose
fastness Hereward the Wake defied the Conqueror. There is
the Thorney Isle, on which Westminster Abbey stands, and
the Isle of Thanet, and I am sure, several others.

I travelled towards Ely in the early morning long before
the first harvester was awake. At this time of year a veil of
white mist lies over the Cambridgeshire fenlands, a pearl
pale thing, thin and chill; and as I went on through it I felt
as though I were sailing on the ghost of a sea. The dimly
seen hedges of this flat chessboard land were like the edges
of poised beakers. Suddenly I saw before me, like a frozen
ship upon a frozen ocean, the Isle of Ely rising in spectral
beauty above the morning mist. This sudden high hill
crowned with its towered cathedral seen above the white
mist of late summer is one of the most beautiful things in the
whole of England. It is a spellbound hill: the creation, it

seems, of a wizard's wand: a floating Camelot spun by the fairies from the mushroom mists and ready to dissolve into the cold air even as a man looks in wonder at it.

As the sun rises and the mists melt, the Isle of Ely – the Isle of Eels is the real name – grows to reality, becomes a little town on a hill clustered round its old cathedral; but even in full sunlight it never quite loses its air of having been built by magic.

There is nothing in Ely but the cathedral; and the cathedral is a lady. W. D. Howells said that Wells Cathedral in Somerset is the feminine cathedral of England, and guide-books have copied this remark to such an extent that most people believe it to be true! I cannot. Wells Cathedral is, to my mind, distinctly masculine. In its strong, decorated, ornate way it seemed to me almost as masculine as Durham. Ely Cathedral, is, to my eye, the only feminine cathedral in England. In fanciful mood one might think of Ely as the wife of Durham: Durham the grim Norman knight; Ely the lovely Norman lady. Ely is delicate, tinted, full of gracious beauty. Her unique octagonal tower helps the argument: no other cathedral wears so remarkable a hat!

Ely Cathedral, I must remind you, was founded by a woman. It was to this windy island that the saintly Etheldreda in the age of saints took refuge one thousand three hundred and fifty-three years ago. After twelve years of unhappy married life as Queen of Northumbria she fled to her native fens and founded a church, living there in great humility and godliness. Memory of her is preserved – how many people know? – in the word 'tawdry'. Her popular name was St Audrey, and the famous Pilgrims' Fair at Ely known as St Audrey's Fair, gathered together a number of cheap-jacks and hucksters who sold neckcloths of silk nicknamed St Audrey's Chains, or vulgarly, 'tawdries'. Another word, by the way, supposed to have come from Ely is 'Billycock'. Centuries later the monks of Ely wore by special licence from the Pope head coverings named 'wilkoks' to protect them from the winds that whipped their little island in the winter.

I must mention the monk, Alan of Walsingham, who built the octagonal tower and many other parts of this lovely church. He was one of the greatest architects of the Middle Ages. On February 22nd, 1322, just as the monks were retiring to their cells, the old Norman tower of Ely fell down into the choir 'with such a shock', says the old chronicler, 'that it was thought an earthquake had taken place'. Alan of Walsingham 'rose up by night and came and stood over the heap of ruins not knowing whither to turn. But recovering his courage, and confident in the help of God and of His kind Mother Mary, and in the merits of the holy virgin Etheldreda, he set his hand to the work.'

How magnificently he did so can be seen today. I suppose no one but an architect can truly appreciate the genius of this monk.

Ely, to me as to most people, means Hereward the Wake. I might say that it means Hereward the Wake to me more than to most people, because about twenty-five years ago I was Hereward the Wake on Saturday afternoons (and with luck, on Sundays), while another boy with wild red hair was William the Conqueror, a rôle that never appealed to me. A fine, upstanding manure heap in a paddock was our Isle of Ely, and I can see in great detail to this day the bony, freckled, furious William the Conqueror (who is now a missionary in West Africa) charging me with a clothes prop! Ely is in general conformation exactly like our old Ely of the paddock; and as I stood on a high spot and looked down over the green sea of the fens I knew from personal experience that Hereward was never seriously worried about the Norman cavalry which blundered unhappily about in the marshes.

But what a great story is that of the Conqueror, who, when Hereward had been betrayed by the monks on the condition that their possessions should be spared, came secretly to Ely when the monks were at dinner. He knew that they expected a gift from him as a reward for their treachery to Hereward. The Conqueror stood in silence and alone before the high altar. He flung down on it a single gold mark (worth about one hundred and fifty pounds of modern money) and walked quietly out to his horse.

In a few moments the monks were surprised by a knight who rushed in to them, crying: 'You wretched drivellers! Can you choose no better time for guzzling than this when the King is here in your very church?' The brethren made a rush for the church, but it was empty! They ran out after the King and caught him three miles off at Witchford. They apologized. He accepted the apology and fined them seven hundred silver marks (about fourteen thousand pounds). They melted down the church ornaments to pay the fine, but the Norman officials reported that the ingots were deficient in weight, which made William fine the monks a further three hundred marks, so that this silent reverie before the high altar cost Ely twenty thousand pounds.

I turned, and from the fens looked back at the hill of good St Audrey, which through centuries has ridden the rough sea of English history as it rides above the biting winds of Cambridgeshire; and about it in these September mornings is the phantom calm of a ship that has left old storms behind it.

7

I stopped at the 'White Hart' in Brandon to drink beer. Brandon is in Suffolk, but Brandon Railway Station is in Norfolk. Now while I was sitting taking stock of the argumentative little groups round the bar there trickled in from outside a curious, insistent tapping – a queer, tinkly, metallic sound for which I could find no name. It was not the sound of a shoeing forge – it was too thin.

'Oh, that!' replied a labourer, 'that is young Mr Edwards knapping gun-flints in the shed at the back. . . .'

Whereon I put down my tankard and went out to find young Mr Edwards.

I suppose thousands of travellers pass through this apparently uninteresting little town every week without the slightest suspicion that it contains the oldest commercial firm on earth. It is that of Fred Snare, who states that his business was established in the tenth century. Before history began men chipped flints at Brandon. They made those beautiful and efficient little arrow-heads which we find buried in the earth; they made flint knives and flint scrapers; they mined Grimes Graves, nearby, for flint; they dug long galleries in the chalk and took out the flint with picks made of red deer antlers.

The lost art of chipping flint has been kept alive in this Suffolk village for tens of thousands of years. Nowhere else is the difficult art of knocking this stubborn stone into shape practised as in Brandon. . . .

The door of the shed was open. A young man was sitting on a low stool with a stout leather guard strapped above the knee of his left leg. On this guard he held a great nodule of flint which he hit sharply with a short-necked hammer, making in the process the peculiar, glassy hard tinkle I had heard. On one side of him lay a great mound of newly mined flint with the chalk still clinging to it, and on the other was a tin tub half full of little square smoky-blue gun-flints – the finished article.

He smiled an invitation, so I went in and sat on an upturned tub watching him.

Have you ever tried to make an arrow-head of flint?

I have, and I have never succeeded. It has always been to me a mystery how our Stone Age ancestors worked this brittle stone; how they made it into small razor-edged arrow-heads and long, thin spear-heads, all neatly chipped as if the steel-hard stone had been nibbled into shape by a mouse.

As I watched young Mr Edwards knap his flints, I realized that flint behaves well if you know exactly where to hit it. Mr Edwards took up a lump of stone, hit it gently, and seemed to listen to the sound. When satisfied by the sound he hit harder, and the flint broke crisply, along the lines of cleavage. He now had a nice flat piece of flint to work on. He struck it near the edges. It flaked, and he proceeded to fashion a little square gun-flint with a series of quick expert blows; and the astonishing thing to me was that the disobedient stone obeyed him. In a few seconds another gun-flint fell into the tin tub and another flake was on his knee.

'You have to learn this trick when you're young,' said Mr Edwards, 'and some can't even learn it then. It's a kind of gift.'

'Handed down from the Stone Age?' I asked.

'Well,' he smiled, 'I have been told so.'

'What happens to all these gun-flints?'

'There's a great trade for them in Africa and places where the natives use the old flint-lock. All the gun-flints used today come from Brandon. They sell 'em in bags of fifty.'

I gather that the flint-knapping trade, like so many ancient trades, may die out with this generation. Young boys do not take kindly to the art; it is too poorly paid and too difficult, and the flint dust is supposed to eat into the lungs. The flint-knappers of Brandon have dwindled to about half a dozen, and most of them regard the job as a spare-time one.

I watched Mr Edwards make without one flaw gun-flint after gun-flint. He worked with astonishing speed, and the glassy hard tinkle of his little metal hammer on the flint was one of the most fascinating sounds I have heard – a sound, I thought, to which the human race won its battle for mastery over the beasts thousands of centuries ago. . . .

'Make me an arrow-head,' I asked.

'That's one thing I can't do,' said Mr Edwards. 'There's only one man here who can, and he probably wouldn't. He lives down the street. He can make arrow-heads and mace-

heads, but he won't tell how he does it! We get Sir Arthur
This and Sir John That down here trying to get him to tell
how he chips his flint implements, but he won't say. For
instance, he made this last week.'

He handed me an axe-head of stone. I know little about
prehistoric antiquities and I would unhesitatingly have
bought this as genuine.

I found this old flint arrow-head maker in his cottage,
and I asked him how he learned this lost art.

'When I was a boy,' he said, 'I used to hear the professors
and such like who came up to the flint-workings say that
they could not think how these old Stone Age men made
their weapons. So I started to practise. And the idea came to
me. It came suddenly! I thought to myself. "This is how
these people worked flint and stone!" and I began to make
arrow-heads and axe-heads and some of them, I'm afraid,
got into museums!'

Mr Spalding looked stubborn.

'It's my secret,' he said. 'I thought it out myself, and I
don't see why I should give it away. . . .'

He opened a drawer in which lay a little collection of
Neolithic arrow-heads beautifully chipped; in a second
drawer lay an identical collection. Mr Spalding pointed to
this second drawer and said simply:

'I made those in my spare time.'

No man looking at these two collections, separated by
who knows how many thousands of years, could doubt that
ancient and modern have been made by the same method,
whatever that may be. The strange thing is that while Mr
Spalding can manufacture Stone Age weapons that puzzle
the antiquary, he cannot fashion a gun-flint! He is not really
one of Brandon's flint-knappers; he is, even to the men who
daily master this brittle stone, a mystery. They know the
difficulties he has overcome in the higher branches of flint-
working, an art which till he remembered it had been lost
these thousands of years.

I left him standing at his cottage door holding a Stone

Age axe to which he had fixed a stout handle bound to the stone with rough strands of untanned ox-hide. He swung the axe and said how perfect the balance was; and it occurred to me that he looked rather like a caveman standing there in the darkness of his cottage door, ready to defy any inquisitive professor, ready to defend his discovery with flint-like tenacity. And I thought that had I been one of those people who cannot disguise a belief in reincarnation he would not have got off so easily.

Neither, perhaps, considering the perfect balance of the prehistoric axe, might I!

CHAPTER TWELVE

I sit beside the Avon at Stratford, meet the new gipsies, go to Coventry, Kenilworth, Warwick, and come, at last, to the end of my journey

I

THESE Warwickshire lanes, deep and banked; these mighty trees; these small, arched bridges over small streams, how well I knew them when I was a boy. There were little villages in which men still spoke Elizabethan English, such as Welford-on-Avon, where there was a maypole, where they grew the most delicious raspberries and took the sweetest honey from straw skeps. Here it was years ago that I saw a man in a smock. There was Bidford – 'drunken Bidford' – where an old woman, with a face like a withered apple under a mauve sun-bonnet, used to point out the crab-tree beneath whose shade Shakespeare, so the legend went, slept off a carouse at the Falcon Inn there. And I knew the eight villages of the rhyme (written, of course, by Shakespeare!):

> *Piping Pebworth, Dancing Marston,*
> *Haunted Hillborough, Hungry Grafton,*
> *Dodging Exhall, Papist Wixford,*
> *Beggarly Broom, and Drunken Bidford.*

I would not dare to revisit them in the time at my command.

Some day I will spend a month there, but it must be in June, when the raspberry canes are heavy in Welford.

It is an amusing error to revisit a place which thrilled us when we were very young. I seem to remember Stratford-on-Avon as a quiet little heaven where it was always May, with the nightingales shaking silver in the dark trees at night and the Avon mooning under Hugh of Clopton's grand old bridge. And I was terribly young. I used to rise with the sun and walk over dripping meadows with their wrong-way-

247

round shadows, the king-cups shaking dew over my boots, and I would read Shakespeare aloud to the astonishment of the cows, pausing transfixed in wonder (on an empty stomach) by such lines as – well, never mind. Only Youth knows; only Youth can achieve that passionate intensity.

And one night I nearly killed Marie Corelli. A moon-struck night just like that which Dido knew upon 'the wild sea banks', so marvellous that I, looking only at the moon, drove a punt with great force into the author's famous gondola. There was Mr Frank Benson – as he was in those days – the local deity, seen often in swift and god-like transit on a decrepit bicycle, the high priest of the Stratford Festival. I remember him waving his arms at me in a storeroom hung with hams, which he used as an office, and telling me, as I sat worshipping him from a sugar crate, that only through Stratford, the common meeting-place of the English-speaking world, could we heal the pains of Industrialism and make England happy again. We were to make the whole world happy, apparently, by teaching it to morris-dance and to sing folk-songs and to go to the Memorial Theatre. With the splendid faith of Youth we pilgrims believed that England could be made 'merrie' again by hand-looms and young women in Liberty gowns who played the harpsichord. Then, I seem to remember, shortly after that war was declared. However . . .

I drove between those well-loved Warwick hedges, through a perfect death-rattle of motor traffic, into Stratford. My quiet old Stratford was suffering from a rash of trippers. Charabancs from everywhere were piled up in the square; half the motor cars of the Midlands were either coming or going; and the hotel was full of long-legged girls from America, and sallow fathers and spectacled mothers.

They gave me a bedroom called 'Love's Labour Lost' – all the rooms in this hotel are Shakespeareanized – and, as it overlooked the street, I sat a while watching more Americans arrive and thinking how amused Shakespeare would have been. Stratford's fame rests on Shakespeare: much of

248

its prosperity rests on the fact that it is a social disgrace in America not to have rushed through Stratford. This town is the very core of the heart of the American's England. The rich American in his touring car, and the poor American doing England on a book of coupons, are alike in this: neither dare show his face at home unless he can honestly say that he has seen Shakespeare's home town.

Stratford-on-Avon is the only town in England which can be compared with the ancient pilgrimage towns; it is, in its way, a kind of lay Glastonbury. I suppose the old religious shrines also received thousands of sheep-like pilgrims who had no idea why they were pilgrims beyond the fact that it was the right thing to do.

How I detest the word 'pilgrim' in its modern sense. Also the word 'shrine'. Whenever I hear them I seem to hear also someone saying, 'Bring a couple of Martinis – quick now – and some ice water!'

I went into Harvard House, which belongs to the American University and is used as a rest room. (It has Yale-blue curtains!) In this house lived Katherine Rogers, who married Robert Harvard and became the mother of the founder of Harvard University. I went to New Place, which, thanks to the energy of Mr Wellstood, the curator of Shakespeare's Birthplace, is becoming an excellent museum. I went, of course, to the Birthplace, where, because Stratford seems to arouse all the instincts of the souvenir hunter, they keep a guardian in every room. I must have exhausted my Shakespeare worship years ago, for I found myself more interested in the moon-like faces of the pilgrims bent above the glass cases than in the fact that here, they say, was born the greatest poetic genius of the English race.

'Say, guide,' asked a pilgrim, 'is it known how much Shakespeare made out of his plays?'

Overlooking the garden of Shakespeare's Birthplace, is, if association and surroundings mean anything to a writer, the most perfect workroom in the world. From his desk in the window Mr Wellstood, the curator, overlooks the garden in which Shakespeare was hushed to sleep, blew bubbles, tried to catch the clouds, and suffered, no doubt, from those alarming facial convulsions common to all infants. Another inspiration is that from May till September every American girl in England passes in review before it.

Mr Wellstood told me that he has discovered Roman Stratford beneath the golf links.

I found two things unchanged in Stratford. One was a mossy seat on the high wall of Holy Trinity churchyard overlooking the Avon. This is, to my mind, one of the supremely English views. It seems as you sit there with the willows dipping to the river, beyond, on the opposite bank, great freckled meadows, and in the air the sound of the water rushing past the old mill, that all the beauty and peace of the Warwickshire countryside have been packed into one riverscape. Between the tombstones grow vast yew-trees. It is so right that Shakespeare's bones should lie in this quiet church . . . now and again from the thin spire a bell tells the time lazily; the tall avenue of lime-trees moves in the wind.

And the woods by the river, they, too, are unchanged. The tourist never goes to them; the tripper knows them not. Here in the spring you can hear the nightingale all night long; here the wild roses light up the hedges; and the tiny blossom of the blackthorn lies over the grass like snow. Just now the brake is feeling the fingers of autumn among the leaves. And this is the place where you will meet Shakespeare, if you want to meet him, in this wood, which I swear is that magic wood 'near Athens'.

It was evening when I went there on a real pilgrimage, and it seemed that Oberon and Titania had just hidden behind the great trees; that Mustard-Seed and Peas-Blossom had withdrawn to their acorn cups at the sound of footsteps. In the middle of the wood, that clings to the high Avon bank, I met an old man going home to Shottery with a sack over his back and an untrimmed ash stick in his hand. We just said 'Good evening', and passed on. But I recognized him! He was one of those homespun Warwickshire yokels whom Shakespeare took to Athens on that magic midsummer night.

2

I was coming out of the village post office when a voice, which I know well, cried:

'The very man! Do you know that my wife wrote three letters to you and never had a reply?'

'No, I didn't.'

'Well, she wants you to write about the new gipsies.'

'Who are the new gipsies?'

'We are. There are heaps more, but we are typical examples. The habit's growing, too. The only way I can keep fit is by getting out of London for weekends. We had a houseboat on the Thames last year, but it sank this spring, so we've taken to weekend camping. Some weekends we go to Devon or Somerset or down to the New Forest, and this is our first Warwickshire camp. . . . Look here, do you know Abbot's Mill? Good! Well, you go past the mill, take the footpath to the left, and carry on till you meet a stream with a little bridge over it. Don't cross the bridge: it isn't safe: there's a plank to the left. Cross the stubble field to the wood, which you will see right ahead, and when you get there shout, and we will hear you. Come to dinner! Sardines, bacon and eggs, and tinned tongue. . . .'

'I can't tonight.'

'Then come when you can after dinner. The stars are simply marvellous. You'll be able to write yards about it. Great Scott, that reminds me! I've got to get a half-yard of elastic. See you later.'

John X the precise London businessman, clipped and neat in everything, was the last person I would have expected to see in a lost village dressed like a rat-catcher. So, of course, I decided to go.

It was growing dark when I passed Abbot's Mill and

struck off along the footpath which, contrary to all my expectations (for directions always lead you astray), led to a small stream and a decayed bridge. A rich gold field of cut corn with rabbits at the edges led on to a ragged line of trees against the sky. Here I shouted. A man's voice answered some way off, there was a crackling of twigs, and in a few moments John X appeared at the edge of the wood with his sleeves rolled up.

'Just been washing up,' he explained with a grin. 'Beastly job! Come on.'

He led the way along a little gamekeeper's track through the wood.

'Can you imagine a greater change from London than this?' asked John X, waving a hand to include the shadowy trees. 'Weekend cottages and houseboats, and all that sort of thing, end in bridge parties and cocktails, and in time you meet all the friends you want to escape from. But this . . . one might be in the middle of the moon. Here we are. . . .'

We stepped into a sudden clearing. A wood fire was burning some way from a green tent. A touring car covered by a tarpaulin was in the background.

'We had an awful job getting the car up here; but it's worth it: we're right off the main track.'

Mrs John X came out of the tent; and I never saw a prettier gipsy.

'You see,' she said, taking me to the tent, 'we have electric light tapped from the car.'

There was a rug on the floor and two camp beds.

'Say when,' said John, approaching with a soda siphon.

We sat round the fire and watched the darkness creep out of the still woods and enfold the little clearing. We found the first star. The light of the camp fire ran up the trunks of the nearest trees.

'This isn't our best camp by any means,' said John X, lighting his pipe, 'but the idea is not to stick in one place. You keep on exploring. Our best spot so far is bang in the middle of the New Forest, with a crystal-clear six-foot swimming pool at the tent door, and nothing for miles. . . .'

'Gorgeous!' said Mrs John X. 'I take a swimming costume with me, but I never use it . . . and we hear the foxes barking, and one night we went with a gamekeeper to smoke out a wild bees' nest. We took over forty-five pounds of honey in a tin bath. . . .'

John X got up and wandered off towards the car.

'I'm thinking,' I said, 'that this must an excellent cure for married life. I suppose you and John quarrel in town now and then?'

'Like hell,' said Mrs John. 'One gets into a groove. Then I think, love them as much as one does, it's a good thing to get away from the children, if you know what I mean. . . .'

'I do. A man and a woman ought to get away alone together like this and fend for themselves and rely on one another. A cottage with servants or a country hotel isn't the same thing.'

'Hear, hear!' cried John X, emerging carrying what at first sight I feared was a large gramophone. 'This gipsying together puts us right for the week after, doesn't it, old girl? Of course, some women would hate it. . . . Mary, give me a hand with this thing. . . .'

She got up, a neat silhouette against the fire, and helped him to fix up on the ground a big wireless set.

'This,' said John X, 'is only to show off to you: we keep it for wet weekends.'

It was a queer experience to sit in front of a fire in the middle of a wood and hear a strong orchestra playing in London.

'It's friendly on a wet night,' said Mrs John X.

It was quite dark. The stars were indeed marvellous, powdered above the clearing. Moths flickered in the light of the fire, and in the outer ring of darkness the tall trees stood unruffled by the slightest wind, the yellow firelight touching their boughs and moving, flinging grotesque shadows. We sat mostly in silence, smoking and hushed by the peace of night.

'Anyone with a car can do this,' said John X, closing a great paw over Mrs John's hand, 'couldn't they, Mary?'

Almost anyone, I thought, watching them. It occurred to me that their short dashes from the responsibilities of their home are a secret worth passing on. The atmosphere of playing a game together is a great one to introduce into married life.

Mrs John went into the tent and switched on the light.

'Oh, John,' she cried, coming into the firelight, 'there's a moth as big as an aeroplane on my pillow!'

'I'll fix him!' said John X, rising and striding to the tent.

'Don't kill him: remove him!' cried Mrs John.

'You're too late,' came the reply.

'My caveman!' said Mrs John X, lighting a cigarette.

John X lit a lantern, took me to the plank over the stream. The stars. The peace of that place. I watched his lantern bob back through the wood, and then there was darkness. I stood a moment thinking that no one would guess how lost together these two London gipsies were; only a few hours from their home and their children, but as alone together on this night of stars as if they were in the heart of the Libyan Desert.

There was a great scurrying of cottontails at the edge of the dark field, and the rush of water at Abbot's Mill drummed loud in the hush of the night.

3

I suppose no one dares to write about Coventry without mentioning motor-cars and bicycles, so, having done this in the first sentence, we will leave it there. The interesting fact about Coventry is, to my mind, not cycles or cylinders, but women. Coventry has always been lucky with women, and should, therefore, be England's happiest city.

It begins with an old legend that when Coventry was in

its infancy, the eleven thousand virgins of Cologne arrived there on a kind of spiritual Cook's tour. They stayed awhile, illuminating the village with their piety, and, departing, left eleven thousand virtues to be shared by successive generations of their own sex in Coventry. If any city in the kingdom has a more beautiful story or has paid a sweeter compliment to its womenfolk I have yet to hear about it.

It is interesting, to descend from fiction to strange fact, that Coventry has a remarkable feminine roll of honour: St Osburg, Lady Godiva, Isabella, Margaret of Anjou, the sisters Botoner, who built the spire, Joan Ward, the Lollard Martyr, Mrs Siddons, George Eliot, Ellen Terry.

I approached by road, admiring the stately, slow dance of the three spires against the sky; and I was not a bit surprised to find, on entering the city, that the eleven thousand virgins seem still in possession. One, shopping with a Scalyham at the corner of Hertford Street, had inherited far more than her fair share, if beauty is a virtue.

Lady Godiva has always attracted me. She is, of course, the leading lady in Coventry's history. I do not care much for the modern version of her ride, which, in an excess of Victorian modesty, makes her agonized by the shame of her ordeal. I prefer the first written account done by Roger of Wendover, somewhere about A.D. 1230, which, to any man who knows and admires the grim recklessness of a woman who has made up her mind, rings down seven centuries with the tone of truth. According to him Godiva wasted no time in remorse, or wondering what the Robinsons would say. She just 'loosened her hair, thus veiling her body, and then, mounting her horse and attended by two knights, she rode through the market seen of none, her white legs nevertheless appearing; and having completed her journey, returned to her husband rejoicing. . . .'

As a matter of fact it seems clear from this first record that if we could witness this ride, which has given the world a thrilled shock for centuries, we should probably find that Lady Godiva's appearance in Coventry market was no

255

more sensational than a modern girl catching an omnibus. . . .

In the Mayoress' parlour of the Guildhall is a statue of Godiva on her white horse. It is a lovely thing. There is another in the Great Hall, set in a niche. There is also a picture of her.

'You really believe this happened?' I asked the keen, well-read caretaker who shows people over the hall.

'Well, we can't prove it,' he said, 'but where there's smoke there's fire. A story that lives as long as this must be true.'

A different opinion was held by a high official in Coventry.

'I don't believe it happened,' he said. 'But don't mention my name or I shall be driven from the city! You have read Sir James Frazer's *Golden Bough*?'

'Surely you are not going to tell me that Lady Godiva was a corn spirit?'

'No; but it is very suggestive! We know Godiva lived and founded a religious house here. Her name was therefore respected. It is not for a hundred and fifty years after she died that we have any documentary evidence of her ride. There is no contemporary reference to it. Now, as Frazer points out, the ride of a naked or bough-clad woman on a white horse occurs in the folklore of many heathen people. I suppose it had something to do with heathen sacrifice. In this part of the country the hobby-horse has played an important part in folk dances. Old men can still remember the Warwickshire May Day revels with the morris dancers and their hobby-horse. I believe that Godiva's famous ride is nothing more than an ancient folk tradition coming down from remote heathen times of the naked woman on the white horse. What would be more obvious than for tale-makers to link up this legend with the admired name of Lady Godiva? . . . However, we can prove nothing. . . .'

I left him impressed and depressed. I hate killing old stories. I like to believe that Alfred burned the cakes; that

Canute had a conversation with the sea. And I shall go on believing that Godiva rode through the market attended by two thanes, and that nobody paid any attention to her. After all, experience tells us that women have a genius for getting the better of their husbands, and when Godiva returned rejoicing to the fiery Leofric, I suppose she said: 'My dear, I *said* I'd do it, and *did* it, and – no one saw me. While I'm dressing you'd better go and take off those taxes as you promised, or I shall be very angry.'

We must remember that Godiva's inheritance from the eleven thousand virtues was obviously the art of managing a headstrong husband.

A corn spirit? Nonsense! She was just an ordinary wife.

Like Norwich, Coventry is a modern manufacturing city which is spread like thick butter over a slice of medievalism. It is a lucky city. Fire, which wiped old London from the map, has spared to Coventry several of the finest buildings of their kind in the world – St Mary's Hall, Ford's Hospital for Aged Women, the Bablake Hospital.

Ford's Hospital appeals to me as the most beautiful and most lovable half-timbered building in England. I know of nothing else quite so fine. When I passed through the gate into the flagged courtyard, with the top-heavy, leaning, black and white house running round the four sides, glowing with a richness of oak beams and yellow plaster work, I entered another world; I was in the Coventry of A.D. 1550.

The narrow square of sky overhead included no reminder of modern Coventry; the usual gasworks or factory stack did not strike the false note; here was the peace and beauty of the Tudor world. For four hundred years this house has protected old women of Coventry who have fallen on bad times. At the present moment it shelters sixteen.

'Many are over eighty,' said the caretaker. 'They get four shillings a week and free coal, and they can do what they like: have friends to tea, visit each other, and so on.'

The rooms in which the old women live have made many a rich American bite his nails in envy.

'Some visitors cannot drag themselves away,' said the caretaker. 'It's very lovely with the flowers out in the window-boxes.'

We entered a large beamed apartment in which a fire was burning in a vast grate.

'She's just moved in today,' explained the caretaker. 'She has just been admitted to the hospital. All the old ladies furnish their own rooms.'

I looked around the high, elegant room, and noticed the little treasures which this old woman had saved at the end of life. Pathetic rooms! The first thing she had done, I noted, was to hang on the wall over her bed pious mottoes in praise of God and His goodness.

'She's out at the moment. She is over seventy, and hale and hearty, too. It's surprising how active they are. . . .'

If good William Ford, merchant stapler of Coventry, who sent his grand gift down the ages, could revisit it nothing would surprise him, I think, except the electric light.

'And what a blessing that is!' remarked the caretaker. 'When I first came here I couldn't sleep at the thought of a possible fire. When you come to think that for nearly four hundred years old women of seventy and eighty have been going to bed by candlelight, it's wonderful that we have had no accidents.'

We entered many of the rooms. Most of the old women had gone out to attend a meeting in the city. Some rooms were prettier than others and better furnished, but all were alike in this: near the bed children and grandchildren looked out from photograph frames.

In the finest room of all was a scene that Rembrandt would have loved. Against a broad Tudor window made of hundreds of small leaded panes of glass sat a wrinkled old woman, with a shawl over her shoulders. Behind her, through the window, we could see the quadrangle, the yellow and black beams of the house, and a little square of sky. The old woman was smiling across the tea-table to her grandchild. The young woman had come with that news of the outside world which old people love to hear.

'I am always sorry for the lonely ones,' said the caretaker. 'They do love to have little presents and to see their children and grandchildren. . . .'

Once a week the old ladies of Ford's House put on their best bonnets, and meet in the room downstairs facing the street. The almoner sits at a little table with a pile of money before him. One by one the old women go up and receive four shillings straight from Elizabethan England.

William Ford needs no statue in Coventry.

4

Warwick Castle. You see it from the bridge, lying low on its cliff bowered among trees, shining in the Avon, the two machicolated towers to the right. Generally the bridge is crowded with trippers. Someone always says: 'That's one of the finest views in England'; which is true.

I stood there alone. I suppose that Warwick Castle is, after Windsor, the most famous and most beautiful in England.

A guide met me at the barbican, and we walked past vivid green lawns such as you will see in no other country in the world, till we came to the grey bulk of the castle, with a blankness about the windows which seemed to say that the earl was not at home.

The Great Hall of Warwick Castle is, although extensively and carefully restored, one of the glories of England. In old days the Earls of Warwick used to ride in on horseback, scattering the rushes, and, dismounting, draw a dagger and help themselves to the ox or the sheep which was roasting before the great log fire.

How many Americans, I wonder, stand in this hall every year with their faith in England justified? It is California's

ideal of an English nobleman's home. Its influence can, I
think, be traced on the films.

We admired the armour, also the giant cooking pot called
Guy's Punch Bowl, an enormous cauldron that holds a
hundred and twenty gallons, made in the fourteenth century
for Sir John Talbot of Swannington. There is a legend that
when an Earl of Warwick comes of age Guy's Punch Bowl
is filled and emptied three times. That must also impress the
American!

'I show thousands over the castle every year,' said the
guide, 'and give me the interested American tourist in
preference to the dull kind of Englishman who seems to
know nothing about the history of his own country. . . .
There's Oliver Cromwell's death mask! I said that to a
visitor once, and she made no reply, so, thinking she was
deaf, I said it a bit louder. "It's all right," she replied. "I
heard you, but – why did Oliver Cromwell wear a mask?" '

Is there a fairer scene in Warwickshire than the view of
the Avon from the drawing-rooms? The river runs far below
between green banks, cascading over a weir.

'Two things are hidden about Warwick Castle,' said the
guide. 'The Avon makes our electric light, but you can see
no signs of it; and hidden beneath the great hall is an
organ.'

These rooms are delicious. They are packed with
treasures. Holbein, Rubens, Van Dyck, Lely are frame to
frame on the walls. The lighting is mellow. Little gilt shields
illuminate the canvases and reflect their richness.

It was growing dark when I entered the Beauchamp
Chapel, which takes the breath away with its beauty. I can
compare it only with Henry VII's Chapel in Westminster
Abbey and King's College, Cambridge. The great Richard
Beauchamp lay with his bare head in a tilting helm and his
hands raised above his breast.

I remember the story of the disaster that overtook the
Earl's body in the seventeenth century. The floor of the
chapel fell in, and the body was found inside the tomb

marvellously preserved. The women of Warwick, it is said, seized the hair and worked it into rings. . . .

The light faded moment by moment. I went out into the streets of Warwick, those quiet, attractive streets that have not lost a look of other days, conscious that a man might spend a month here and not exhaust the memories that lie so thickly beside the green banks of the Avon.

5

It is difficult to know in Kenilworth where Elizabeth ends and Walter Scott begins. I went there on one of those hot sleepy midsummer afternoons, when the heat throws a haze low over the meadows and stones are hot to the hand.

This rambling, chocolate-red ruin fills me with a greater sense of desolation than any other ruin I have seen in England. Tudor England, in which it reached its prime, is, as time goes, only yesterday. The faces, the philosophy, the poetry, the deeds, even the love letters, of the people who moved through that age are still as fresh in our memories as the faces and the thoughts of friends. While many a Saxon and a Norman building stands perfect in England with the mistakes of the builders' axes still clean in the stone, this Kenilworth flings its tattered walls to the skies, and its once grand stairways end in thin air, and the green grass lies in great hummocks over the tilt yard.

This ruin is one of the tragedies. Had it only survived, as other Tudor buildings contemporary with it have survived, Kenilworth Castle would be without a peer of its kind in the historic monuments of England.

Near Leicester's Gatehouse I met an elderly man in a black coat who was saying goodbye to a crowd of American trippers. He waved his stick in the air and stamped his feet on the ground, and instead of smiling at his vehemence, they appeared to treat him with considerable deference. He was, I learnt, the official guide, and I was soon to find that he is the best guide in England.

He collected a new flock, and certain members of it, having no proof as yet of his virtues, laughed behind his back as he waved his dramatic stick. He started off and we trooped behind like sheep. He kept turning round to face us and to wave his stick at us, then he would move on a few paces and suddenly wheel round again, as if to assault our ignorance, sometimes giving us in a phrase the essential importance of a turret or a tumbled wall.

This old man has soaked himself in Kenilworth. He lives Kenilworth, he loves Kenilworth. He took us to a high place, waited with raised stick until the giddiest college girl had stopped giggling, and then from the mouth of this extraordinary guide there flowed a magnificent oration. He built up the tattered walls of Kenilworth for us, he took us through the Middle Ages and he brought us through Tudor Warwickshire in the train of Queen Elizabeth. There was not a sound now from his flock.

The little old man in the black coat standing there on the hill-top, with a great dip beyond, where the meadows lay flat to the sky, and near him a jagged red sandstone tower, seemed to our astonished eyes to be the spirit of the place. He was so dramatic. His expression changed as he described the various men of that time, Leicester, Burleigh, Shakespeare, Cecil. He spoke of Queen Elizabeth, threw his head up stiffly until I swear I saw the ghost of a ruff round his neck, and then he led us into that pageant which Scott has not described better than he did.

Turning to face the meadows below, he waved his magic stick and filled the fields with the water of the famous lake of Kenilworth, another wave and barges sailed there, another wave and he rebuilt the castle, filled its gaunt corridors with the sound of laughter and the thin sweet sound of the virginals.

It was a remarkable *tour de force*. He left us rather bewildered, rather like children when the story has been told. Then sweeping that dramatic stick of his round the landscape he ordered us to admire it, he dropped his voice to a whisper and moved his hands in time to his well-balanced sentences. He spoke about the long pageant of history that is England, the evil and the good that have marched side by side down the centuries, ending with:

'England! You now stand in the heart of England. Are you proud of her, of your share in her? . . . I know that I am.'

An emotional Boston woman on the edge of the crowd wiped tears from her eyes.

I went thoughtfully over the bumpy grass cursing Colonel Hawkesworth and his Roundhead troopers who made Kenilworth a ruin, and at the gate I met the old man, waving his magic wand at a new flock. I stopped him and complimented him on the dramatic genius of his address.

'Ah,' he said, peering at me, and I then saw that he was partially blind, 'I am glad you feel like that. I was an actor once. I am one of the original members of Sir Frank Benson's company, but' – and here he pointed to his eyes – 'my career ended before it began!'

He waved his stick and moved off over the ruins.

6

I met him in the churchyard. He was carrying a basket of eggs, and I could see that he was, although not wearing a clerical collar, the vicar; a man, I judged, about sixty, red-faced, muscular, white-haired.

'Dreadful, dreadful!' he said sadly, looking out over the tombstones, some cut with eighteenth-century inscriptions, some leaning together, some propped up with posts, many covered with green lichen or half-obscured by the long grass that grew between grave and grave. I thought it rather strange that a man whose mission in life is to teach the joys of the world to come should express painful emotion at the sight of his own graveyard; and I ventured to tell him so.

'Well, you see,' he said, 'my trouble is that the people of this parish lie buried ten and twelve deep in this little plot of earth; and the worst of it is that they like it! If you look over the wall you will observe a fine meadow. That is our new graveyard, and it has been ready for use for us for twelve years, but no one will hear of being buried in it. I greatly fear that I must take legal measures to shut the old churchyard – an Order in Council or something – and make them accept the new meadow. I hate to do it. I do really. A great blow to them. A terrible blow to them!'

'But what,' I said, 'is their objection?'

He looked at me and smiled.

'It is, perhaps, difficult for you, a stranger, to understand. You see, we are, in this little hamlet, untouched by modern ideas, in spite of the wireless and the charabanc. We use words long since abandoned – why, only today I heard a little girl use the word "boughten" for "bought". My parishioners believe firmly in a physical resurrection! They believe that a trumpet will herald the end of the world, and that the bones in this churchyard will join together. So you see they like to be buried on top of their fathers and grandfathers, because they will rise together as a family. It is, to them, more friendly. Clannish in life and clannish in death. It is a very old and primitive idea. I know other country clergy who are in the same, as it were, box.'

We walked slowly through the churchyard towards a grey house that stood smothered in trees.

'Do come in and drink a glass of cider. I make it myself; my own apples, my own brandy cask.'

It was cool in the dark hall, and we went into a long room. Beyond the windows was one of the loveliest gardens imaginable, a tangle of magnificence; roses falling in white cascades from old walls, pink roses flinging their rich sprays over arbours, and the air was heavy with the scent of flowers and loud with the sound of bees. There was a movement on the lawn.

'Was that a hare?'

'That wicked little beggar again!' cried the vicar. 'He comes and dances there every evening, confound him, for

264

he makes a dreadful hash of my garden. Really I must think about finding him a good home, the little rascal!'

He cast a quick glance towards a gun rack.

'How do you like the cider?'

'It's rather like Sauterne.'

'Ah, you have a palate! It is good; it is, in fact, excellent. The bouquet is delicious – just smell – and hold the glass against the window – look at that cloudy amber! My own apples; my own brandy cask. Have another glass?'

'It is, I believe, stronger than Sauterne.'

'Indeed it is.'

We walked through the garden talking about the modern difficulty of being happy.

'Happiness,' said the old man, 'is a compound of simplicity, love, and philosophy and, of course, faith. One must believe in something. I'm not preaching at you, am I? If so tell me to stop! Lack of faith is a modern spiritual disease, and people, it seems, are only just becoming aware of it. How happy I am; how glad I am to be alive to work here among children, flowers, and fruit. I love the children of this parish; I watch over them like a benevolent eagle, if that is a permissible simile. To me, of course,' he added whimsically, 'all of them up to the age of forty are children, for I have held them all in my arms when they were babies. How old do you think I am?'

'I should have said sixty.'

'I am nearly eighty. Then I have my flowers, my fruits, and my fishing rods. What more can an old man want? It is very quiet here. We are far from the pain of cities, the complexities. Life is reduced here to a simple common denominator. The men are on the land. Now and then a girl goes away to service or to marry a man in a town and she returns with skirts up to her knees to astonish us for a bit, thinking us old-fashioned and stodgy. But are we? Our foundation is so solid. We are rooted in something firmer than fashion. We believe things too, I see to that! Our simple sins, such as they are, are sins all flesh is heir to, and like all human beings, we need kindness sometimes more than advice or censure. Oh, I know that so well. . . . How the greenfly has got into those roses, damn them!'

'You must have seen great changes here in your time?'

'Yes and no. It's easier to get about now. We go to London once in a blue moon. You must have seen us with our mouths wide open in Piccadilly. . . . Unless I net those cherries there won't be one left! Look at those birds!'

Over the meadows drifted the smell of hay. We could see in the field beyond the garden a man and a woman knee deep on the stack.

'My churchwarden! I often rocked that great, big, hulking fellow to sleep in an old wooden cradle shaped like an ark!'

We walked round, and beyond the garden field lay against field, marching together to the hills. The church bell struck the hour as we came unexpectedly to the little Norman porch.

A shaft of light fell through the western windows across a stiff company of knights lying spurred in full mail, their hands at rest upon their breasts. There were ladies, too: alabaster pale ladies whose hair was dressed in a forgotten mode, whose ringed fingers were held together in prayer.

'The Jocelyns,' said the vicar, with his hand on a stone sword hilt. 'They died fighting long ago. There is a man of the same name working on a farm near, but he spells it differently. I often think he looks a bit like Sir Gervais who went on the third Crusade.'

There were coloured coats of arms on the wall, and, high up, hanging precariously by a nail, an ancient helmet with a badly dented visor. The sunlight slanted upward till it lay in a bar across the face of the nearest knight and lit the thin, long fingers of his lady.

'Would you care to stay the night, and we could have a talk?' said the old man. 'Tomorrow is our harvest festival and you might like to . . .'

I told him that nothing would give me greater joy, and I think that my sincerity pleased him. My room in the old vicarage was small and white. There was a coloured picture of the Duke of Wellington on the wall dated 1812, put there in a moment of patriotism over a hundred years ago on the eve of the last great war but one. When I looked out of the window I saw the hare dancing on the lawn, beyond lay the stubble field, gold in the late sunlight with a few rabbits lolloping on the edges. Over the window drooped a screen of tight red roses, full of a sound of wings and swinging slightly with the weight of bees.

In a warm twilight we sat down to dinner with the windows open to the lawn, he at one end of the long oak table that had fed his family, I at the other. Half-way through the meal the aged housekeeper paused in her services to light two candles on the table. We saw outside the hush of evening deepen. There came into the sky that rich gold flush that precedes a harvest moon. A moth fluttered in and charged the candle. In the silence we could hear a dog barking miles off. It seemed that all the beauty of the world had been gathered up into the Hand of God.

'And they heard the voice of the Lord God walking in the garden in the cool of the day.'

His voice came slowly and softly beyond the candlelight, and we both looked again out to the fields.

'I am rarely honoured with a visitor,' he said, rising, 'so we will celebrate our meeting.'

Slowly, and with a reverence that was habitual to him, he carried from the sideboard a cradle in which lay a very ancient bottle:

'This port,' he explained, 'is older than I am. I have only a few dozen bottles left. I keep it to cheer me in my solitude. An inheritance.'

He then removed the glasses from the table and replaced them by two elegant Georgian wine glasses.

'A good wine,' he said with a smile, 'must not be insulted by a young glass.'

We held the wine to the candlelight, bowed slightly to

one another and drank. I thought that I had never seen a finer picture than his kind, experienced face in the glow of the two candles, the dark oak panelling behind his white head, as he lifted the little glass of dark red wine to his lips.

He talked of his people, of their fields, of the lord of the manor, poor now as a church mouse but rooted to the land. He would have liked me to have met him, but he was away healing the sins of his ancestors at a spa. But an old type. He loved his acres. He could not afford his birthright in society unless he sold land; and he could not sell his mother, could he?

'When he dies,' said the vicar, 'I suppose they will sell to pay the death duties and then . . .'

He did not finish.

'I suppose,' he went on, 'I have lived for so long in old England that I cannot visualize a change. Nothing has changed here. Our last real big sensation was in 1066, when the first Jocelyn grabbed the manor. But we soon got over that. We even followed him on a crusade or two and joined his descendants under the walls of Harfleur. Now and then we sent a son to the city to represent us in the larger life – by the way, I wonder if it is really larger? For centuries we have prized the same prejudices – we still hate a man from Spennithorpe – and we have grown up as naturally as my currant bushes out there, century after century. We were, you see, locked up here together with our fields and our imaginations, making our own songs and dances until the world outside sent us a gramophone and the latest murders every Sunday morning. Even that has not altered us much: the newspapers are only another kind of fairy story about the world outside. Our fields are the same as they always were, and we are the servants of our fields. We are happy because we have rarely known discontent. And, as I told you, we believe every word that proceedeth out of the mouth of God.'

We walked out into the garden, and the moon was up.

7

A Sunday hush lay over field and wood: a silence broken only by the song of birds and the drone of insects. The church bell rang.

The little church was full of corn sheaves. Apples, picked for their size and colour, washed and polished, stood in a line against the altar rails. Above the empty pew of the absent squire, barley nodded its gold beard. The church smelt of ripe corn and fruit. Someone, I wonder if consciously, or just by chance, had placed a posy of flowers in the stiff, stone hands of Sir Gervais. He lay there with his thin, mailed toes to the vaulting, his sword at his side and in his hands this offering from his own land to warm his heart in a Norman heaven.

There was a discreet procession up the nave, until the tiny church was full, the women in black, the men unhappy in collars, their great hands burnt red with the harvest sun. The children made eyes at the apples and whispered.

The old vicar mounted into the pulpit and talked to his people about the harvest and God's harvest, as I knew he would. His wise eyes, that knew all their sins and the sins of their fathers, and loved them perhaps because of those sins, moved over them as he spoke; and I noticed a subtle change in his manner. As he addressed them he talked with a faint country accent and I realized then better than before how well he knew his people. The little organ whispered down the nave:

> *To Thee, O Lord, our hearts we raise*
> *In hymns of adoration,*
> *To Thee bring sacrifice of praise*
> *With shouts of exultation;*
> *Bright robes of gold the fields adorn,*
> *The hills with joy are ringing,*
> *The valleys stand so thick with corn*
> *That even they are singing.*
>
> *We bear the burden of the day,*
> *And often toil seems dreary*
> *But labour ends with sunset ray,*

IN SEARCH OF ENGLAND

And rest comes for the weary;
May we, the Angel-reaping o'er,
Stand at the last accepted,
Christ's golden sheaves for evermore
To garners bright elected. . . .

The church emptied. The noon sun fell in bright spears of colour over the old Jocelyns; beyond the porch was a picture of harvest set in a Norman frame. The rich earth had borne its children, and over the fields was that same smile which a man sees only on the face of a woman when she looks down to the child at her breast.

I went out into the churchyard where the green stones nodded together, and I took up a handful of earth and felt it crumble and run through my fingers, thinking that as long as one English field lies against another there is something left in the world for a man to love.

'Well,' smiled the vicar, as he walked towards me between the yew trees, 'that, I am afraid, is all we have.'

'You have England,' I said.

INDEX